# The Origins of Development Economics

## How Schools of Economic Thought

## Have Addressed Development

Edited by
**JOMO K.S.**
**ERIK S. REINERT**

Tulika Books

Zed Books
London and New York

First published in India in 2005 by
Tulika Books
35 A/1 (third floor), Shahpur Jat, New Delhi 110 049, India

First published outside South Asia in 2005 by
Zed Books
7 Cynthia Street, London N1 9JF, UK, and Room 400, 175 Fifth
Avenue, New York, NY 10010, USA. www.zedbooks.demon.co.uk

© Jomo K.S. and Erik S. Reinert, 2005

The rights of Jomo K.S. and Erik S. Reinert to be identified as the editors
of this work have been asserted by them in accordance with the
Copyright, Designs and Patents Act, 1988

ISBN (Tulika Books edition): 81-85229-98-8

ISBN (Zed Books edition): 1 84277 646 0 hb     1 84277 647 9 pb

A catalogue record for this book is available from the British Library.
US CIP data is available from the Library of Congress

Distributed in the USA exclusively by Palgrave, a division of
St. Martin's Press, LLC, 175 Fifth Avenue, New York 10010

Cover designed by Ram Rahman; typeset in Sabon and Univers at
Tulika Print Communication Services, New Delhi, India; printed and
bound at Chaman Enterprises, 1603 Pataudi House, Daryaganj, New
Delhi 110 002, India

# Contents

*Introduction*  JOMO K.S. and ERIK S. REINERT      vii

*Contributors*      xxiii

Mercantilism and Economic Development:
Schumpeterian Dynamics, Institution-building
and International Benchmarking
ERIK S. REINERT and SOPHUS A. REINERT      1

The Italian Tradition of Political Economy:
Theories and Policies of Development in the
Semi-Periphery of the Enlightenment
SOPHUS A. REINERT      24

German Economics as Development Economics:
From the Thirty Years' War to World War II
ERIK S. REINERT      48

The Capitalist Transformation
MUSHTAQ HUSAIN KHAN      69

The Pioneers of Development Economics
and Modern Growth Theory
JAIME ROS      81

International Trade in Early Development Economics
AMITAVA K. DUTT      99

The Rise and Decline of Latin American Structuralism
and Dependency Theory
ALFREDO SAAD–FILHO      128

Development in the History of Economics
TAMÁS SZENTES      146

*Index*      159

# Introduction

*Jomo K.S. and Erik S. Reinert*

'Despite many currents and cross-currents, continuity is perhaps the most impressive phenomenon in the history of economic doctrines.' These words by historian Raymond de Roover (1955: 182) appear more correct, the more one extends the study of the history of development economics back in time. For centuries, economics was – at its very core – an art, a practice and a science devoted to 'economic development', albeit under a variety of labels: from an idealistic promotion of 'public happiness' to the nationalistic creation of wealth and greatness of nations and rulers, and the winning of wars. One purpose of this volume is to demonstrate the continuity of thinking on economic development from pre-Smithian times to the classical development economics of the post-World War II era.

This continuity does not manifest itself in smooth incremental transitions but, rather, in the recurrence of similar ideas in similar contexts. There are no paradigm shifts in the Kuhnian sense but, rather, parallel streams, often at different levels of abstraction, which compete for the attention of economists and policy-makers. When similar economic situations reappear – even centuries apart – similar approaches tend to be reinvented, with or without reference to previous theories addressing similar problems. Periods of profound understanding alternate with periods dominated by abstract theories, as knowledge previously recognized as valuable becomes devalued. As we shall describe below, since the 1760s, two different approaches – or parallel streams – to economics have competed for attention and prominence. Sometimes one dominates, while at other times the two streams are seen as complementary and theoretical pluralism is seen as natural. During such times of pluralism, the economist's toolbox is at its largest.

The two types of social theory are built differently. Theory may be built by induction from observations of reality towards higher levels of abstraction. Alternatively, theory may be built from above, through deductive *a priori* analysis. These two methods tend to depend on different metaphors[1] – the theory that builds from below uses metaphors from biology, like the human body, while the more abstract *a priori* method has normally used metaphors from physics, but recently also from biology. The former builds theory on observations of facts and of history, where human wit and will – the kind of 'human capital' Friedrich

Nietzsche called *Geist und Willens-Kapital* – are important elements. This type of theory is relatively inaccurate for predictive purposes and its conclusions are often open-ended. The latter builds social theory by comparing society to matter (physics) or to abstract biological models; it is therefore more sophisticated, but only at the risk of being less relevant.

During some historical periods, one of these two types of economics rules. During other periods, they coexist, sometimes fighting each other and sometimes in relative peace, recognized as complementary approaches and tools. The 1890s started such a notable period of pluralism, when virtually every economist agreed with Alfred Marshall (1842–1924) that both induction and deduction are needed in economics, just as both legs are needed for walking. The famous *Methodenstreit* in economics, the late nineteenth-century methodological fight between the German and Austrian schools, was not about excluding analysis based on history but about induction or deduction sitting in the driver's seat (Reinert 2003).

By comparing economic history, the history of economic thought and that virtually non-existent field, of the history of economic policy, an interesting pattern appears. We can observe gaps between rhetoric and reality in ostensibly grand schemes based on abstract theory but actually modified in practice. Adam Smith, in his *Wealth of Nations* (1776), urged conversion to free trade. However, historical evidence tells us that for most of the following century, tariffs as a percentage of total imports were higher in 'free trade England' than in the notorious 'fortress France'. The conflict between British theory and British practice produced a rhetoric–reality gap that US economists had already pointed to, in 1820, when they recommended: 'Don't do as the English tell you to do, do as the English do.'

We can observe the same rhetoric–reality gap today. While the theories of economists recommending minimal or no government intervention are exported to, or even imposed on, the rest of the world, in practice, the United States spends billions of dollars on advanced research. George Bush preaches the benefits of free trade, while his own government gives tariff protection and subsidies to the world's biggest farmers and to a host of industries. Paul Krugman, a guru of trade policy, complains that orthodox theories are not listened to in his country, the United States: 'the view of trade as a quasi-military competition is the conventional wisdom among policy-makers, business leaders, and influential intellectuals. . . . It is not just that economics have lost control of the discourse; the kind of ideas that are offered in a standard economics textbook do not enter into that discourse at all' (quoted in Reder 1999: 6).

This conflict between rhetoric and reality can be seen as a conflict between what Thorstein Veblen calls esoteric theory, a theory for the initiated few, and exoteric theory, a theory for the many. One important problem – as the examples above testify – is that the grand theories tend to be exported, while 'common sense' modifications are made closer to home. In the 1820s, a member of the US House of Representatives remarked that the theories of David Ricardo, like so many English products, seemed to be produced exclusively for export markets. 'Don't do like the English tell you to do, do as the English do' thus became a nineteenth-century dictum for economic policy-making. Therefore, the conflict between the two different types of economic theory – in reality, between *theory* and *praxis* – also involves important dimensions of politics and power.

*Types of Economic Theory* is the title of two books on the history of economic thought by people who had their formative years in the pluralistic 1890s. One is a two-volume work on the history of economic thought by Wesley Claire Mitchell (1874–1948), the US economist most famous for his studies of the business cycle. The English edition of German economist Othmar Spann's (1878– 1950) best-selling book[2] on the same subject was also published with the same title. To Mitchell's and Spann's generation of economists, it was obvious that there are, indeed, different types of economics, not just the one monolithic canon, with some scattered dissenters, that we are used to today.

In trying to make order of the history of thought on economic development – on the origins of development economics – I suggest that creating a taxonomy, albeit a crude one, of the existing *types of economics* will assist in understanding the vicissitudes of both theory and history. The basic types of economics can be seen as the following.

*Based on metaphors from biology:*
- The human body (from the Greek tradition and Roman law through the Renaissance to German economist Albert Schäffle in the 1880s).
- Darwinian and Lamarckian evolution. Thorstein Veblen. Schumpeterian and evolutionary economics. Nelson and Winter (1982). The OECD Technology and Economy Programme of the early 1990s.

*Based on metaphors from physics:*
- The invisible hand that maintains the planets' trajectory in the solar system, the Enlightenment 'mechanization of the world picture' (Adam Smith).
- Equilibrium (physics of the 1880s).

The body metaphor for society is found in the codification of Roman law ordered by Justinian in the sixth century, creating a tradition that came to be known as the *body politic*.[3] The most celebrated manifestation of the body metaphor is probably Hobbes' *Leviathan*: from its impressive frontispiece, showing the incarnation of the state literally formed from its citizens, to its intricate taxonomy of man's ills and their respective counterparts in the commonwealth. This 'organic' social system was described by Max Weber as an attempt to understand social interaction by using – as a point of departure – the 'whole' within which the individual acts. The last example of this is German economist Albert Schäffle's four-volume *Bau und Leben der Sozialen Körper*, published in the 1880s, also representing a transition to a Darwinian metaphor.

There were two broad traditions in Renaissance or pre-physics economics, what can be called proto-economics. One was the *descriptive tradition*, dating back to the *De magnalibus urbis mediolani* by Bonvesin de la Riva (1288) of Milan and later works on the Florentine state. The other was an equally ancient *prescriptive tradition* – for example, the *Fürstenspiegel*, or the Princes' primers on how to rule. Examples of the descriptive tradition are the extensive fact-finding missions, like the *visitas* in the Spanish provinces of the New World, which yielded us a wealth of information. Veit von Seckendorff (1626–1692), the first German economist, represented a fusion of these two traditions in his *Teutsche Fürstenstaat* (1656) – a primer on how to rule based on an extensive descriptive survey of the context in which the ruler was to act. Seckendorff's best-selling book, which remained in print for more than 90 years, was preceded by fact-finding missions in the Duchy of Gotha, where the author participated. As discussed in the chapter on German economics in this volume, the important *Additiones* to this book were published after a new fact-finding mission to the Dutch Republic.

Early economics was built on facts: principles were abstracted from praxis and *best practices* defined. This methodology yielded inaccurate tools, such as Weber's *ideal types* or Kaldor's *stylized facts,* but also created important qualitative distinctions between economic activities like increasing and diminishing returns. This type of economics started out as praxis long before it became theory, and the truly great early works in development economics are those that abstract general theories from good practice and create theories explaining why a particular praxis is successful. The best examples in this category are Antonio Serra's *Breve Trattato* (1613), James Steuart's *Inquiry into the Principles of Political Economy* (1757) and Friedrich List's *National System of Political Economy* (1841). Later, with a somewhat different aim, Werner Sombart's six-volume qualitative description of capitalism (1927) represented a crowning achievement in this now virtually defunct tradition.

Explanation, however, was done with varying degrees of sophistication as to the underlying mechanisms at work. To use a metaphor from medicine, some, like Friedrich List, tell us to take an aspirin, while others, like Antonio Serra, tell us much better why aspirin works. While giving us much wider historical evidence of why his aspirin did the job, List – clearly a founding father of the 'national innovation system' approach – was not that clear on the mechanisms that made his formula so successful.

For Schumpeter, Antonio Serra's book was the first scientific treatise in economics. Serra abstracts, from observed practice, the mechanisms that made Venice, virtually devoid of raw materials, so wealthy, and Naples, wealthy in raw materials, so poor. He attributed this contrast in wealth and poverty to inherent differences between economic activities, to geographical differences as they related to trading routes, to the 'quality of the people' and to government policies. At the core of the wealth-producing machinery of Venice, Serra described cumulative causations produced by increasing returns and a large division of labour. This contrasted with the diminishing returns and minimal division of labour in Naples. This qualitative distinction between raw materials and manufacturing production represents a key continuity from Antonio Serra to all later development economics.

Around 150 years later, James Steuart abstracted his theories from English economic practice. He added an extremely important discovery of the 1700s: the synergies between manufacturing and agriculture, also present in David Hume's work. The idea seems to have originated with Leibniz in Germany – where Steuart lived for many years – but Steuart was important in spreading the idea internationally. The discovery of the *synergies* between agriculture and manufacturing – that the proximity of manufacturing greatly improved agricultural practices – represented a great leap forward, and, once described, it was an easy sell. People who travelled in Europe could observe with their own eyes the backward agriculture around an administrative city like Madrid, and the prosperous agriculture around a manufacturing city like Milan. Later, US economists would particularly emphasize the role of manufacturing in creating a market for agricultural goods.

James Steuart's work was immediately translated into German and French, and was much more influential in the catching-up continental European nations than with the English, who were forging ahead at the time. Although they were both Scotsmen and members of the same social clubs, Adam Smith made it a point not to mention Steuart's work in his *Wealth of Nations*. Steuart's work, based on more than twenty years' residence on the European continent, was a manual for catching up and, therefore, at best, to be ignored by the leader.

While the Renaissance understanding was largely qualitative, a mechanization and quantification of the world picture accompanied the rise of the Enlightenment. This invited 'natural' forces of nature and metaphors from physics into economics, starting with the physiocrats (physiocracy – rule of nature, as democracy – rule of the people) and also with Adam Smith's invisible hand. However, there is a significant amnesia about what the 'invisible hand' actually accomplished on the one occasion it is mentioned in *Wealth of Nations* – it made import substitution tariffs unnecessary: 'By preferring the support of domestic to that of foreign industry, he intends only his own security; and he is in this, as in many other cases, led by an invisible hand to promote an end which was not part of his intention.'

While many periods have been characterized by methodological pluralism in economics, there have been at least three periods when metaphors from physics dominated.

| School | Starting point | Peak | Loss of influence |
| --- | --- | --- | --- |
| Physiocracy ('rule of nature') | Quesnay 1758 | 1760s | *c.* 1770 |
| Classical economics | Ricardo 1817 | 1840s | *c.* 1895 |
| Neoclassical synthesis | Samuelson 1948 | 1990s | ?[4] |

The seeming accuracy of physics-based theories has been acquired at the cost of excluding *qualitative differences, diversity, synergies* and *novelty* – all factors present in economic theory from the late 1500s. The exclusion of these factors has made economics into what Lionel Robbins called a *Harmonielehre* – a system where economic harmony is already built into the assumptions. The guiding insight of Derrida's deconstruction was, as far as I understand, that every structure – be it literary, psychological, social, economic, political or religious – that organizes our experience is constituted and maintained through acts of *exclusion*. In the process of including and creating some things, something else inevitably gets left out. The focus on classical and neoclassical economics should therefore be what these theories left out, factors that were generally already there.

The unifying theme in development economics after Adam Smith and David Ricardo has, therefore, been to insist on the re-inclusion of factors that became exogenous with physics-based metaphors. Development was understood as a process of cumulative causations that were the joint effects of factors left out by these metaphors: (i) qualitative differences between economic activities (for example, increasing or diminishing returns, windows of opportunity for innovation); (ii) diversity (the *degree* of division of labour); (iii) synergies (linkages, clusters); (iv) institutions (present from twelfth-century Florence); and (v) novelty (innovations, learning, science, all strongly present from Francis Bacon to James Steuart, but exogenized by Smith). Themes that appeared with Giovanni Botero's study on *The Greatness of Cities* (Italian 1588, English 1607) – that the windows of opportunity for innovations vary greatly from activity to activity, and that it is important for a nation to produce where technological change is greatest – were still explicit in Alfred Marshall's work.

Development economics can, therefore, be seen as a field of study that refuses to yield to the metaphors from physics which portray the market as a mechanism creating automatic harmony. The factors focused on are generally qualitative and rarely quantifiable. When what appeared to be progress in economics increasingly came to follow the path of least mathematical resistance, development economics fought a losing game. 'Hardening the paradigm' carried with it the exclusion of qualitative factors, but the effects of this exclusion vary between rich and poor countries. Wealthy economies are characterized by the very factors that the metaphors from physics leave out: increasing returns, specialization in activities where the opportunities for innovation are the largest, the division of labour and diversity the greatest, synergies and institutions the strongest, and innovation the most intense. Physics-based metaphors – and the set of assumptions they carry with them – therefore tend to not harm rich economies.

Adam Smith made colonialism ethically acceptable. Earlier economists knew that manufacturing was a key to wealth, and Friedrich List's metaphor that Smith's type of economics kicked away the ladder was a most appropriate one. The use of a metaphor that raised the level of abstraction above all qualitative differences – what James Buchanan calls 'the equality assumption' – was an innovation that had enormous political consequences. Clearly, there were also elements of development economics in Adam Smith; the question is, to what extent one accepts the basic metaphor of a harmony-ensuring market or, instead, pursues his many qualifications. Smith the development economist is more clearly present in his earlier work, *A Theory of Moral Sentiments* – especially on the role of the state and on increasing the number of branches of manufacturing – than in *The Wealth of Nations,* written after his meetings with the French physiocrats.

As described in the chapter titled 'Mercantilism and Economic Development' of this volume, economic activities were seen as qualitatively different in contributing to economic growth. In other words, growth is activity-specific. The pre-Ricardian logic worked as follows – if stockbrokers are wealthier than farmers, a nation of stockbrokers would be wealthier than a nation of farmers. In addition, diversity was in itself important, as when Antonio Serra saw maximizing wealth as maximizing the number of professions in a city. Contrasting the huge number of professions in wealthy Venice or Holland with the poverty, monoculture and self-sufficiency in the poor parts of Europe brought that point home.

Diversity creates trade and specialization, generating the synergies that were already referred to as *il ben commune,* or the common weal, in the 1200s. These synergies were seen as key to explaining the wealth of some cities and the poverty of the rural areas. Antonio Serra emphasized the qualitative differences between activities of increasing and diminishing returns as the bases for cumulative causations. Serra is quoted by List and by Wilhelm Roscher, who brought increasing returns back into economics in the mid-nineteenth century, when this distinction became a key argument for the countries that industrialized after England. A 1923 article by Frank Graham prominently raised the issue from a theoretical viewpoint, and this qualitative distinction between increasing and diminishing returns activities – between specialization in raw materials and in manufacturing – underlay early development economics in the 1940s.

Since Henry VII and the 'Tudor Plan' to industrialize England, starting in 1485, the core theme of development economics has been industrialization: *to achieve a diversified economic sector besides agriculture and raw materials.* With this new sector created, agriculture may even serve as an engine of growth, but not alone in monoculture without a manufacturing sector. Underlying the industrialization logic is often – as it was very explicitly with the US economists Daniel Raymond (1820) and Mathew Carey (1821) – a trade-off between 'man the consumer' and 'man the producer' over time. In the short run, pro-industry policies cause man the consumer to pay more for industrial goods. In the long term, however, as a wage-earner, the same person receives wage increases that more than compensate the initial costs, a result of the cumulative causations rooted in increasing returns and a large division of labour. Raymond compares the sacrifice of a nation doing this to a young man sacrificing his wages short-term in order to get an education that will hugely increase his life income as compared to staying in an unskilled job. As the mid-nineteenth century US economists argued, England would have him specialize in being a 'hewer of wood and drawer of water' while she kept her own position as the workshop of the world. Again, we see that the qualitative differences between economic activities – in terms of their ability to absorb skills and education – are key to development theory.

This volume documents the truly impressive continuity of manufacturing industry being key to economic development, and, as argued in the chapter titled 'Development in the History of Economics', the basic toolbox of economic policy used to achieve this goal also presents a remarkable continuity. This volume shows that development economists may, like Paul Rosenstein–Rodan and Albert Hirschman did, disagree over whether industrialization can be achieved through a big push in a large number of sectors or by unbalanced growth pulling the rest of the economy with it. They may focus, as Hans Singer and others did, on how the fruits of technological change are distributed differently in raw materials production than in manufacturing industry. They may, as many did, focus on price fluctuations in the primary sector and price stability in the manufacturing sector. They may, like Gunnar Myrdal and Ragnar Nurkse did, argue that the distinction between increasing and diminishing returns is important because virtuous circles originate in increasing returns industries, while vicious circles begin in diminishing returns industries. They may argue about the role played by foreign trade, an issue that necessarily will vary, both according to the size of the nation in question and its relative degree of development, as List so lucidly pointed out. They may put more or less emphasis on the role and sources of finance, but they never disagree that industrialization should be financed.

Development economists may argue, as John Kenneth Galbraith did when observing the United States of the 1930s, that wages in the primary sector are reversible, while wages in the manufacturing sector are 'sticky'. The distinction between the two sectors may be defined in terms of different elasticities of demand and/or development of the terms of trade. The distinction between agriculture and manufacturing may be explained in terms of how technological change affects the two types of activities differently, through product or process innovations, which again explains Singer's main point that the fruits of technological change can either be harvested in the producing country, as higher wages, or in the consuming country, as lower prices. Like Friedrich List, Hans Singer and George Marshall (when presenting the Marshall Plan), some development economists argue that urbanization with increasing returns industries, and the resulting division of labour between city and countryside, are the basis for western civilization itself. What they all agree on – viewing different aspects of the phenomenon from different angles – is that a combination of manufacturing activities and a large division of labour is a mandatory passage point in order to create a wealthy nation. As pointed out in the chapters two to four, virtually in all these respects, classical development economics recalled influential voices present in economics long before Adam Smith. The pre-Smithian armoury of arguments also added the reduction of unemployment, increasing the tax base by creating high-income individuals, helping solve balance of payments problems, and increasing the velocity of circulation of coinage as arguments in favour of creating a manufacturing sector.

Today, knowledge-intensive services may play much the same role as manufacturing once did. However, this service sector cannot grow and thrive without demand from a diversified manufacturing base. In this sense, synergies among economic sectors – the great eighteenth-century discovery – are also important today for manufacturing and services.

Based on 500 years of development economics, the deindustrialization that has accompanied the Washington Consensus policies since the mid-1980s is particularly grim, and could, with a good understanding of history, have been avoided. 'A strong case could be made for the proposition that ideas about economics had led close to half the world's population to untold suffering', says Joseph Stiglitz. We could argue that at the root of this lies an excessive dependence on an inappropriate physics-based metaphor, rather than on a more diversified economics toolbox.

From this point of view, the World Bank and the International Monetary Fund (IMF) fail to come to grips with the basic problems of physics-based models: its inability to account for diversity, novelty and synergies. Since the late 1980s, in growing recognition of their failure to create wealth, the Washington Consensus prescriptions have gone through the following stages:
- 'get prices right'
- 'get property rights right'
- 'get institutions right'
- 'get governance right'
- 'get competitiveness right'
- 'get national innovation systems right'
- 'get entrepreneurship right'.

All these slogans have been created without leaving behind the mother of all assumptions: the assumption of no diversity and no qualitative differences among economic activities. The Washington Consensus prescriptions represent a sequence of what Michael Porter calls 'single issue management', a simplistic type of management that fails to account for the complexities and interdependencies of real life, and which is therefore doomed to fail. The slogan that is still missing is 'get the economic activities right', which requires allowing for diversity and discarding the equilibrium metaphor. If economic development depends, as may be argued from observing history, on synergies and linkages that can only be created in a dense and finely knit web of diversified increasing returns activities, the sequence of 'insights' and policy prescriptions by the Washington institutions misses the key point.

The previous periods of excess of physics-based economics were both abandoned because of the social problems created. The brief reign of physiocracy in France came to an end when scarcity and dearth caused famines. The social contract – for the French king to feed his people adequately – had been broken, opening the path to the French revolution. The excesses of market optimism in the mid-1840s came to an end with the revolutions of 1848 and 'the social question' that dominated European politics for more than fifty years. The current social problems in the global periphery may start a global version of 1848. In that year, in a speech in Belgium, Marx had insisted that his sole reason for supporting free trade was that it hastened the revolution, and we can imagine that today's revolutionaries are of the same opinion. The lessons from 500 years of development economics are about to be rediscovered. As in the late nineteenth century, it will require a group of dedicated economists, who were surprisingly diverse in their approaches at the time, and perhaps a new Bismarck to accept their views.

Much to the satisfaction of US and German economists of the time, after 1848, John Stuart Mill recanted on the Siamese twin of physics-based economics – the wage funds doctrine (essentially that wages cannot be raised) and the claim that free trade is always preferable. Mill (1848: 3) also described the collective wake-up call when inappropriate theory is rejected:

> It often happens that the universal beliefs of one age of mankind – a belief from which no one *was*, nor without an extraordinary effort of genius and courage *could* at the time be free – become to a subsequent age so palpable an absurdity, that the only difficulty then is to imagine how such a thing can ever have appeared credible. . . . It looks like one of the crude fancies of childhood, instantly corrected by a word from any grown person.

One purpose of this volume is to capture much of the long tradition of development economics and, as already mentioned, to link the early economics traditions with classical development economics from the 1940s onwards. The link between development economics and the theories of Friedrich List is sometimes alluded to, but the connections are rarely traced further back. It will be shown that pre-Smithian economics has much in common with classical development economics. The emphasis on the role of manufacturing, going back to practical policy of the late 1400s and theory of the late 1500s, is one important common element. The editors feel the importance of re-establishing this link to successful strategies of the past. In the perspective of 500 years of successful development strategy, from when Henry VII came to power in England in 1485 to the East Asian 'miracle', physics-based economics merely represented three historical parentheses that inevitably came to an end because of the damage they caused to the poor.

The organizational principle of the volume is mainly chronological, but also going from the general to the particular. In the first chapter, titled 'Mercantilism and Economic Development', Erik S. Reinert and Sophus A. Reinert trace the origins of development economics as a *praxis* originating in the changing world of the Renaissance. As Etienne Laspeyres (1863) so convincingly shows in his work on the history of Dutch economic thought, economic *theory* – as opposed to economic *praxis* – originated in the poor periphery of Europe, not in the rich nations. The poor periphery tried to emulate the economic structure, rather than the economic policies, of the rich nations. It was clear that a key to understanding the wealth of the states most copied – the Dutch Republic and the Republic of Venice – was the absence of agriculture, which had forced the inhabitants into other activities that obviously yielded better standards of living.

In chapter two, titled 'The Italian Tradition of Political Economy', Sophus A. Reinert traces the Italian economic tradition back to its early Renaissance roots, but focuses on the developments of the 1600s and 1700s. Antonio Serra (1613) of Naples, whom Schumpeter refers to as the first economist to have written a scientific treatise on the subject, also ought to be recognized as the first development economist and a precursor of the 'national innovation systems' approach (Reinert and Reinert 2003). An important feature of Italian economic thought in the eighteenth century was the general recognition, by economists representing all regions of the country, that Italy had fallen behind and that the English were beating them at their own game. Sophus A. Reinert argues that these economists were generally in favour of state support for competitive individual initiative in increasing returns manufacturing industries, an approach inspired by earlier thinkers such as Giovanni Botero and Antonio Serra.

In 'German Economics as Development Economics', Erik S. Reinert reviews some enduring characteristics of the German economic tradition over time. After surveying the early cameralist economic policy tradition starting with Veit von Seckendorff (1626–1692), he considers the emergence of academic economics and academic specialization in the eighteenth century. He then turns his attention to the development of the 'German Historical School' in the nineteenth and twentieth centuries, before considering the discourse around the 'Social Problem' involving the Verein für Sozialpolitik from 1872 to 1932.[5] Finally, he suggests that the immediate post-war German experience during 1945–47, when the Morgenthau Plan sought to 'pastoralize', and thus pacify, Germany, following its involvement in the two world wars of the first half of the twentieth century, validates the German economics tradition. He argues that the German economics tradition has consistently been development economics, in the sense that its approach always produced a theory where economic growth is both activity-specific and uneven.

In the chapter titled 'The Capitalist Transformation', Mushtaq Husain Khan explores the importance of social and institutional factors in capitalist transformation. Successful latecomers such as Taiwan and South Korea clearly show that the role of the state is important in economic development, but there is still little consensus on the details. The dominant theories of development, Khan argues, emphasize the need for stable property rights and similar preconditions for efficient markets. Yet, they often fail to account for the larger social transformation necessary to ensure the timely development of 'state capacities to push technological progress through systems of conditional incentives and compulsion'. As he puts it, 'successful catching up has required a range of institutions and interventions that are quite different from classical capitalism'; and an important task facing economists today is not only to identify them, but also to understand the social and institutional structure from which they can arise.

In 'The Pioneers of Development Economics and Modern Growth Theory', Jaime Ros discusses the treatment of modern growth theory by pioneers of development economics, focusing especially on the writings of Paul Rosenstein–Rodan, Ragnar Nurkse and W. Arthur Lewis. He correctly points out that the new interest in modelling uneven development has drawn little from what Paul Krugman has called 'high development theory'. Ros compares these new approaches to those of classical development economics, and casts doubt on the possibility of explaining differences in economic growth among nations by reference to differences in rates of human capital formation.

One of the founders of the American System of Manufactures, Daniel Raymond (1820), who so inspired Friedrich List, would immediately have responded that modern growth theory misses the crucial issue, that is, that different economic activities differ greatly in their ability to absorb new knowledge and technology. Today, the world's most efficient producers of baseballs for the US national sport – a product which all the human capital of the USA has not been able to mechanize – are paid between 30 and 60 cents per hour to hand-sew baseballs in Haiti or the Honduras. On the other hand, the world's most efficient producers of golf balls – a high-tech product – are located in New Bedford, Massachusetts, and are paid 12 to 14 dollars an hour. This unequal exchange – that around forty hours of labour in Haiti are exchanged for an hour of labour in Massachusetts – has been observed since the early days of mercantilism. This reasoning is not made to defend a labour theory of value but is merely intended to show how technology, and its absence, influences differences in rates of growth, wages and welfare. Diversity[6] – as some economic activities cannot be mechanized – opens up new possibilities in a world where some specialize in being poor and uneducated, such as the Haitian baseball sewers.

Educating, without creating a demand for education, is a recipe for mass migration. In Korea, the development of human resources was accompanied by the creation of a local demand for the same human resources. History shows that economic development requires coordination of education policy, industrial policy, innovation policy, trade policy and competition policy. When the Washington institutions and the accompanying research funds succeed, as they now do, in moving our collective focus ahead in a piecemeal and sequential 'single issue management' fashion, as outlined above, it becomes exceedingly difficult to make the case for policy coordination.

Mercantilists generally understood the differences among economic activities, and therefore understood that trade could also be 'war by other means', rather than a system creating world economic harmony. As long as standard economics manages to maintain what James Buchanan calls 'the equality assumption' – that all economic activities are qualitatively alike in contributing to economic growth – mathematical modelling will amount to little more than what the Danish economist Birck, in the 1920s, called 'economic scholasticism' (Reinert 2000).

The chapter on 'International Trade in Early Development Economics' by Amitava Dutt discusses the all-important issue of international trade, which has been seen to produce both factor-price equalization and factor-price polarization, depending on the historical context. He provides an important survey of the writings of early development economists – Paul Rosenstein–Rodan, Ragnar Nurkse, W. Arthur Lewis and particularly Gunnar Myrdal – on the global economy, and the role of the less developed countries. The approaches of these early development economists are discussed both in the framework of standard international trade theory, and in light of subsequent events and contributions.

In 'The Rise and Decline of Latin American Structuralism and Dependency Theory', Alfredo Saad–Filho reviews two influential Latin American theories of development and underdevelopment – structuralism and dependency theory – as well as their principal claims and most important limitations. The theories challenged the hegemony of mainstream (neoclassical) economic thought and argued that its linear interpretation of development was inadequate. Instead, the world economy is divided into centre and periphery, and the periphery does not tend to follow the trajectory of those in the centre. While the structuralists claimed that better economic policies could foster development in the periphery, the dependency theorists argued that genuine development was impossible under capitalism.

Dependency theory reflects the mercantilist theories of 'good' and 'bad' trade, that exporting raw materials while importing manufactured goods was 'bad trade'. Ultimately, however, these Latin American processes ran out of steam. We can speculate as to why. Friedrich List certainly would have faulted the Latin Americans for not taking the next logical step to regional integration. While East Asia temporarily protected new industries from the world markets while encouraging them to export, Latin America created a technological backwater by permanently protecting old industries for small home markets. These greenhouse industries could not survive opening up to world markets without an intermediate 'creative destruction' of a Latin American regional market. Instead, the immediate opening up to the world market has created a destructive destruction in most Latin American countries.

As a postscript to the volume, Tamás Szentes, one of the grand old men of development economics, offers a retrospective view of development in the history of economics. He outlines development economics as a separate field of study, 'born' after World War II. Since its beginning, the major concerns of development economics have been about the sources of economic development, the origins of the 'wealth of nations', and the conditions and factors promoting development. However, Szentes emphasizes, long before the birth of 'development economics', the question of economic development loomed large to writers of the classical, Marxian, historical, institutional, Keynesian and neoclassical schools. As he pertinently points out, *a priori* assumptions about the nature of man and the market often play an important role in formulating theories as well as critiques.

*Reality Economics: The Knowledge- and Production-based Other Canon of Economics*

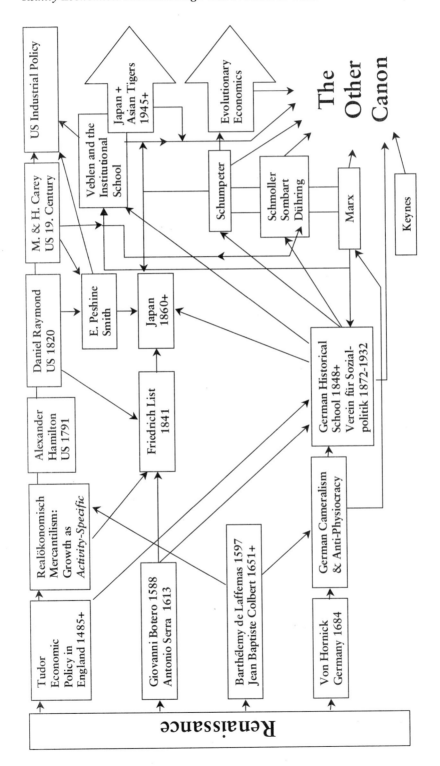

This volume is intended to contribute to the recognition of a long tradition of thought where economic growth and development are, by the very nature of things, an uneven process – as a consequence of the diversity among humans, among firms and among technologies. Figure 1 attempts to capture the filiations of this type of theory, from the Renaissance through to the modern day, showing how generations of economists have influenced each other in sequence (see Reinert and Daastøl 2004 for a discussion). Curiously, in all cases but that of Keynes, it is fairly easy to trace how one generation influences the next, or – as in the case of Antonio Serra – how a reprint, almost two centuries after the first edition, influenced important development economists like Friedrich List and Wilhelm Roscher. The long traditions of non-physics economics merge into what I call The Other Canon, which, in the perspective of five centuries of the practice of economic development, has been the type of theory that has lifted nations out of poverty, starting with England in 1485.

**Notes**

[1] For a discussion of the use of metaphors in economics, see McCloskey (1985), Mirowski (1989, 1994).

[2] Spann's *Die Haupttheorien der Volkswirtschaftslehre* first appeared in 1911. By 1936, this book had reached twenty-four editions and a total of 1,20,000 copies were printed in German. There were numerous translations, including different editions with different titles in the US and the UK.

[3] Catherine de Pizan's description from 1406 exemplifies this approach. 'For just as the human body is not whole, but defective and deformed when it lacks any of its members, so the body politic cannot be perfect, whole, nor healthy if all the estates of which we speak are not well joined and united together. Thus, they can help and aid each other, each exercising the office which it has to, which diverse offices ought to serve only for the conservation of the whole community, just as the members of the human body aid to guide and nourish the whole body. And in so far as one of them fails, the whole feels it and is deprived by it.' (Pizan 1994: 90)

[4] Paul Samuelson's own 2004 article in *Journal of Economic Perspectives* (Samuelson 2004), at the age of 89, can be seen as beginning a revision of the neoclassical synthesis similar to that of John Stuart Mill's recanting on the main principles of Ricardo and the classical economists.

[5] Literally, 'The Association for Social Policy', an association in which most German economists were active.

[6] This is a key aspect discussed in many of the papers in Reinert, ed. (2004).

**References**

de Roover, Raymond (1955), 'Scholastic Economics: Survival and Lasting Influence from the 16th Century to Adam Smith', *Quarterly Journal of Economics*, 69: 161–90.

Laspeyres, Etienne (1863), *Geschichte der Volkswirthschaftlichen Anschauungen der Niederländer und ihrer Litteratur zur Zeit der Republik*, 'Preisschriften gekrönt und herausgegeben von der Fürstlich Jablonowski'schen Gesellschaft zu Leipzig', Vol. 11. (Leipzig: Härtel). Reprinted in 1961 (Nieuwkoop: De Graaf) and 1999 (Dillenburg: Wissenschaftliches Antiquariat Lothar Gruber).

McCloskey, Donald (1985), *The Rhetoric of Economics* (Madison: University of Wisconsin Press).

Mill, John Stuart (1848), *The Principles of Political Economy* (London: Longmans, Green and Co.).

Mirowski, Philip (1989), *More Heat than Light: Economics as Social Physics, Physics as Nature's Economics* (Cambridge: Cambridge University Press).

———, ed. (1994), *Natural Images in Economic Thought: 'Markets Read in Tooth and Claw'* (Cambridge: Cambridge University Press).

Pizan, Catherine de (1994), *The Book of the Body Politic* (Cambridge: Cambridge University Press).

Reder, Melvin (1999), *Economics: The Culture of a Controversial Science* (Chicago: University of Chicago Press).

Reinert, Erik S. (2000), 'Full Circle: Economics from Scholasticism through Innovation and back into Mathematical Scholasticism; Reflections around a 1769 price essay: "Why is it that Economics so far has Gained so Few Advantages from Physics and Mathematics?"', *Journal of Economic Studies,* 27 (4–5).

——— (2003), 'Austrian Economics and the Other Canon: The Austrians between the Activistic–Idealistic and the Passivistic–Materialistic Tradition of Economics', in Jürgen Backhaus, ed., *Evolutionary Economic Thought, European Contributions and Concepts* (Cheltenham: Edward Elgar).

———, ed. (2004), *Globalization, Economic Development and Inequality: An Alternative Perspective* (Cheltenham: Edward Elgar).

Reinert, Erik S. and Arno Daastøl (2004), 'The Other Canon: The History of Renaissance Economics, Its Role as an Immaterial and Production-Based Canon in the History of Economic Thought and in the History of Economic Policy', in Reinert, ed. (2004).

Reinert, Sophus A. and Erik S. Reinert (2003), 'An Early National Innovation System: The Case of Antonio Serra's 1613 *Breve Trattato'*, *Institutions and Economic Development,* 1 (3): 87–119.

Samuelson, Paul (2004), 'Where Ricardo and Mill Rebut and Confirm Arguments of Mainstream Economics Supporting Globalization', *Journal of Economic Perspectives,* 18 (3): 135–46.

# Contributors

AMITAVA K. DUTT is Professor, Economics Department, Notre Dame University.

MUSHTAQ HUSAIN KHAN is Senior Lecturer, Economics Department, School of Oriental and African Studies, University of London.

ERIK S. REINERT is Professor of Economics at the University of Oslo, and heads The Other Canon Foundation, Oslo, Norway.

SOPHUS A. REINERT is Carl Schurz Fellow, Krupp Chair of Public Finance and Fiscal Sociology, University of Erfurt.

JAIME ROS is Professor of Economics, Notre Dame University.

ALFREDO SAAD–FILHO is Senior Lecturer in Political Economy of Development, School of Oriental and African Studies, University of London.

TAMÁS SZENTES is Professor Emeritus, Budapest University of Economic Science and Public Administration, and a member of the Hungarian Academy of Sciences.

# Mercantilism and Economic Development

## Schumpeterian Dynamics, Institution-building and International Benchmarking

*Erik S. Reinert and Sophus A. Reinert*

In most of the arts and sciences – from astronomy to zoology – the Renaissance represents a qualitative watershed in human history, and historians are generally united in considering it a period of unprecedented intellectual ferment. Echoes of da Vinci, Galileo and Machiavelli still resound in the way we approach art, science and human coexistence, and it is noticeable how these developments came 'out of Italy' (Braudel 1991). As a precondition for this, the Renaissance was also a period when the productive powers of small European city-states allowed a large part of the population to live free from poverty. Where feudalism had provided wealth for the very few and misery for most, the city-states of the Renaissance for the first time witnessed a situation where artisans, merchants and public employees filled the ranks of a new middle class.

### The Debate on Mercantilism: A Brief Overview

In this picture, the economics profession stands out with a completely different view of the period. The fact that 300 years of economic theory and practice tend to be lumped together under the label of 'mercantilism', as if it were a homogeneous mass, alone points to a rather superficial treatment of a long period with much variety. The common view today is that mercantilism was 'an irrational social order' (Ekelund and Tollison 1981: 6), the basic feature of which was that economists collectively made the serious mistake of confusing gold with wealth. This practice is referred to as the 'Midas fallacy' (*chrysohedonism*), after the mythological king whose touch converted everything to gold. Starting with Adam Smith, this Midas fallacy has been the common interpretation of mercantilism, and is also found in today's histories of economic thought. The Midas legend had, however, been known as a warning since Roman times, and the mercantilists themselves had used it to explicitly refute this view of wealth (Barbon 1696). Fairly recently, two American authors have offered what appears to be an alternative interpretation of mercantilism, that of a society seeking rents, presumed to be non-productive (Ekelund and Tollison 1981).

Both these standard interpretations, of mercantilism and of pre-Smithian economics in general, present us with serious problems. How is it possible that human civilization as we know it, from the birth of modern cities to the Industrial Revolution, is recognized as a product of genius in all human endeavours but economics? A field whose practitioners supposedly 'did not rely on any "true" empirical knowledge of economic reality whatsoever' (Magnusson on Heckscher, in Magnusson 1994: 15), but were committed to hideous methodological errors, wrong economic policies and false goals? Mercantilism has, in a sense, been set up like an irrational 'hell', a strawman against which classical and neoclassical economic rationality increases its splendour. But is it possible that the Industrial Revolution, which Adam Smith lived through without even noticing it, came into being *in spite of* the stupid and irrational economic policies of the preceding period? Only in the bigoted historiographical tradition of 'manifest destiny' – that the greatness of the United States is God-given, regardless of policy – is it possible to ignore the fact that the US economy was built on the key principles of mercantilism for well over 100 years, starting with Alexander Hamilton in 1791.[1] The titles of the most influential US economics books of the time testify to their mercantilist origins (Carey 1822).

Or, do we dare think that the mercantilist policies actually carried out, to a large extent, were in fact wise policies, given the circumstances? In this chapter, we claim that the latter is the case; indeed, we argue that production-focused mercantilist policies have been a mandatory passage point for nations that have taken the step from poor to wealthy, from England starting in 1485 to South Korea in the 1980s. This 'mercantilist' toolbox of the generic developmental state, the basic principles of which, we claim, have changed very little over the years – gaining somewhat in sophistication over time but keeping to the same basic doctrines – is reproduced in Appendix 1. We argue that this represents a collection of economic principles and policy tools typical of mercantilism across Europe, including its local variants – Cameralism in Germany and Colbertism in France.

One fundamental problem of interpreting mercantilism is that few historians of economic thought actually read the original texts. Magnusson (1994: 50), discussing the previously mentioned work of Ekelund and Tollison, argues, 'They also seem totally uninterested in what the mercantilist writers actually wrote' – a criticism that may be extended to many histories of economic thought. Furthermore, the analysis of mercantilism frequently suffers from what Perrotta (1993: 21) calls 'percursorism': that any idea, instead of being judged by its relevance in a given context, is either hailed as a surprising early anticipation of a healthy neoclassical economic principle or as an example of hopelessly ill-conceived theories (Ashley 1920: II, 381).

Additionally, few studies of mercantilism cover more than one or two language areas. The truly pan-European distribution of common principles and policies, particularly in the period from 1650 to 1770, is therefore seldom noticed. The matter is further complicated by the fact that the long-recognized authority on the mercantilist system, the Swede, Eli Filip Heckscher (1931),[2] made a rather static analysis of a tradition for which he had little sympathy, and therefore depicted as primitive and pre-analytical. Likewise, the first compiler of

Spanish mercantilist literature, Manuel Colmeiro, was a recent convert to economic liberalism and was therefore also fundamentally opposed to the system he was attempting to describe. All in all, the modern history of mercantilism has largely been written as if Attila and his Huns had been put in charge of writing the history of the Roman empire.

Our interpretation of mercantilism relies on the insights provided when the mercantilist texts themselves are studied in the historical context in which they were written. It coincides with recent views from the European periphery, by Cosimo Perrotta (1988, 1991, 1993) in Italy, Ernest Lluch (1973, 1997, 2000) and others in Spain, and Lars Magnusson (1991, 1994) in Sweden. This 'new' and context-specific interpretation largely corresponds to the view of mercantilism held by the German Historical School, in that most of them acknowledge the interdependency of mercantilism and state-building.[3]

We shall, however, grant some validity to the two other theories of mercantilism – although both arrive at conclusions that, in our view, are fundamentally incorrect – because they grab different ends of the problems that mercantilists attempted to address. This applies both to Smith's Midas fallacy approach and to the rent-seeking approach of Ekelund and Tollison. Indeed, the outflow of bullion in the form of gold and silver was an acute *symptom* of a set of economic problems that affected most nations and, therefore, a matter that contemporary writers had to attend to.[4] Early mercantilist policy advice falls into two broad categories – the simplistic and populist one that attempted to cure the symptoms evident in the financial sphere simply by manipulating financial variables; and the one advanced by what we have called 'mercantilists of the real economy' (*realökonomische Merkantilisten*), who sought the underlying causes of the problems in the sphere of production.[5] The most heated of all mercantilist debates were between these two types of theorists – the 'monetarists' and the 'productionists' – between de Santis and Serra in Naples (1610–13), and between Misselden and Malynes in England (1622–23). By the late 1600s, however, the emphasis was clearly more on the 'real economy'. John Locke ([1691] 1696) was one of the latest pure monetarists. Recurrent financial bubbles nevertheless recreated relatively shortlived floods of books on speculation, as was the case in the 1720s.

In this chapter, we focus on the 'productionists' who were everywhere the great majority; in fact, most mercantilists are extremely clear in their analysis that the key to wealth lies in the sphere of production rather than finance.[6] In this sense, present-day economics suits the standard accusation made against mercantilism, due to its predominant focus on financial and monetary values, much better than mercantilism itself does. The recent handling of the economic crisis in Argentina, deindustrializing the nation and halving its wage bill in order to pursue an arbitrarily chosen monetary goal, is the kind of policy against which the majority of mercantilists would have protested vehemently.

One of the more curious aspects of capitalist economic theory is that it does not allow for other than a 'normal' profit, identifying 'perfect competition' or 'commodity competition' as both the normal state of affairs and the goal of the system. The 'normal' participant in the economy is the farmer who has no influence over price, and the success stories of history, from the steel magnates to Henry Ford and Bill Gates, are, in this view, abhorred as 'rent-seekers', by definition a negative concept. The Ekelund and Tollison view of mercantilism can only be understood from this neoclassical/neo-Austrian point of view and, in a sense, they do identify an important aspect of mercantilism: the 'perfect competition' of the farmers did not and still does not produce significant wealth. Even the most efficient farmers in the world today, those in the United States and in the European Community, need heavy subsidies in order to achieve a decent income. Pre-Smithian economics can only be understood as system-building, 'Schumpeterian', dynamic imperfect competition. Two of its most successful economic institutions, *patents* and *protection* (for industrialization, rather than for revenue) were both created during the late 1400s in order to achieve this dynamic imperfect competition through artificial creation of time-limited market power. Like any businessman today, the mercantilists understood that 'perfect competition' is a situation where serious wealth cannot be accumulated and economic development cannot take place.

It has previously been argued (Reinert and Daastøl 2004) that dynamic rents spread in the economy at three levels: (i) to the entrepreneur in the form of profit; (ii) to the employee in terms of employment; and (iii) through the government in terms of increased taxes. Under conditions of rapid technological change, as with the 'productivity explosions' of new technologies (Perez 2004), this 'triple-level rent-seeking' represents a hugely positive-sum game in the producing country. We argue that a core objective of mercantilism was achieving this 'triple-level rent-seeking'. Institutions like patents, protection and apprenticeship, created 300 years before Adam Smith, and scientific academies, created almost a century before his writings, would help increase the size of the economic pie, increasing profits, the wage bill and governments' ability to tax.

### Changing Mentality and the Origins of Renaissance Wealth Creation

The very idea of economic development, however, was an early mercantilist innovation. When George Soros recently claimed that 'globalization is not a zero sum game' (Soros 2002), he unwittingly touched upon the very problem that faced economic thinkers as the idea of development emerged at the end of the Renaissance. For the longest time, the world was considered a finite place, locked in a cyclical system of cosmic equilibrium. This traditional zero-sum model of the universe was codified by Aristotle (*Politics* 1328b, vii, ix, 3) and, channelled by the scholastics, came to dominate the European cosmology into the early modern period.[7] Sir Thomas Browne (1605–1682) encapsulated this view when he argued that 'all cannot be happy at once for, because the glory of one state depends upon the ruins of another, there is a revolution and vicissitude of their greatness' (Browne 1643: xvii), and the early 'balance of trade' argument was strongly related to this theory that 'one man's gain must be another man's loss' (St Jerome in Finkelstein 2000: 89). Economic thought and, in many ways, economic development, were thus shackled by fear of social instability. This, however, slowly eroded in the late Renaissance.

Several factors combined to unlock this zero-sum world view.[8] Many of the necessary elements can be traced far back in time, but only during the Renaissance did they achieve a critical mass sufficient to profoundly change society in the whole of the Italian peninsula and, later, the rest of Europe. First of all, the undeniable urban bias of wealth creation was, at the time, identified as a result of *synergic effects*, what the Florentine chancellor Brunetto Latini (*c.* 1210–1294) had called the 'common good'. This *ben comune* that made some cities so wealthy (Machiavelli in Reinert and Daastøl 1997) sprang from an organic social harmony – seeing the body as the metaphor for society – which was also an inheritance from the scholastics.[9] This idea of a synergic *common good* forms the axis around which many mercantilists wrote. It must be emphasized that the important discovery of the role of the individual during the Renaissance was superimposed upon the idea of a synergic common weal of society. Mercantilism, like later German economics, had a dual vision where the interests both of society and of the individual had to be considered, and, at times, had to be traded off against one another (see the chapter titled 'The Italian Tradition of Political Economy' in this volume).

Secondly, the Aristotelian view of society as a zero-sum game slowly gave way to an understanding that new wealth could be *created* through innovations. Indeed, the very meaning of the word *innovations* changed from being a potentially heretical activity (as when Roger Bacon was arrested for 'suspicious innovations' in 1277 in Oxford) to being the new carrier of human welfare and happiness, when Francis Bacon wrote *An Essay on Innovations* a little more than 300 years later (Reinert and Daastøl 1997). New scientific breakthroughs, and geographical and scientific explorations slowly changed the static medieval world view. This growing understanding of an infinite and expanding cosmos was a precondition for the mercantilist reinterpretation of the economic sphere: as cosmos expanded unendingly, so could the economy. A remarkable synergy could be observed between *innovation* and *exploration*, between theory and practice, in weaving the new European cosmology.

Thirdly, religion loosened its grip on society and opened up to innovations. With the fall of Constantinople to the Turks, Byzantine philosophers moved to Italy and brought with them religious views that were more open to man's role as a co-creator, rather than merely a caretaker, in God's plan. Man's creation in the image of God indeed made a life of invention and innovation *a pleasurable duty* (Reinert and Daastøl 1997). Thus, around 1600, as in Francis Bacon's *New Atlantis*, a never-ending frontier of new knowledge was drawn up for mankind, transformed 'from a spectator into an owner and master of nature' (Koyré 1957: vii).

The Italian economic historian and many times prime minister, Amintore Fanfani, encapsulated the shift from scholasticism to mercantilism: 'while scholasticism thinks of an order in equilibrium, mercantilism thinks of an order in growth' (Fanfani 1955: 149). We would argue that neoclassical economics, with its focus on the allocation of scarce resources and equilibrium, in many ways, represents a return to scholasticism (Reinert 2000a).

### Observing Spain and the Dutch Republic: Mercantilism as National Benchmarking

'Mercantilism was born in response to the failure of Spain', says Perrotta (1993: 19), referring to the 1500s. We could add that mercantilism further developed, during the 1600s and 1700s, in reaction to the successes of the Dutch Republic and Colbert's France. The best mercantilist writers were practical men, not people dedicated to what used to be called 'metaphysical speculations'. One logical approach to establishing a national economic policy was to look for what had worked, and not worked, in other nations. The European scene provided examples of both poor and rich areas, and the observations of these successful and unsuccessful economies became a major source of inspiration for the economic theory and policy of laggard nations. Economics as a science was therefore not born in wealthy and successful areas – in Venice or in the Dutch Republic, where wealth only seemed 'natural' – but in the poorer cities and nation-states (Laspeyres 1863) that were trying to understand what factors had created the few 'islands' of wealth in an otherwise poor Europe (some were islands in more than one sense, which is part of the clue).

We argue, then, that one of the key tools of mercantilism, as well as its inspiration, was benchmarking successful and less successful nations, a practice already existent in the late 1400s (Defoe 1728). Starting from around 1550, Europe provided one outstanding experience of national economic failure – Spain, and two examples of unquestionable economic success – Venice and the Dutch Republic. The basic question was a relatively simple one. Everyone knew that huge amounts of gold and silver flowed into Spain from the Americas. Starting around 1550, however, it became increasingly clear that this flow of bullion did not cause generalized wealth in Spain. The gold and silver ended up elsewhere, in nations that generally had no mines. Wealth left nations producing raw materials, even if the raw materials were gold and silver, and accumulated in nations housing a diversified manufacturing sector.

Spain became increasingly indebted to foreign bankers after about 1550, and gradually lost its financial independence. The monopolies of Spanish agricultural supplies, like wine and olive oil for the American colonies, caused very high food prices in the peninsula and, with the inflow of species, contributed to rampant inflation. Spanish industries like silk, iron and steel, which had previously been competitive in European markets, died out. The country was deindustrialized and flooded with imports, which caused the species that flowed in from the American colonies to leave the country at the same speed, or even faster. Wealthy farmers, protected by a monopoly and very inelastic supply of wine and oil, could purchase noble titles that exempted them from paying taxes. Church property and organizations were also exempt from taxes, leaving the tax burden on the few artisans and industrialists who survived the flood of imports. The powerful *Mesta*, an organization of sheep farmers, fortified its power with loans to the crown, and worked like a state within a state. Large tracts of mort-main[10] land belonging to the church remained uncultivated. A huge clerical class added to a general contempt for manual work; huge unemployment, underemployment and large numbers of beggars complete this brief picture of Spain in rapid decay. Money was made in Spain from financial transactions that did not promote the productive system, from *censos,* that is, financial loans and mortgages, and from *juros,* that is, privileges, titles and rights granted by the king in exchange for loans. A very interesting aspect here is the extent to which Spanish economists at the time clearly saw the forces behind the economic ills of the country, and provided theoretical and practical remedies. 'History records few instances of either such able diagnosis of fatal social ills by any group of moral philosophers or of any such utter disregard by statesmen of sound advice', said the American historian Earl Hamilton (Hamilton 1932: 237).

On the other side of the European economic spectrum, we find the united Dutch provinces. Many mercantilist tracts, starting with Giovanni Botero (1590), contain descriptions of their wealth and, after the death of 'the great Colbert' in 1683, similarly, of the success of French policies. In various forms, the statement that manufactures were the real gold mines, much more valuable than the actual gold mines themselves, is found all over Europe during the 1600s and 1700s, from Giovanni Botero (1590), Tommaso Campanella (1602) and Antonio Genovesi (1770s) in Italy, to Anders Berch, the first economics professor outside Germany in Sweden (Berch 1747). The Spanish mercantilist Geronymo de Uztariz ([1724] 1752), in the Foreword to Goyeneche (1717), whose main work was translated into both French and English, commented from a particularly good vantage point, being a Spaniard and having lived in Holland and Italy for twenty-three years. Uztariz's conclusion is in line with the contemporary mainstream: '[Manufactures] is a mine more fruitful of gain, riches, and plenty, than those of Potosi.'[11]

Josuah Child, a governor of the British East India Company and one of the more famous mercantilists, encapsulated this benchmarking attitude to economic policy by arguing: 'If we intend to have the Trade of the World, we must imitate the Dutch, who make the worst as well as the best of all manufactures, that we may be in a capacity of serving all Markets, and all Humors' (Child 1693: 90). Similarly, Child opens his 1668 book with a comment on 'the prodigious increase of the Netherlanders' which is 'the envy of the present and may be the wonder of all future generations'. 'And yet,' he adds, 'the means whereby they have thus advanced themselves, are sufficiently obvious, and in a great measure imitable by most other nations . . . which I shall endeavour to demonstrate in the following discourse' (Child 1668). The French observers of the period, Huet (1722) perhaps being the most detailed, found not only a country specialized in manufacturing – where close to 30 per cent of the labour force was already engaged in manufacturing in the early 1500s – but also a system of synergies that brings to mind the old Italian idea of a *ben comune.* It was clear to most astute observers that the wealth of Holland rested on the synergic interdependence of manufacturing, long-distance trade and fisheries, where 'one factor gave strength to the other and vice versa', as Antonio Serra explained the Venetian system.

A brief case study of the Dutch city of Delft in the seventeenth century shows how synergies created by a diversified base of activities created knowledge and spill-overs between seemingly unrelated activities. In Delft, it is indeed possible to identify a closely knit maritime–scientific–artistic cluster, where innovations leapt to and from very different sectors of the economy. The case of Delft brings together, in the very same productive–scientific cluster, the sectors and elements that are seen, in the German tradition, as being the important driving forces of capitalism, all in an interwoven whole:

- the quest for military power, in this case through the navy, as in Werner Sombart's *War and Capitalism* (Sombart 1913a)
- the quest for luxury, in this case art, as in Sombart's *Luxury and Capitalism* (Sombart 1913b).
- The quest for scientific knowledge, as in Sombart's work on capitalism (Sombart 1902) and Thorstein Veblen's 'idle curiosity'.

These three forces interacted in creating serendipitous economic development in Delft, and a profession curiously uniting the three seemingly unrelated fields – maritime warfare, art and scientific development – was that of the producer of glass lenses, *the lens grinder.*

Dutch artists invented oil painting and painting on canvases. The raw materials for these inventions – linseed oil, linen and hemp fibre – were widely used in Dutch shipbuilding and were readily available, but not as readily to artists of other schools. Taking over the leadership from Florence, in the seventeenth century, Delft emerged as a centre for the scientific production of glass lenses. Important improvements to the microscope were also made there (Ruestow 1996). Delft's natural scientist and microscope-maker, Antoni van Leeuwenhoek (1632–1723), found a synergy between the production of woollen cloth, the main industry of the day, and his scientific work, because the hand lenses he developed were used extensively to inspect cloth (Huerta 2003: 33). Similarly, lens-making was integrated with the development of Flemish art – bringing together the history of art and the history of science – through the work of the Delft painter Jan Vermeer (1632–1675), whose painting techniques included seeing his motifs through lenses and the *camera obscura*, an apparatus similar to a primitive camera (Steadman 2001). Vermeer also keenly participated in aspects of the discoveries surrounding him in Delft: the geographical discoveries of the Dutch navy and the discoveries in the natural sciences made possible by improvements of the microscope by Leeuwenhoek and his colleagues.[12] The navy and the merchant marine constituted the largest demand for lenses for binoculars but, as mentioned, lenses were also in demand among natural scientists and producers of early microscopes. The Delft lens grinders thus formed the core of an extremely dynamic and path-breaking cluster including such diverse actors as the navy, the woollen industry, painters like Vermeer, natural scientists and microscope builders.

Another product linking the three clusters – war (navy), luxury (art) and 'idle curiosity' (science) – in Holland at the time was map-making. Holland's position as a seafaring power demanded not only binoculars and naval instruments, but also up-to-date maps.[13] Vermeer's fascination with maps and explorations is clear in many of his paintings; one author has commented on his 'mania for maps'. Such synergic cumulative causations and the path dependency they created were, no doubt, at the core of knowledge creation and the process of economic growth (Arthur 1989). They were, however, neither possible to reproduce in any meaningful way by quantitative methods only, nor apparent through the lenses of methodological individualism.

The enormous diversity of economic activities was observed and commented on by all contemporary economists who wrote about the Dutch Republic. This is also apparent in the early economic journals (Zincke 1746–67). The role of diversity and the resulting creative serendipity bring back the issue of 'monoculture' in traditional development economics and in agricultural societies, where such creative linkages do not appear among professions that trade with each other. A community of milk producers and a nation of banana producers have very little to sell to each other. By emulating the Dutch economic structure rather than Dutch economic policies necessarily, and by avoiding the pitfalls of Spain, the mercantilists revealed their conviction in common economic principles:

- Economic development is *activity-specific*, created by some economic activities (manufacturing) rather than others. (Due to stagnant productivity, diminishing returns and monoculture, without synergies in agriculture.[14])
- Economic development is a *synergic* process: the greater the division of labour and the number of professions, the greater the wealth (already very clear in Serra 1613).
- The targeting, support and protection of *manufacturing* were argued in terms of its ability to:
  (i) create wealth
  (ii) create employment
  (iii) solve balance of payments problems
  (iv) increase the velocity of circulation of money.
- Starting in the 1700s, great emphasis was put on the beneficial synergies between manufacturing and agriculture: only where there was manufacturing, was there successful agriculture (Justi in Germany, Galiani in Italy, Hume in England).[15]

The mercantilists are generally accused of not having a 'model' for development. In our view, the model comes out clearly and consistently both across time – from the first Spanish and Italian writers in the 1500s to Friedrich List in the 1840s, and across the European continent. The economic essence of mercantilism was to line up private and public vested interests by getting nations into increasing return industries that create virtuous circles of development.

We would argue that adherence to the above principles has been a *man-*

*datory passage point* for all nations progressing from poor to rich, including Korea in the 1960s and 1970s. When classical and neoclassical economics disallowed their *de jure* or *de facto* colonies from following these principles, they were, as Friedrich List put it, in reality, 'kicking away the ladder' that they themselves had used to climb to wealth.

The most fundamental difference between mercantilist economics and neoclassical economics is that the mercantilist policy recommendations were highly context-dependent – protecting manufacturing industry could be the right thing to do in one context, while promoting free trade could be right in another, whereas the policy recommendations of neoclassical economics are independent of context.

### Mercantilist Dynamics and Institutions:
### Activity-Specific Growth and Context-Specific Policy

Economic institutions have been brought to the forefront in the development debate during the last decade. It is generally agreed that economic activities and their institutions co-evolve, and attempts at establishing causality – to what extent institutions are created through *demand-pull* or *supply-push* – can therefore easily run into a chicken-and-egg type of problem. The mercantilist view of institutions, from very early on, was that institution-building was fundamentally a *demand-pull* phenomenon, that *the mode of production of a society* would determine its institutions. In 1620, Francis Bacon formulated a view that was to dominate the social sciences for almost the next two centuries: 'There is a startling difference between the life of men in the most civilized province of Europe, and in the wildest and most barbarous districts of New India. This difference comes not from the soil, not from climate, not from race, but from *the arts.*' Francis Bacon was crystal clear on the causality in question: man's activities, his mode of production, determine his institutions. In a similar vein, Carlota Perez (2004) recently argued the relationship between technological change and human institutions.

When Johan Jacob Meyen, a German scientist, stated in 1769, 'It is known that a primitive people does not improve its customs and institutions later to find useful industries, but the other way around' (Reinert 2000a), he expressed an understanding of causality that was considered common sense at the time. This would appear to run counter to the standard World Bank view that the lack of institutions *per se* can be blamed for the poor performance of so many third world countries. To the mercantilists, it would not be meaningful to attempt to understand the institutional development of Europe independently of the underlying strategy of industrialization that prompted the establishment of so many key institutions. The patent system was invented in Venice in the late 1400s with this purpose, and the establishment of an apprentice system in England under Elizabeth I cannot be understood outside the context of a highly successful Tudor strategy of building English woollen manufactures during the 1500s. The establishment of scientific academies in the 1700s, promoted particularly by Gottfried

Wilhelm von Leibniz and Christian Wolff, cannot be understood independently of their strategy of building German economic activities outside agriculture. The success of these diversification strategies, in turn, created new institutional arrangements.

These mercantilist institutions cannot be understood outside a context of nations seeking to escape a comparative advantage in producing raw materials, a strategy that cannot be understood in the neoclassical framework of the Washington Consensus. We would argue that the present focus on institutions views them as outside the context of what they were created to accomplish. In reality, a large number of these institutions are part of a much broader process of economic development that is incompatible with the internal logic of current mainstream economics. Seeing institutions independently of the productive system they support and sustain is not meaningful, and attempting to establish scientific academies in hunting and gathering tribes is, therefore, attacking the problem from the wrong end. History shows that only societies that have achieved a certain level of manufacturing and/or other increasing return activities have ever achieved the 'right' institutions or any degree of 'competitiveness'. Experience accumulated over hundreds of years shows that today's maxim of 'getting institutions right' cannot be solved independently of 'getting into the right kinds of economic activities'.

Perhaps the most fundamental methodological difference between mercantilism and neoclassical economics is that the mercantilists, like any successful businessman today, see economic activities as being qualitatively different. The whole colonial system was based on this crucial insight. 'Linen industry is proper only for countries where they can have flax and hemp cheap, and where the common people work at very easy rates', wrote the English mercantilist Charles Davenant (1696: 42). The woollen industry, on the other hand, was able to maintain much higher wages. When the English king prohibited the Irish from exporting woollen manufactures in 1699, he therefore knew that England was 'underdeveloping' its Irish colony: 'No Wise State, if it has the Means of preventing the Mischief, will leave its Ruin in the Power of another Country' Davenant (1699: 125).

As also indicated in this volume's chapter on German Cameralism, the mercantilists were clearly aware that they were keeping the colonies poor. Most saw this as a natural part of the world power game, while a few defended the practice by saying that since everyone else did so, England had to follow the same policy. Some, like Justi in Germany in the 1750s, thought colonialism would soon end because the people in the colonies knew they were being fooled. This was, of course, what happened in the United States, which suffered from not being allowed to establish manufacturing industries.

By establishing itself as the workshop of the world, importing raw materials and exporting manufactured goods, England experienced the most dramatic increase in wealth the world had yet seen. It was therefore of vital importance to keep things that way:

> That all Negroes shall be prohibited from weaving either Linnen or Woollen, or spinning or combing of Wooll, or working at any Manufacture of Iron, further than making it into Pig or Bar iron: That they be also prohibited from manufacturing of Hats, Stockings, or Leather of any Kind. . . . Indeed, if they set up Manufactures, and the Government afterwards shall be under a Necessity of stopping their Progress, we must not expect that it will be done with the same Ease that now it may (Gee 1729: 81).

When the colonies demanded to establish their own manufactures, their attention could be diverted by allowing them to export their raw materials to other European countries:

> Because People in the Plantations, being tempted with a free Market for their Growths all over *Europe*, will all betake themselves to raise them, to answer the prodigious Demand of that extensive Free Trade, and their Heads be quite taken off from Manufactures, the only thing which our Interest can clash with theirs. . . . (Decker [1744] 1751)

In our view, the parallel to today's situation is clear. A large number of third world countries have been deindustrialized during the last decades (Reinert 2003, 2004b), but they are kept politically at bay with promises of being able to export their agricultural products to Europe and the United States.

As already mentioned, two important mercantilist institutions, both invented in the late 1400s, are *patents* (in order to protect new knowledge) and *protection* (for industry-building, rather than for revenue purposes). Both institutions, of course, go against the basic tenets of neoclassical economics. It is curious to how the twin institutions, *patents* and *protection* – children of the same basic understanding of the dynamics of a knowledge-based economy – are today considered to be heroes and villains, respectively. Patents and their rights, creating artificial rents in order to promote new knowledge, are heralded as an indispensable ingredient of world growth, while protection, creating manufacturing rents in order to spread this production to new geographical areas, is considered the greatest of all evils. This is particularly problematic since all historically successful catching-up strategies, starting with England's in 1485 and lasting there for more than 300 years, have depended on the nourishing, promotion and protection of economic activities subject to increasing returns. The Bretton Woods institutions now defend the mercantilist institution that helps rich countries (that is, patents) but seek to eliminate its twin institution that could help the poor (that is, protection).

The main institution that the mercantilists built was, of course, the state (Reinert 1999). Cosimo Perrotta saw mercantilism as an import substitution strategy, while Gustav Schmoller saw mercantilism as an exercise in state-building and nation-building. These are complementary, rather than contradictory views of mercantilism. As Schmoller describes mercantilism: 'The essence of the system lies not in some doctrine of money, or of the balance of trade; not in tariff barriers, protective duties, or navigation laws; but in something far greater – namely in the total transformation of society and its organizations, as well as of the state and its institutions, in the replacing of a local and territorial economy by that of the national state' (Schmoller [1896] 1967: 51).

Mercantilist economic policy therefore became highly context-specific. From a mercantilist standpoint, neoclassical economic policy suffers from the same weakness as cure-all medicines in the old US west; they come across as what used to be referred to as 'snake oil'. Steuart (1767) is the most mature English mercantilist work, where important elements like technology, innovations and institutions, later to be removed from economics by Adam Smith, were still intact. Two immediate translations into German testify to its popularity at the time.

### Why Successful Mercantilism Carries the Seeds of its Own Destruction, or Adam Smith, the Misunderstood Mercantilist

We agree with Cosimo Perrotta that mercantilism, at its core, is an import substitution policy (Perrotta 1988, 1993), a policy aimed at establishing national comparative advantage in increasing return areas.[16] In the language of Thomas Mun (1664), the transition is from 'natural activities' to 'artificial activities' or, in the language of Michael Porter, from a 'natural comparative advantage' to a 'created comparative advantage'. Porter (1990) provides a stage theory of economic development that is perfectly compatible with mercantilism (Reinert 2000b).

If this was the strategy, we should expect mercantilists to stop arguing for protectionism once this goal of industrialization has been reached. And, indeed, this is what we see. Most mercantilists, and all the most sophisticated ones from Jean–Baptiste Colbert (1619–1683) to Friedrich List (1789–1846) and the nineteenth- century American economists,[17] saw the end of industrial protection, and argued that international trade between nations specialized in manufactures was a positive-sum game. After the Tudor plan in England, the first successful system – originating in the writings of Laffemas (1597) – was that of Colbert during the reign of Louis XIV. The many volumes of Colbert's collected papers (Clément, ed. 1861–72) show the manager of 'France Inc.' building manufacturing and infrastructure, facilitating internal trade, and attempting to recreate, on a national level, the synergies that earlier observers (Botero 1590) had confined to city-states (Cole 1931, 1937). Already, however, Colbert saw mercantilist policies as temporary, and 'spoke of protective duties as crutches by the help of which manufacturers might learn to walk and then throw them away' (Ingram 1888: 41). The contemporaries could observe that for long periods of time, the leading nation of the period, the Dutch Republic, had relatively low tariffs, raising its tariff barriers only when its decay was obvious and advanced in the 1720s.

The English mercantilists John Cary (1696), Theodore Janssen (1713) and Charles King (1721) spelt out a system of 'good' and 'bad' trade that is completely in line with Paul Krugman's (1980) trade theory – later recanted,[18] based on increasing and diminishing returns (see also Graham 1923). Janssen and King's system was very influential throughout the eighteenth century. This was judged on a nation-by-nation basis. 'Good trade' is with nations from which you import raw materials and export manufactured goods; 'bad trade' is with nations from which you import manufactured goods and export raw materials. And, finally, exchanging manufactured goods for other manufactured goods is 'good trade' for both nations involved. This is also Friedrich List's principle (List 1841), which explains why List is, at the same time, both an important mercantilist and the first supporter of a European Union with free trade between manufacturing nations (Reinert 1998). List too saw mercantilism as a mandatory passage point on the road towards global free trade among equals. In other words, successful mercantilism carried with it the seeds of its own destruction: the type of protection that would initially help manufacturing, would later, by limiting production only to the national market, be an obstacle to manufacturing success. The assumption of increasing returns in manufacturing underlies most mercantilist writings, and is clearly spelt out by Antonio Serra (1613).

Throughout the early modern 'mercantilist' period, it was clear to all that universal free trade was only in the interest of the wealthiest nations – Venice and the Dutch Republic in the sixteenth and seventeenth centuries, England later. In the United States, the same type of economic analysis that recommended industrial protection in the 1820s (Raymond 1820; Carey 1822) recommended free trade for that country in the 1880s and 1890s. The new and changed message is clear from the book title, *The Destructive Influence of the Tariff upon Manufacture and Commerce* (Schoenhof 1885). Writing in the United States, Friedrich List foresaw this development around 1830: some time in the future, when the United States had industrialized after a century of protection, when its population had reached 100 million and its navy was the most powerful in the world, then the period would come when the United States would proclaim free trade to the world (Reinert 1998). It is impossible to understand Friedrich List's work without seeing that his 'mercantilism' was only a mandatory passage point towards free trade, which would be desirable when a symmetrical situation had been created in which all nations had a comparative advantage in dynamic, increasing return activities.

Normally, one would see Friedrich List and Adam Smith as opposite poles when it comes to economic policy – one the archetypal protectionist and the other the archetypal free trader. However, Adam Smith can be read in a variety of ways, and he is an author who is more quoted than read. Not only are there important differences between Smith's views before and after his meetings with the French physiocrats, *The Wealth of Nations* also contains passages that are more or less 'mercantilist'. The inconsistencies between the early and later Smith have, since the mid-nineteenth century, led to a debate under the German heading, *Das Adam Smith Problem*. The variation within *The Wealth of Nations* opened the way for selective translations, as in the case of Sweden, where the most mercantilist Smith was translated first. As a result, there is at least one Adam Smith interpretation for every European nation.

In his early work, *The Theory of Moral Sentiments* (Smith [1759] 1810), Adam Smith argued passionately for 'the great system of government' which is helped by adding new manufactures. Interestingly, he argued that new manufactures are to be promoted to help neither suppliers or consumers but to improve 'the great system of government' (ibid., Vol. 1: 320).

In fact, it is possible to argue that Adam Smith was also a 'misunderstood mercantilist', someone who firmly supported the mercantilist policies of the past, but then argued that they were no longer necessary for England. In other words, Adam Smith played the same role later played by Schoenhof in the United States. Policies like patents and protection, which had once been established in order to further innovation, were, in the 1770s, partly used to hinder innovations and sold to finance the crown. Adam Smith praised the Navigation Acts protecting English manufacturing against Holland, arguing 'they are as wise . . . as if they had all been dictated by the most deliberate wisdom' and holding them to be 'perhaps, the wisest of all the commercial regulations of England' (Smith [1776] 1976: I, 486–87). All in all, Smith described a development that had become successfully self-sustained, a kind of snowballing effect, originating in the wise protectionist measures of the past. Only once did Smith use the term 'invisible hand' in *The Wealth of Nations*: when it sustained the key import substitution goal of mercantilist policies, when the consumer preferred domestic industry to foreign industry (ibid.: 477). This is when 'the market' had taken over the role previously played by protective measures and national manufacturing no longer needed such protection. If one cared to look, Adam Smith also argued for mercantilist policies as a mandatory passage point, like Charles King and Friedrich List.

But Adam Smith was contradictory, and it is possible to read British vested interests into his contradictions. Undoubtedly, Alexander Hamilton, the first US Treasury Secretary, who had read Smith, noticed that, at one point, Smith argued that it would be very foolish for the people of the United States, with whom England was at war when his book appeared, to attempt to establish manufactures. In a different part of the same book, Smith convincingly argued that only nations with manufacturing industries are able to win wars. English classical economists are first Englishmen and then economists, is the implication of a remarkable passage by Lord Lionel Robbins: 'we get our picture wrong if we suppose that the English Classical economists would have recommended, because it was good for the world at large, a measure which they thought would be harmful to their own community' (Robbins 1952: 10–11). It is not surprising, then, that Alexander Hamilton let the English mercantilists (in particular, Malachy Postlethwayt), and not Adam Smith, be his inspiration for US industrial policy (Hamilton 1791). 'Don't do as the English tell you to do, do as the English do' became a maxim in the young United States. Today, a wise maxim for economic policy would similarly be 'Don't do as the Americans tell you to do, do as the Americans did.'

### Conclusion: Mercantilism as a Mandatory Passage Point for Development

Most economists show clear mercantilist tendencies when they advice their own children. Even the most convinced neoclassical economist will not tell his or her children that it does not matter what profession they choose – picking tomatoes or becoming a lawyer – because factor-price equalization, when wages and interest rates will be equal across the planet, is around the corner. However, when pontificating on children in the third world, the same economists recommend that nations specialize according to their comparative advantage, which will normally mean specializing in providing cheap labour to produce raw materials for simple assembly operations. If a job is available at all, that is.

When the future of their own children is at stake, economists understand that a career picking cucumbers and tomatoes will provide much less wealth than a skilled job in industry or in services. Why, then, is the mercantilist argument so unheard that a nation where *everyone* specializes in picking cucumbers and tomatoes – growth industries in Mexico today – will be poorer than a manufacturing nation? We are tempted to refer to Thorstein Veblen, who claimed that education tends to contaminate and ruin many healthy human instincts. Of course, the enlightened economist today will add that Mexico should invest more in education. But Mexico's comparative advantage lies in economic activities that do not require much knowledge. Its comparative advantage lies in providing cheap and uneducated labour. Investing in education therefore means training either for unemployment or for migration.

In this chapter, we have argued that the mercantilists who influenced economic policy were obsessed with strengthening domestic production. It must be kept in mind that the 1500s were a particularly cosmopolitan era, when the percentage of foreign students in European universities was much higher than today. As early as 1550, this cosmopolitan European theatre presented economic theorists and policy-makers with two fascinating and revealing case studies of success and failure respectively. 'A spectre haunted Europe in the mercantilist period,' says Perrotta, 'the fear of ending up like Spain, rich in gold, poor in production, and with a frighteningly unfavourable balance of trade' (Perrotta 1993: 18). Fortunately, two other cases – Venice and the Dutch Republic – as successful as Spain's case was unsuccessful, were also at hand.

Daniel Defoe (1728) tells how the first and hugely successful import substitution strategy, the English Tudor plan during 1485–1603, was based on King Henry VII benchmarking the poverty of England and the wealth of Burgundy, a wealth based exclusively on English raw material. The success of England's 'Tudor plan' in building a woollen manufacturing sector showed the world that even if the success of Venice and the Dutch Republic, in a certain sense, were products of the invisible hand of providence – a lack of raw materials had forced them into manufacturing – it was possible, through enlightened policy, to achieve the same results, even from a very different starting point.

Standard business strategy aims at maximizing market share without necessarily spelling out the theory of increasing returns and lowered unit costs, in everything from production to finance and advertising that underlies this strategy. In the same way, the mercantilists did not necessarily explain the underlying mechanisms behind the success or failure they observed. The identification of cumulative and synergic elements behind wealth creation is what makes Antonio Serra's 1613 work so remarkable and, we would argue, theoretically much superior to other theorists like Myrdal, who worked on the same problems much later. In order to learn from the mercantilists, it is therefore necessary to spell out the mechanisms that they utilized but often did not explain.

We argue that some basic economic mechanisms are as timeless as gravity. The effects of compound interest were the same in Babylonia in 2000 BC as with third world debt today.[19] The conditions of a commercial enterprise with cash flow problems would be fairly similar today as 500 years ago, and whether costs of production would increase (diminishing returns) or fall (increasing returns) as a nation specialized will have very similar results today as when Serra wrote in 1613.[20] In fact, we would argue that the basic policy recommendations of *realökonomisch* mercantilism – investment in manufacturing, an extensive division of labour, importing raw materials and exporting manufactured goods, increasing the population of the cities – all aim at creating dynamic synergies based on what Schumpeter called 'historical increasing returns',[21] in order to create sustainable wealth, employment and balance of payments.

Martin Wolf (2003: 49), associate editor and chief economic commentator of the *Financial Times*, recently wrote an article for *Foreign Policy* where he argued the 'gap' between rich and poor countries 'reflects the success of those countries that embraced capitalism and the failure of those that did not'. The fact that mercantilism lies at the root of all successful capitalism is not considered. Harvard economist Robert J. Barro, writing for *Business Week*, recently dismissed worries about unemployment resulting from China's growing textile exports by arguing 'we should not be swayed by seventeenth-century mercantilism, which viewed imports as bad and exports as good'. When taken together, these statements, appearing in two of the world's most influential publications on economic policy matters, frame real historical fallacies fuelling contemporary economic debates: liberalism is always 'right' and protectionism is always 'wrong'. Mercantilism, probably the most contested 'ism' in the historiography of economic analysis (Magnusson 1994), is mostly summoned as a strawman of irrational folly representing a system of destructive rent-seekers that supposedly made the fundamental mistake of confusing gold with wealth. The diffusion of this view reflects the extent to which the economics profession is virtually united in a common misconception of its own past, both as regards theory and policy.

We argue that the basic mercantilist insights – in the right contexts – have been proved right, again and again. These are: (i) national wealth cannot be created or based on raw material production in the absence of a manufacturing/increasing returns sector; (ii) an inefficient manufacturing/increasing returns sector provides a much higher standard of living than no manufacturing sector. Large-scale deindustrialization is therefore a crime to posterity (Reinert 2003,

2004b). Time after time, these principles have been resurrected in times of need: with increasing poverty in Spain after 1550, with the economic downturn of Italy in the following century (see the chapter titled 'The Italian Tradition of Political Economy' in this volume), during the famines in Paris in the 1770s, with the misery in France following the Napoleonic Wars, as the basis for solving serious economic problems in the United States in the early 1820s, solving the 'social problem' in nineteenth-century continental Europe, aiding Korea, poorer than Tanzania in 1950, in creating wealth, and after the devastation of the Morgenthau plan in Germany after World War II (see the chapter titled 'German Economics as Development Economics' in this volume). We argue that although increasing return activities may partly shift from manufacturing to services, the fundamental insights about the activity-specific and synergic nature of economic development remain valid. These are, however, blind spots in standard economics. The blind spots are products of David Ricardo's approach to economic theory, based on *a priori* assumptions rather than on factual observations as in the Baconian method, today fossilized into an ideology impervious to observations of economic reality. To those nations that have not yet been through a successful mercantilist phase, generally due to a colonial past, these blind spots of economic theory create untold human suffering on a daily basis.

### Appendix 1
*'Mercantilist' Economic Policies of the Generic Developmental State: Continuity of Policy Measures and Tool Kit from England in 1485 (Henry VII) to Korea in the 1960s: A Mandatory Passage for Economic Development*

> . . . the fundamental things apply, as time goes by.
>
> Sam, the pianist, in *Casablanca*.

1. Observation of wealth synergies clustered around increasing return activities and continuous mechanization in general. Recognition that 'we are in the wrong business'. Conscious *targeting, support* and *protection* of these increasing return activities.
2. Temporary monopolies/patents/protection given to targeted activities in a certain geographical area.
3. Recognizing development as a synergic phenomenon and, consequently, the need for a diversified manufacturing sector ('maximizing the division of labour' [Serra 1613] plus observations of the Dutch Republic and Venice).
4. Accumulated empirical evidence shows that the manufacturing sector solves three policy problems endemic to the third world in one go: increasing national value added (GDP), increasing employment and solving balance of payments problems.
5. Attracting foreigners to work in targeted activities (historically, religious prosecutions have been important).
6. Relative suppression of landed nobility (from Henry VII to Korea). (Physiocracy as a landowners' rebellion against this policy.)
7. Tax breaks for targeted activities.

8. Cheap credit for targeted activities.
9. Export bounties for targeted activities.
10. Strong support for the agricultural sector, in spite of this sector being clearly seen as incapable of independently bringing the nation out of poverty.
11. Emphasis on learning/education (UK apprentice system under Elizabeth I, Child [1693]; Leibniz, Wolff and Justi in Germany).
12. Patent protection for valuable knowledge (Venice from the 1490s).
13. Frequent export tax/export ban on raw materials in order to make raw materials more expensive to competing nations (starting with Henry VII in the late 1400s, whose policy was very efficient in severely damaging the woollen industry in Medici Florence).

### Notes

[1] Even the chapter on this issue in the *Cambridge Economic History of the United States* must be considered as belonging to the 'manifest destiny' tradition (Engerman and Sokoloff 2000).

[2] Also the father of the Heckscher–Ohlin trade theory.

[3] Brentano (1827–29), Eisenhart (1881), Laspeyres ([1863] 1961), Schmoller ([1897] 1967), Sombart ([1902] 1928, 1913a, 1913b).

[4] This would be similar to a balance of payments problem in third world countries today, what Celso Furtado once called 'the break-down of the capacity to import'.

[5] Schumpeter's recognition of Antonio Serra's 1613 treatise is particularly clarifying on this point: 'the implication being that if the economic process as a whole functions properly, the monetary element will take care of itself and not require any specific therapy' (Schumpeter 1954: 195; see also the chapter on 'The Italian Tradition of Political Economy' in this volume).

[6] See Seligman (1920), and Reinert and Reinert (2004), for a discussion of these debates between the 'monetarists' and 'the mercantilists of the real economy'.

[7] See, for example, the important and influential works of Paracelsus (1951: 38–44) and Michel de Montaigne ([1580] 1958: 48).

[8] We discuss the factors in more detail in Reinert and Reinert (2004).

[9] Schumpeter (1954: 177) refers to 'the old scholastic Public Good'. See also Sophus A. Reinert (2003).

[10] Mortmain is land that cannot be sold.

[11] Potosi, at about 4,000 metres above sea-level in present-day Bolivia, was the richest of all mines in the world. At the time, it was the second largest city in the world after London.

[12] Leeuwenhoek was to be the executor of his neighbour Vermeer's estate.

[13] With the technology of map-making changing from wood-cuts to copper plates, the same copper used by instrument-makers, the Dutch took over its production from the Italians.

[14] The wisdom of taxing diminishing return activities and paying bounties to increasing return activities was also recognized by Alfred Marshall, the founder of neoclassical economics (Marshall 1890: 452). Similarly, the different effects of technological change in agriculture (lower prices) and industry (higher wages) in Hans W. Singer ([1950] 1964) supported arguments for the key role of manufacturing industry in development. See also Reinert (1980, 1996).

[15] Modern economic historians agree with the mercantilist explanation of causality here: 'The bulk of the evidence points to urbanization being the cause of agricultural productivity gain, not a result.' Philip Hoffman quoted in Prak (2001).

[16] This is a fundamental *leitmotif* in sixteenth, seventeenth and eighteenth-century economic thought, and formed the basis of successful industrialization policies across Europe. It appears in English mercantilist texts, for example, Misselden (1623), Mun (1664), Child (1693: 3, 18, 100–01), Cary ([1695] 1745: 1), Barbon (1696), Davenant

(1696), King (1721) and William Petty. See also the chapters on 'The Italian Tradition of Political Economy' and 'German Economics as Development Economics' in this volume.

[17] See Hudson (2004) for a discussion of nineteenth-century US industrial strategy.

[18] Bhagwati (2002: 31) confirms '[Krugman's] firm retreat back to free trade'.

[19] When asked what power could be stronger than the atomic bomb, Albert Einstein reputedly answered 'compound interest'. It can, in fact, be argued that the ancient Babylonians institutionalized a better solution to this problem than we have today. At varying and unforeseeable intervals, the king would cancel all non-commercial debt, thus creating a 'clean slate' for everyone. Remnants of this practice, the Jubilee Years, are found in the Old Testament, becoming the basis for the Jubilee 2000 movement to forgive third world debt.

[20] Reinert (1980) documents that developing countries tend to produce well into the area of diminishing returns, revealed when costs decrease as production is reduced. See also Reinert (1996).

[21] With this term, Schumpeter refers to the combined effects of technological change and increasing returns, which are separable in theory, but often not in practice, because new technology is not available in the former scale.

### References

Arthur, Brian (1989), 'Competing Technologies, Increasing Returns and Lock-in by Historical Events', *Economic Journal*, 99 (394): 116–31.

Ashley, William (1920), *An Introduction to English Economic History and Theory* (New York: Putnam).

Barbon, Nicholas (1696), A *Discourse Concerning Coining the New Money Lighter* (London: Richard Chiswell).

Berch, Anders (1747), *Inledning til Almänna Hushålningen, innefattande Grunden til Politie, Oeconomie och Cameralwetenskaperna* (Stockholm: Lars Salvius).

Botero, Giovanni (1590), *Della Ragione di Stato. Libri Dieci*, this work also contains *Delle Cause della Grandezza delle Città, libri tre* (Rome: Vicenzio Pellagalo).

Bhagwati, Jagdish (2002), *Free Trade Today* (Princeton: Princeton University Press).

Bouwsma, William James (2000), *The Waning of the Renaissance, 1550–1640* (New Haven: Yale University Press).

Braudel, Fernand (1991), *Out of Italy, 1450–1650* (Paris: Flammarion).

Brentano, Lujo (1927–29), *Eine Geschichte der wirtschaftlichen Entwicklung Englands*, 3 volumes (Jena: Gustav Fischer).

Browne, Thomas (1643), *Religio Medici* (London: Andrew Crooke).

Carey, Mathew (1822), *Essays on Political Economy; Or, The Most Certain Means of Promoting the Wealth, Power, Resources and Happiness of Nations: Applied Particularly to the United States* (Philadelphia: H.C. Carey & I. Lea).

Cary, John ([1695] 1745), *An Essay on the State of England* (Bristol: W. Bonny).

Child, Josuah (1668), *Brief Observations Concerning Trade and Interest of Money* (London: Elizabeth Calvert).

—— (1693), *A New Discourse on Trade* (London: John Furringham).

Clément, Pierre, ed. (1861–72), *Lettres, Instructiones et Mémoires de Colbert*, 7 volumes in 10 + 1 volume, 'Errata Général et Table Analytique' (Paris: Imprimerie Impériale/ Imprimerie Nationale).

Cole, Charles Woolsey (1931), *French Mercantilist Doctrines Before Colbert* (New York: R.R. Smith).

—— (1937), *Colbert and a Century of French Mercantilism* (New York: Columbia University Press).

Davenant, Charles (1696), *An Essay on the East-India Trade* (London).

—— (1699), *An Essay upon the Probable Methods of Making a People Gainers in the Balance of Trade* (London: James Knapton).

Decker, Mathew ([1744] 1751), *An Essay on the Causes of the Decline of the Foreign Trade* (Dublin: George Faulkner).

Defoe, Daniel (1728), *A Plan of English Commerce* (London: printed for Charles Rivington).

Eisenhart, Hugo (1881), *Geschichte der Nationaloekonomie* (Jena: Gustav Fischer).

Ekelund, Robert B. and Robert D. Tollison (1981), *Mercantilism as a Rent-seeking Society: Economic Regulation in Historical Perspective* (College Station: Texas A&M University Press).

Engerman, Stanley L. and Kenneth L. Sokoloff (2000), 'Technology and Industrialization, 1790–1914', in Stanley L. Engerman and Robert E. Gallman, *The Cambridge Economic History of the United States* (Cambridge: Cambridge University Press): 367–401.

Fanfani, Amintore (1955), *Storia delle dottrine economiche dall'antichità al XIX secolo* (Milan: Giuseppe Principato).

Finkelstein, Andrea (2000), *Harmony and the Balance: An Intellectual History of Seventeenth-Century English Economic Thought* (Ann Arbor: University of Michigan Press).

Gee, Joshua (1729), *Trade and Navigation of Great Britain Considered* (London: Bettesworth & Hitch).

Goyeneche, Pedro Francisco (1717), *Comercio de Holanda, o el gran thesoro historial y político del floreciente comercio, que los holandeses tienen en todos sus estados y señorios del mundo* (Madrid: Imprenta Real, por J. Rodríguez Escobar).

Graham, Frank (1923), 'Some Aspects of Protection Further Considered', *Quarterly Journal of Economics*, 37: 199–227.

Hamilton, Alexander (1791), *A Report on the Manufactures of the United States*, on www.juntosociety.com/i_documents/ah_rom.htm.

Hamilton, Earl (1932), 'Spanish Mercantilism before 1700', in *Facts and Factors in Economic History, Articles by Former Students of Edwin Francis Gay* (Cambridge, Mass.: Harvard University Press): 214–39.

Heckscher, Eli Filip (1931), *Merkantilismen: Ett Led i den Ekonomiska Politikens Historia* (Stockholm: P.A. Norstedt).

Hudson, Michael (2004), 'Technical Progress and Obsolescence of Capitals and Skills: Theoretical Foundations of Nineteenth-Century US Industrial Policy', in Reinert, ed. (2004b).

Huerta, Robert D. (2003), *Giants of Delft, Johannes Vermeer and the Natural Philosophers: The Parallel Search for Knowledge During the Age of Discovery* (Lewisburg: Bucknell University Press).

Huet, Pierre Daniel (1722), *A View of the Durch Trade in all the States, Empires, and Kingdoms of the World* second edition (London: C. King and J. Stagg); first edition 1717, original French edition 1712.

Hume, David (1767), *The History of England from the Invasion of Julius Caesar to the Revolution in 1688*, 6 volumes (London: A. Millar).

Ingram, John Kells (1888), A *History of Political Economy* (Edinburgh: Black).

Justi, Johann Heinrich Gottlob von (1760), *Die Natur und das Wesen der Staaten, als die Grundwissenschaft der Staatskunst, der Policey, und aller Regierungswissenschaften, desgleichen als die Quelle aller Gesetze, abgehandelt* (Berlin: Johann Heinrich Rüdigers).

Janssen, Theodore (1713), 'General Maxims in Trade, Particularly Applied to the Commerce between Great Britain and France', in King (1721).

King, Charles (1721), *The British Merchant; or, Commerce Preserv'd*, 3 volumes (London: John Darby).

Koyré, Alexandre (1957), *From the Closed World to the Infinite Universe* (Baltimore: Johns Hopkins University Press).

Krugman, Paul (1980), *Rethinking International Trade* (Cambridge: MIT Press).

Laspeyres, Etienne ([1863] 1961), *Geschichte der volkswirtschaftlichen Anschauungen der Niederländer und ihrer Litteratur zur Zeit der Republik* (Nieuwkoop: de Graaf).

Laffemas, Barthélemy (1597), *Reiglement (sic) general pour dresser les manufactures en ce rayaume, et couper le cours des draps de soye, & autres merchandises qui perdent & ruynent l'Estat: qui est le vray moyen de remettre la France en sa splendeur, & de faire gaigner les pauvres. . . .* (Paris: Claude de Monstr'oil and Jean Richter).

Latini, Brunetto (1993), *The Book of the Treasure (Li livres dou tresor)* (New York: Garland Publishing).

List, Friedrich ([1841] 1959), *Das nationale System der Politischen Ökonomie* (Basel: Kyklos Verlag): 12. (This part of the Foreword was not translated in the English translation of 1885.)

Lluch, Ernest (1973), *El pensament econòmic a Catalunya*, Edicions 62 (Barcelona, in Catalan).

—— (1997), 'Cameralism Beyond the Germanic World: A Note of Tribe', in *History of Economic Ideas*, 5 (2).

—— (2000), 'El Cameralismo en España', in Enrique Fuentes Quintana, ed., *Economía y Economistas Españoles*, Vol. 3 (Barcelona: Galaxia Gutenberg): 721–28.

Locke, John ([1691] 1696), *Some Considerations of the Consequences of the Lowering of Interests, and Raising the Value of Money* (London: Awnsham and Churchill).

Magnusson, Lars (1991), *Merkantilismen: Ett ekonomiskt tänkande formuleras* (Stockholm: SNS Förlag); English edition: *Mercantilism: The Shaping of an Economic Language* (London: Routledge).

——, ed. (1993), *Mercantilist Economics* (Boston: Kluwer).

—— (1994), *Mercantilism: The Shaping of an Economic Language* (London: Routledge).

Marshall, Alfred (1890), *Principles of Economics* (London: Macmillan).

Misselden, Edward (1623), *The Circle of Commerce or the Balance of Trade* (London: printed by Iohn Dawson for Nicholas Bourne).

Montaigne, Michel de ([1580] 1958), *Essays*; translated by J.M. Cohen (London: Penguin).

Mun, Thomas (1664), *England's Treasure by Foreign Trade* (London: J.G. for T. Clark).

[Paracelsus] Hohenheim, Aureolus Theophrastus Bombastus von (1951), *Selected Writings of Paracelsus*, edited by Joland Jacobi (Princeton: Princeton University Press).

Perez, Carlota (2004), 'Technological Revolutions, Paradigm Shift and Socio-Institutional Change', in Reinert, ed. (2004b).

Perrotta, Cosimo (1988), *Produzione e Lavoro Produttivo nel Mercantilismo e nell'Illuminismo* (Galatina: Congedo Editore).

—— (1991), 'Is the Mercantilist Theory of the Favorable Balance of Trade Really Erroneous?', *History of Political Economy*, 23 (2): 301–36.

—— (1993), 'Early Spanish Mercantilism: A First Analysis of Underdevelopment' in Lars Magnusson, ed., *Mercantilist Economics* (Boston: Kluwer): 17–58.

Porter, Michael (1990), *The Competitive Advantage of Nations* (London: Macmillan).

Prak, Maarten (2001), 'Early Modern Capitalism: An Introduction', in Maarten Prak, ed., *Early Modern Capitalism: Economic and Social Change in Europe 1400–1800* (London: Routledge): 1–21.

Raymond, Daniel (1820), *Principles of Political Economy* (Baltimore: Fielding Lucas).

Reinert, Erik S. (1980), *International Trade and the Economic Mechanisms of Underdevelopment* (Ann Arbor: University Microfilms).

—— (1996), 'Diminishing Returns and Economic Sustainability: The Dilemma of Resource-Based Economies under a Free Trade Regime', in Stein Hansen, Jan Hesselberg and Helge Hveem, eds, *International Trade Regulation, National Development Strategies and the Environment: Towards Sustainable Development?*, (Oslo: Centre for Development and the Environment, University of Oslo), available on www.othercanon.org.

—— (1998), 'Raw Materials in the History of Economic Thought: or, Why List (the Protectionist) and Cobden (the Free Trader) Both Agreed on Free Trade in Corn', in G. Parry, ed., *Freedom and Trade, 1846–1996* (London: Routledge).

—— (1999), 'The Role of the State in Economic Growth', *Journal of Economic Studies*, 26 (4/5); a shorter version was published in Pier Angelo Toninelli, ed. (2000), *The Rise and Fall of State-Owned Enterprises in the Western World* (Cambridge: Cambridge University Press).

—— (2000a), 'Full Circle: Economics from Scholasticism through Innovation and Back into Mathematical Scholasticism; Reflections around a 1769 price essay: "Why is it that Economics so far has Gained so Few Advantages from Physics and Mathematics?"', *Journal of Economic Studies*, 27 (4/5), available on www.othercanon.org.

—— (2000b), 'Karl Bücher and the Geographical Dimensions of Techno-Economic Change', in Jürgen Backhaus, ed., *Karl Bücher: Theory, History Anthropology, Non-Market Economies* (Marburg: Metropolis Verlag).

—— (2003), 'Increasing Poverty in a Globalized World: Marshall Plans and Morgenthau

Plans as Mechanisms of Polarization of World Incomes', in Chang Ha-Joon, ed., *Rethinking Economic Development* (London: Anthem Press).

—— (2004a), *Globalization in the Periphery as a Morgenthau Plan: The Underdevelopment of Mongolia in the 1990s*, in Reinert, ed. (2004b).

——, ed. (2004b), *Globalization, Economic Development and Inequality: An Alternative Perspective* (Cheltenham: Edward Elgar).

—— (forthcoming), 'Benchmarking Success: The Dutch Republic (1500–1750) as Seen by Contemporary European Economists', in Oscar Gelderblom, ed., *The Political Economy of the Dutch Republic*.

Reinert, Erik S. and Arno Daastøl (1997), 'Exploring the Genesis of Economic Innovations: The Religious Gestalt-Switch and the Duty to Invent as Preconditions for Economic Growth', *European Journal of Law and Economics*, 4 (2/3): 233–83.

—— (2004), 'The Other Canon: The History of Renaissance Economics; Its Role as an Immaterial and Production-Based Canon in the History of Economic Thought and in the History of Economic Policy', in Reinert, ed. (2004b).

Reinert, Sophus A. (2003), 'Darwin and the Body Politic: Schäffle, Veblen and the Biological Metaphor Shift in Economics', paper presented at the 17th Heilbronn Conference in the Social Sciences, June, on www.othercanon.org.

Reinert, Sophus A. and Erik S. Reinert (2004), 'An Early National Innovation System: The Case of Antono Serra (1613)', *Institutions and Economic Development*, 2 (1).

Robbins, Lionel (1952), *The Theory of Economic Policy in English Classical Political Economy* (London: Macmillan).

Ruestow, Edward G. (1996), *The Microscope in the Dutch Republic: The Shaping of Discovery* (Cambridge: Cambridge University Press).

Schoenhof, Jacob (1885), *The Destructive Influence of the Tariff upon Manufacture and Commerce and the Figures and Facts Relating Thereto*, second edition (New York: New York Free Trade Club).

Serra, Antonio (1613), *Breve Trattato delle Cause che Possono far Abbondare l'Oro e l'Argento dove non sono Miniere* (Naples: Lazzaro Scorriggio).

Schmoller, Gustav ([1896] 1967), *The Mercantile System and its Historical Significance* (New York: Macmillan): 50–51; reprinted, Kelley, 1967.

Schumpeter, Joseph Alois (1954), *The History of Economic Analysis* (New York: Oxford University Press).

Singer, Hans W. ([1950] 1964), 'The Distribution of Gains between Investing and Borrowing Countries', in *International Development: Growth and Change* (New York: McGraw-Hill).

Smith, Adam ([1759] 1812), *The Theory of Moral Sentiments*, in *Collected Works* (London: Cadell and Davies).

—— ([1776] 1976), *The Wealth of Nations* (Chicago: Chicago University Press).

—— ([1902] 1928), *Der moderne Kapitalismus* (Munich and Leipzig: Duncker and Humblot).

Sombart, Werner (1913a), *Krieg und Kapitalismus* (Munich and Leipzig: Duncker and Humblot).

—— (1913b), *Luxus und Kapitalismus* (Munich and Leipzig: Duncker and Humblot).

Soros, George (2002), *George Soros on Globalization* (New York: Public Affairs).

Steadman, Philip (2001), *Vermeer's Camera* (Oxford: Oxford University Press).

Steuart, James (1767), *An Inquiry into the Principles of Political Economy: Being an Essay on the Science of Domestic Policy in Free Nations. In which are particularly considered population, agriculture, trade, industry, money, coin, interest, circulation, banks, exchange, public credit, and taxes*, 2 volumes (London: A. Millar & T. Cadell).

Uztariz, Geronymo de ([1724] 1751), *The Theory and Practice of Commerce and Maritime Affairs*, 2 volumes (London: John and James Rivington).

Wolf, Martin (2003), 'The Morality of the Market', *Foreign Policy*, September–October: 47–50.

Zincke, Georg Heinrich, editor (1746–67), *Leipziger Sammlungen von Wirthschafftlichen Policey-, Cammer- und Finantz-Sachen*, 192 issues in 17 volumes (Leipzig: Erster (bis) Sechzehender Band (und) General-Register).

# The Italian Tradition of Political Economy

## Theories and Policies of Development in the

## Semi-Periphery of the Enlightenment

*Sophus A. Reinert*

Around the thirteenth century the Florentines, Pisans, Amalfitans, Venetians, and Genoese began adopting a different policy for enhancing their wealth and power because they noticed that the sciences, the cultivation of land, the application of the arts and of industry, and the introduction of extensive trade could produce a large population, provide for their countless needs, sustain great luxury and gain immense riches without having to add more territories.

Sebastiano Franci, writing a 1764 article for the Milanese newsletter *Il Caffè*, here describes how Italians, first among the Europeans, circumvented the Malthusian trap of poverty by nurturing activities yielding increasing returns to scale. More people, they observed, could be supported on a given piece of land by manufactures and trade than by sheer agricultural surplus. Manufactures did not, however, merely produce wealth, but were also pivotal in unleashing a cultural and political revolution. 'Liberty and industry', Cesare Beccaria taught in his inaugural lecture, 'together arose from amid the marshes of the Adriatick' ([1769] 1970: 31). Of the four largest European cities in 1500, only Paris was not in Italy (Vries 1984: 35) and, indeed, as Franci says, 'so happy was their success that the world for the second time turned its gaze towards Italy . . . and their example was quickly imitated' (Franci [1764] 1998: 144).[1] However, as the other countries of Europe adopted the economic practices of the Italian city-states, Italy itself fell behind, gradually moving to the semi-periphery of the world system (Cipolla 1970; Wallerstein 1974: 214; Wallerstein 1980: 171–72, 196).

Franci was a sworn member of *L'Accademia dei Pugni*, a coterie of young upper-class Milanese intellectuals and reformers embodying many of the ideals of their age, and the medium of their message, *Il Caffè*, is widely regarded as 'the most eminent and influential periodical of the Italian Enlightenment' (Messbarger 1999: 355). Together, they sought to address some of the main social and political questions of the day; among them, why Italy, already twice in history at the very centre of the world's attention – during the Roman empire and during the Renaissance (see also Ruffolo 2004) – was languishing in the wake of Britain, France and Holland, and what one could do about it. The very same question of how to 'catch up', to adopt Abramowitz' phraseology (Abramowitz

1986), was confronted by writers all across the peninsula with largely similar results.

During the Italian Enlightenment of the late eighteenth century, economists – from Ferdinando Galiani and Antonio Genovesi in Naples to Pietro Verri and Cesare Beccaria in Milan, Andrea Tron in Venice and Carlo Salerni in Otranto – were systematically exploring and codifying the mechanisms of economic development. The challenge facing them all was one of underdevelopment, of reversing the process of 'falling behind' in the face of active English, French and Dutch economic policy. The basic rules of economic development were clear for everybody to see, as Salerni wrote: 'the English model provides . . . the precedent for anyone aspiring to perfect and make their own manufactures useful' (Salerni [1782] 1996: 83). The question was how to adapt the basic model so successfully pursued by England and Holland to the peculiarities of the Italian city-states. This chapter will present a survey of these distinct Italian contributions to the field of economic development.

Joseph A. Schumpeter mentions many of these thinkers, and, opening a section on the 'High Level of the Italian Contribution' in his seminal *History of Economic Analysis,* he argues that 'the honors of the field of pre-Smithian system production should go to the eighteenth-century Italians' (Schumpeter 1954: 176). Still, the English-language historiography of these contributions is surprisingly anaemic, and the tradition they represent remains overshadowed by the pall of physiocracy. While Schumpeter segregates the Italian contributions of the period into two schools, the Milanese and the Neapolitan, divided by the 'regionalism of Italian life' (ibid.: 177), for the purpose of this chapter, this might not be the most fruitful way to approach their tradition. The fact that Italy was not unified did not mean its states did not share common institutions. Just as economists in the many small German states, starting with Seckendorff (1626–1692), were acutely aware of their *Deutschtum,* the economists of the Italian city-states explicitly shared a common *italianitá* (Carli [1765] 1998). It therefore remains viable, in light of the documentary and material evidence, to talk of a pan-peninsular economic discourse that developed in response to the evolution of the European economy. Indeed, surveying the field, the same recurring themes appear, some common to the larger European exchange of ideas, others unique to their Italian context. Most pertinent from the perspective of economic development was the need for an appropriate institutional infrastructure for the market to function properly, the fortuitous material and moral effects of manufactures, the role of the state in economic growth, and the discrepancies, at times evident, between the mechanisms of growth identified by writers in the core and in the periphery.

The aim of this chapter is thus to explore the tradition of Italian economic thought in the early modern period as it relates to both questions of economic development or, in the Italian case, underdevelopment, and to the dissemination of theory and practice from core areas of the world system. In other words, how did economists of a previously rich but now underdeveloped region consider their own loss of economic power, what mechanisms did they identify as causes of this change, and how did they receive the economic theories of the developed countries? Hopefully, this survey will not only shed light on some aspects of the field of economic development as it was first formulated, but also address certain historical processes relevant to current concerns.

### Italy from Core to Semi-Periphery in the Early Modern Period: The Case of the Medici Grand Dukes and the Tudor Plan

Cities such as Florence, Genoa, Milan and Venice soared economically during the Middle Ages and the early Renaissance due to their fortuitous location as mandatory passage points for trade and travel between east and west, and investments made in manufactures and infrastructure cemented the region's role as a centre of commercial gravity in Europe. Florentine banking families such as the Bardi supplied foreign sovereigns with credit for more than a century before the Medici rose to prominence in the late fourteenth century, and the unearthly splendour of Venice still bears witness to the inflow of riches from its near-monopoly over the eastern spice trade. Double-entry book-keeping, patents and tariffs to nurture infant industries were all institutional inventions of the Italian Renaissance, and Raymond de Roover, the great historian of the Medici bankers, has argued that:

> Modern capitalism . . . has its roots in Italy during the Middle Ages and the Renaissance. From the Crusades to the Great Discoveries, Italy was the domi-nant economic power in the western world, and its merchants were the leading businessmen. . . . The hegemony of the Italians rested largely upon superior business organization. As a matter of fact, they laid the foundations for most of the business institutions of today. (Roover 1963)

This foundation, however, was not enough to sustain the growth during the sixteenth and seventeenth centuries, when several factors coalesced to rearr-ange the European economic arena. As the Atlantic and Baltic seaways were domesticated, the economic linkages between the old and the new world mat-ured, and the circumnavigation of Africa opened the eastern markets to Dutch and Portuguese influences; the international economic system underwent a deep structural change. Foreign aggressors ravaged the factionalized Italian city-states. Added to this was the gradual spread of Italian-born capitalist institutions and practices to the emerging European economies of England, France and Holland. The first two had the advantage of a larger domestic market as well, but eco-nomic development in all three consistently reflected the synergy between a strong base of manufactured exports and a privileged position in the international net-work of commerce pioneered by the Italian city-states (Zanden 2001: 76, 85). Sebastiano Franci was not the only eighteenth-century Italian to argue that for-eigners learnt their ways from the Italians, as it was almost unanimously agreed from one end of the peninsula to the other that certain countries began to 'imi-tate' Italian customs, practices and products in the late fifteenth century – in the end, practically beating the Italians at their own game (Beccaria [1769] 1970:

31–40; P. Verri [1771] 1986: 2–3; Salerni [1782] 1996: 80–89; Tron [1784] 1994: 106). Italy's first university professor of economics, Antonio Genovesi, encapsulated this view when he argued, in his lecture notes of 1773, that 'the nations to which Italy communicated the arts and manufactures have indeed left us behind' (in Venturi 1969: 574–75). As would happen to Holland, a major reason for Italy's decline was the gradual end of city-state mercantilism. The successful economies of later periods developed in the context of nation-states (List [1841] 1959; Schmoller [1897] 1967: 50–51; Ruffolo 2004). The result was both a relative and, in certain areas, an absolute decline of economic power in Italy.

Immanuel Wallerstein, among others, has argued how the old economic powerhouses of northern Italy were left behind in the semi-periphery of the world system as the core moved northwest to Holland and England, and never recovered their one-time standing. The causes of this dynamic did not, however, escape the Italian political economists, who, throughout the early modern period, wrote from a standpoint of catching up, of regaining lost economic territory. Genovesi and others were exceedingly aware of the problems facing what they called 'latecomers' in the economic system, and their theories are therefore valuable for understanding the mechanisms of economic development when the modern world system was first established (Genovesi 1757: 17–24). To better illustrate the impact of these fundamental changes in the economic make-up of Europe on individual economies, the case of Grand Ducal Tuscany might be illuminating.

One of the most notorious of the 'imitations', which had huge consequences for the north Italian manufacturing sector and the Florentine one in particular, was the so-called 'Tudor plan'. Under this policy, started by Henry VII in 1485 and reaching its perfection with Queen Elizabeth in 1587, the Tudor monarchy began to impose export duties on raw wool and import duties on finished woollen cloth (Defoe [1730] 1969: 131; Salerni [1782] 1996: 85; Reinert 1995). When sufficient manufacturing capacity had been built up in England, all export of raw wool was prohibited. England had been the largest source of raw wool for European markets for centuries and this drastic change of policy had wide-reaching consequences for the pan-European economy. The Florentine wool trade was not only gradually cut off from its main supplier of raw wool in the late sixteenth century, but also lost one of its most important customers.[2] As a result of the highly successful Tudor plan – laying the basis for England's subsequent development – the Florentine wool trade found itself unable to compete with the lower-priced English manufactured goods, its urban artisan work force underbid by the low wage earners of rural England. Tuscany subsequently lost her staple economic activity and had to reorganize the very foundations of her economy. To enumerate the decline, it can be mentioned that from an apex of 152 wool workshops in 1561, the number declined steadily to 100 in 1596 and a mere 49 in 1626. Likewise, the number of pieces produced yearly fell from a high average of 30,000 in the period 1560–72 to a mere 9,000 during 1620–29 (Malanima 1982: 292–95).

Starting in 1537, the Medici Grand Dukes, pre-dating what is generally accepted to be the period of mercantilist theory, already operated the practice that was later called mercantilist and cameralist (Brown 1983; Litchfield 1986: 203), basically continuing many of the practices pioneered in the thirteenth century. Tariffs and prohibitions were set to limit the export of raw materials while ducal decrees facilitated their import. The textile industry was both the best protected and the most conducive to economic growth because it was characterized by mechanization, high demand and increasing returns to scale, combined with a high degree of division of labour in the productive process (Rolova 1983: 310; Goldthwaite 1993: 19, 44). Other manufactures, ranging from glass to foodstuffs, were likewise protected, and domestic supplies of important raw materials were developed through mining activities and through the cultivation of mulberry trees for silkworms (Morelli 1976: 135; Malanima 1982: 104, 111–12; Malanima 1988: 67; Ilardi 1993: 534). Furthermore, Cosimo I (1519–1574) personally imported German engineers for the nascent silver mines at Pietrasanta. Similarly, Flemish tapestry workers were hired to teach Florentines their craft, glass-makers from Murano were paid high premiums to violate Venetian laws and set up shop in Florence, and silk weavers were brought in from Lucca (Morelli 1976: 123; Adelson 1983: 904; Ilardi 1993: 535; McCray 1999: 127–28). The case of the silk industry, in particular, bordered on 'state capitalism', as the Duke entered as an entrepreneur of last resort in a sector of the economy suffering from high barriers to entry (Malanima 1983: 299; Parigino 1999: 84–85; Reinert 1999; Molá, Mueller and Zanier 2000: 415). The contemporary growth of the luxury industries did stem the tide of economic depression but was ultimately unable to keep relative decline at bay (Albertini 1970: 286; Malanima 1983: 296–99; Malanima 1988: 70). The southern, less 'mercantilist' states, however, fared much worse in the transition from core to semi-periphery.

### The Post-Scholastic Predecessors: Botero and Serra

While the theories of economic development most relevant to our *problematique* only flourished in Italy in the eighteenth century, there are a few earlier contributions worthy of mention, both for their own analysis of the Italian economy on the eve of decline and for their influence on later writers. The influence of the scholastic writers resounded throughout the period, yet they mainly approached the problem of distribution, rather than production, and we must therefore move forward to the turn of the sixteenth century to find our first key protagonists. Much of the groundwork for later Italian contributions was, in fact, laid out in the works of Giovanni Botero (1544–1617) and Antonio Serra (fl. 1613), which had repercussions throughout the entire early modern period. Whereas Botero was an international phenomenon, in many ways setting the scene for later writings, Serra's lone treatise had no influence in his own time and was indeed almost lost. It resurfaced in the eighteenth century, however, and passed, according to the great historian and philosopher Benedetto Croce, like a 'proverbial lamp of life' from hand to hand among the greatest Italian economists of the time, disseminating its message (Croce 1925: 160; Reinert and Reinert 2004).

Schumpeter called Botero the 'intellectual stepping stone' between Machiavelli (1469–1527) and Montesquieu (1689–1755) in the history of political philosophy, and the renegade Jesuit is indeed best known for adding his *Reason of State* to that venerable literary tradition of offering advice to rulers (Schumpeter 1954: 164; Gilbert 1968). A true cosmopolitan, Botero was born in the Italian region of Piedmont, but published his first books in Krakow, Poland and Würzburg, Germany, respectively. He wrote on a variety of subjects but, apart from *Reason of State,* is best known for his *On the Greatness of Cities* and *Universal Relations*, a handbook of geography describing the institutions and inhabitants of the world (1599). Surveying the countries of Christendom and beyond, he observed that industries, rather than mines, were the real source of wealth, establishing a baseline of sorts not only for later Italian writers, but also for mercantilist texts from Spain to Sweden:

> Such is the power of industry that no mine of silver or gold in New Spain or Peru can compare with it, and the duties from the merchandise of Milan are worth more to the Catholic King than the mines of Potosi and Jalisco. Italy is a country in which . . . there is no important gold or silver mine, and so is France: yet both countries are rich in money and treasure, thanks to industry. (Botero [1589] 1956: 152).[3]

Botero found economic growth to result from fortuitous legislature encouraging the expansion of manufactures, and was a pioneer in identifying the capacity of industry to support larger populations than agriculture, but seemingly did not delve deeper to uncover the mechanisms of development (ibid.: 155–56).[4] One could almost argue that Antonio Serra's *Breve Trattato* of 1613 (a short treatise on the causes that can make gold and silver abound where there are no mines) specifically sought to unpack this very passage.

Serra, writing in the Spanish viceroyalty of Naples, observed that countries rich in natural resources, like Naples, were poor and were supplying raw materials to countries like Venice, which, paradoxically, were rich, because their lack of natural endowments forced them to rely on manufacturing industry.[5] Serra's city, at the turn of the seventeenth century, was the fourth largest city in Europe, after London, Istanbul and Paris. Since wrestling the territorial possession from the Angevines in 1442, the Aragon dynasty had incorporated Naples into its system of viceroyalties, and southern Italy was thus subject to the same economic mismanagement observable in Spain (Calabria 1991: 131). Much like its metropolis, Naples was ravaged by rampant inequalities as luxury and leisure met suffering and starvation within its enclosed walls (Porter 2000), and the viceroy was no more receptive to Serra's advice than the crown was to that of his Spanish equivalents.

While mercantilists are today accused of worrying solely about gold, Serra based his thesis about why Venice became rich while Naples remained poor on the relationships between different sectors of the economy. To him, different economic activities were subject to different economic laws. More specifically, manufacturing was subject to increasing returns as production expanded while agriculture was not, and Serra thus sought to uncover the underlying causes in the *Realökonomie* that determined the flow of gold in and out of nations. To him, a deficit of gold was but a symptom of other ills that could only be explained in the realm of production. Approaching the question of economic development from a holistic perspective, Serra argued that it is not enough to have industry, as one must also have the right institutions to nurture and support it. The industriousness of the population had to be encouraged through laws against idleness, favourable inventions and innovations were to be promoted, imports of manufactured goods were to be limited to the bare minimum, and importation of raw materials was to be encouraged (Reinert and Reinert 2004).

In more modern terms, Serra very explicitly argued for import-substituting industrialization, which, one should add, has run through the history of economic development like a red thread, from sixth-century BC Solonic Athens to the twentieth century (Sombart 1902: Book II, 55–56; Reinert 1999). Part of the theory was based on the belief that the amount of labour invested in a good had to be maximized in the case of exports and minimized in that of imports, but this was just its static element. Raw materials were to be imported, refined and exported as finished goods, and the process of adding value to a product was thus to be performed by domestic rather than foreign labour; this was also known as the 'foreign-paid-income theory', later common to the mercantilist discourse (Perrotta 1991: 318; Magnusson 1994: 167). The virtuous circles started accumulating in cities with a large division of labour between manufacturing activities, all subject to increasing returns. In this way, increasing return activities were maximized at home, while diminishing return activities were concentrated abroad, as in contemporary colonial systems.

Employment and wealth were simultaneously created by this policy, and the importation of foreign human capital was a natural progression of this philosophy. Serra, like Cosimo I before him, thus argued for laws and decrees to attract the international flow of expertise by emulating Venetian policies. Foreign experts were paid considerable sums by monarchs all over Europe to ease the transmission of technological innovations across national borders throughout the early modern period, and states would often attempt to counteract this flow of expertise through heavy-handed legislation. Venice, which in many ways had pioneered this practice, experienced the flip side of the process as even instituting capital punishment for wayward craftsmen proved unable to stem the tide of material and institutional plagiarism in England, France, Holland and the other Italian city-states (McCray 1999: 164).

Serra's unique insight, however, was in conceptualizing the economy as an organic and synergetic interdependency of parts, its engine of development driven by cumulative causations between them:

But the number of manufactures also benefits the city, in which diverse causes produce a great gathering of people, not only because of the manufactures (which would then be the cause of it all), but insofar as the two causes reinforce one another: that is to say that the number of manufactures increases the desirability of the place, as well as the volume of the urban traffic, while on the other hand the number of manufactures in turn is a product of the said traffic and gathering of people (Serra 1613: 18).

While Serra's text had little influence in its own time, it was rediscovered in the eighteenth century and, from there, spread its influence to later Italians. It also had a direct influence on the German Historical School through Friedrich List and Wilhelm Roscher, both of whom quote Serra, before Nobel Laureate Gunnar Myrdal unknowingly resurrected Serra's theory (Myrdal 1956, 1957). Serra's holistic approach to identifying the role of increasing return activities in economic development is present in explicit and implicit form in the writings of major Italian economists throughout the early modern period.

### The Naples and Milan Schools of Political Economy in the Eighteenth Century: Galiani, Genovesi, Verri and Beccaria

As already mentioned, Schumpeter identified two distinct 'schools' of economic thought in eighteenth-century Italy. Strong linkages, both intellectual and personal, existed between writers of the north and south. While, of course, their world views and the nuances of their theories at times differed greatly, the fact remains that, from the perspective of economic development, their policy proposals were remarkably uniform across the period and the peninsula. For the purpose of this chapter, it suffices to focus on the contributions to development economics of the four major writers of the period – Ferdinando Galiani (1728–1787) and Antonio Genovesi (1712–1769) in Naples, and Cesare Beccaria (1738–1794) and Pietro Verri (1728–1797) in Milan. Chronologically, the Neapolitan school developed first, with the 1750 publication of Abbé Galiani's *Della Moneta (On Money)* being both the first great economic work of the Italian Enlightenment and, not coincidentally, also the first to explicitly resurrect Serra's theories of development (Galiani [1752] 1977: 315).

Intellectually and professionally, the little Abbé exemplified the European Enlightenment: a Neapolitan diplomat in Paris, he was an active member of the cosmopolitan republic of letters, a favourite in the Parisian salons, a reformer, philosopher and economist. Galiani was educated in the church, and his character was further moulded by his personal experience with the atrocious famines of Naples in 1764 and France in 1768. He was appointed Secretary of the Neapolitan Embassy in Paris in 1759, where he remained until 1769. Galiani was thus an eyewitness to the calamitous 'flour wars' and other direct consequences of the Physiocratic influence at court in the 1760s. It is quite possible that he – like Denis Diderot and even Cesare Beccaria – was sympathetic to French liberalism at the beginning of his career, but his experiences with the rift between economic theory and practice made him one of the most vitriolic opponents of Quesnay's school (Kaplan 1976: 590–611). Interestingly enough, Friedrich Nietzsche thought Galiani was the 'most profound, discerning and perhaps also the filthiest man of his century', and Galiani was also well known for his sharp wit and buffoonish manner (Nietzsche [1886] 2002: 28).[6] The good Abbé is remembered in the historiography of economic analysis mainly for his contributions to marginal utility theory and his vicious polemic with the Physiocrats (Kauder 1953a: 644–45; Kauder 1953b: 565; Spooner 1956). A lifelong friend of Galiani, Antonio Genovesi was also an Abbé, a philosopher and a reformer, but of a more academic inclination than Galiani. Indeed, he was appointed to the chair of political economy at the University of Naples in 1754, the first such chair outside of Germany, Austria, Sweden and Finland. From this position, he came to dominate the Neapolitan Enlightenment; his students, such as Giuseppe Palmieri and Gaetano Filangieri, continued his legacy across Italy.

In Milan, Count Pietro Verri and Marquis Cesare Bonesana Beccaria were both born to aristocratic families and benefited from the social and educational privileges associated with that. They were the kernel of the *Academia dei pugni,* and Verri served as the editor and main driving force behind the journal *Il Caffè*. Although they fell out of friendship later in life, the two Milanese noblemen and reformers had a very formative influence on each other. Their journal was modelled on the English *Spectator,* and presented a series of articles – some direct translations from the French *Encyclopedie,* others of their own writing – discussing matters of society and reform, among them political economy (see Capra 2002; Darnton 1979). Their group proved to be one of the instrumental forerunners of the Italian *Risorgimento* – the nineteenth-century unification of the peninsula (Noether 1951: 89–107). While Cesare Beccaria is best known for his *On Crimes and Punishments,* his lifelong devotion to the Milanese administration exposed him to the economic aspect of social reform. His *Elements of Political Economy,* written in 1769–70 but only published in 1804 in Baron Custodi's collection of early Italian economists, was originally presented as a series of lectures at the University of Milan, and was thus never refined for publication the way the contemporary *Wealth of Nations* was (Groenewegen 2002: 2–47). Nonetheless, he was hailed by Schumpeter (1954: 176) as 'the Italian A. Smith'. Verri, too, was a lifelong civil servant, whose direct experiences with real economic problems instilled in him a realism typical of continental mercantilism.

Beccaria, Verri and Galiani, all travelled extensively in Italy and beyond, conversing with the luminaries of their age (see, for example, Venturi 1972). Genovesi seldom left Naples, but his work and the students he trained spread his message to the far corners of the peninsula. Verri indeed wrote a letter to Genovesi thanking him for his work on political economy and insisting that 'all Italians owe you homage' (P. Verri, no date). The development of Italian economics in the period cannot, however, be properly understood outside of its dialogue with the French *economistes*, or Physiocrats. A voluminous scholarship in a variety of languages exists on the Physiocrats and their doctrines, but, given the focus of this essay, it seems sufficient to elucidate the basic mechanisms they identified for economic development and the policy proposals they extrapolated from them.

### Physiocracy and Its Italian Reception

While the school founded by François Quesnay certainly evolved from its incipience in the mid-1750s to its fall from grace in the late 1760s, its fundamental 'maxims of economic government' remained largely unchanged from Quesnay's 1756–57 articles on 'Farmers' and 'Grains' in *L'Encyclopedie* through his more systematic 1759 *Tableau Economique* to his followers' later works. Physiocracy, literally 'the rule of nature', famously envisioned the economy as a self-equilibrating system, and its insistence on the 'sterility' of the non-agricultural sectors is notorious. This doctrine was born from the theory that manufactures did not contribute to increasing the 'net product', as they could add no value to raw materials beyond what was consumed by the costs of production and the profits of the merchant. (For the survival of this idea in Smith, see Reinert 1999: 309–14.) Therefore, Quesnay and his school concluded with policy proposals such as 'only import luxury goods, and export raw materials', and 'favour the exportation of the immediate fruits of the earth by the importation of manufactures' (Quesnay [1758] 2003: 471–77; Quesnay [1759] 1968: 173; Miller 2000: 499–500; Groenewegen 2002: 222–62). The Physiocrats were instrumental in liberating the French grain trade in the 1760s, and the disorganizing consequences of this measure, intertwined with a series of bad harvests, created a human and political crisis at the end of the 1760s (Kaplan 1982: 52–57). While the Physiocrats have led a spoilt life in the history of economic analysis, many of their contemporaries were less impressed with their work and its very real consequences. While Adam Smith wrote very favourably of them, his best friend David Hume thought one should 'crush them, and pound them, and reduce them to ashes', and Louis Sébastien Mercier similarly hoped that 'equitable history' would 'punish' the Physiocrats (in Kaplan 1976: 591, 603). It has not.

The major eighteenth-century Italian economists seemed almost unanimously opposed to the policy conclusions offered by Physiocracy. While parts of Quesnay's nomenclature entered the economic vocabulary of the Milanese school, for example, in the famous grain question, they uniformly resisted the developmental degradation of the manufacturing sector (Will 1782: 48; Capra 2002: 292, 356). Pietro Verri, who joined Quesnay's brood in advocating free trade in grain, polemically attacked the Physiocratic stance on the role of industry in economic development, arguing, like most of his countrymen, that manufactures added more to the 'net product' of a nation than agriculture alone, and that transforming 'a few pieces of metal into a reproducing machine' was no more sterile than growing grain from 'the fields, soil, air, and water' (P. Verri [1771] 1986: 10; Capra 2002: 371). It has been suggested that the coherence of this Italian opposition to Physiocracy can be explained by the fact that their theories were received alongside Galiani's ferocious critiques (Ferrara 1889: 179), but the two traditions differed greatly even in their pre-analytical 'visions', while fuelling their respective economic methodologies. While the Italians were all too aware of the historical mechanisms that had let them fall behind, Quesnay found few lessons of relevance in the dustbin of history. 'Let us not seek into the history of nations or the mistakes of men,' Quesnay said, 'for that only presents an abyss of confusion . . . [these] do not serve to throw a light which can illuminate the darkness' (in Olson 1993: 132). Similarly, the Italians were, as a whole, less prone to accept theoretical abstractions out of hand, particularly when these manifestly failed to reflect the reality of the situation. The two things went hand-in-hand to a certain extent, and the Italians were generally more interested in understanding how countries had developed and what policies had worked, than in formulating utopian theories. It was exactly the paradox of extolling 'natural equilibrium' while untold thousands died of hunger that had angered Abbé Galiani, whose practicality was born from real-world policy failures (Venturi 1960: 48).

### Mathematics, Methodology, and 'Econo-Mystification'
From the humble beginnings of double-entry book-keeping in Venice, the numerical rendering of reality has given an immeasurable impetus to the progress of economic science. During the Enlightenment, the flow of mathematical ideas in economics increased, and it should therefore not come as a surprise that econo-mists often refer to the period as 'the birth of scientific economics' (Djiksterhuis and Dikshoorn 1969; Crosby 1997; Groenewegen 2002: 48–96). While Petty introduced the use of statistics and the Physiocrats helped render the economy in abstract terms, the eighteenth-century Italians pioneered the introduction of adv-anced mathematical methods, such as differential calculus, into the science (Tubaro 2000, 2002). Their work might, however, present one of the few exceptions to Paul Krugman's dictum that 'economics tends . . . to follow the line of least mathematical resistance' (Krugman 1991: 6).

Galiani, perhaps being the least systematic of the four major Italian economists of the period, never taught economics and was very critical of what he referred to as 'econo-mystification' (Galiani in Kaplan 1976: 601).[7] Writing largely in the immediate context of famine and Physiocracy, it is not surprising that he had little patience with hypothetical utopias. He was averse to the adap-tation of absolute principles in economics, instead arguing for 'empirical, flex-ible and contingent administration'. According to historian Steven L. Kaplan, Galiani 'detested absolute prohibitions as much as he loathed absolute liberty' (Kaplan 1976: 601, 594–96).[8] Galiani's sentiments on the matter were shared by even the most academic of Italian economists. While Genovesi's theories showed the characteristics of a theoretical system, its basic tenets differed little from those of Galiani and Serra before him. Indeed, Genovesi's 1764 *Discourse on the Utility of Sciences and the Arts* presented a systematic vision of science and society where disciplines addressing social reality had 'absolute pre-eminence' over theoretical ones. He argued consistently for propagation of the sciences among the general population, but refused to support theory for theory's sake (Genovesi [1753] 1977; Genovesi 1772; Mazzotti 1998: 684).

The Milanese school was initially much more analytical than its Neapolitan counterpart, but eventually came to adopt a very similar approach. Beccaria, attempting to calculate the tariff levels best balanced between effectiveness and smuggling, wrote in 1764 that 'algebra, as it pertains to everything that in some way can increase or diminish and to all things that have paragonal relationships to each other . . . can also, up to a certain point, find entry to the political sciences'. The results of such analytical endeavours could 'enlighten the creation of a tariff', but the usefulness of the 'geometrical approach' should never be exaggerated, as 'a political science full of numbers and calculations' was 'more adaptable to the inhabitants of *Laputa* than to our Europeans' (Beccaria [1764] 1998a: 173–74).[9] Verri, also writing for *Il Caffè*, similarly thought that the 'spirit of geometry saturated and perfected all sciences' (P. Verri [1764] 1998d: 314), and the 1772 sixth edition of his *Meditations on Political Economy* included a full mathematical rendering of his theory in an appendix by a fellow member of the *Academia dei pugni*, Paolo Frisi.

Later in life, however, Beccaria and Verri both abandoned even this very qualified mathematical exuberance because, as Beccaria wrote, it served 'no other purpose but that of rendering science mysterious and inaccessible' (Beccaria [1769] 1970: 45–46). As one contemporary commented to Frisi, 'you will do with political economy what the scholastics did with philosophy. In making things more and more subtle, you do not know where to stop' (in Tubaro 2000: 215; see also Reinert 2000). Whereas the English economists of the period were primarily merchants who took to the pen, most of the Italians arrived at economics from philosophy, jurisprudence and civil service. The Italians had a fundamentally more holistic perspective on what factors of society contributed to economic development, and refused to adopt methods that limited this vision. The bottom line was that economics had to be relevant, and Alessandro Verri, Pietro's younger brother and co-founder of the *Academia dei pugni,* seemed to have reached this conclusion before his brother when he noted that it is 'better to confess ignorance in certain things than to fabricate chimeras' (A. Verri 1998: 812).

### Human Capital, Institutions and Civil Society
The Milanese economists thus turned away from excessive analytical rigour because mathematical methods proved unable to decipher the complex institutional framework in which economic activities were embedded (Beccaria [1764] 1998a: 173–74; Tubaro 2000: 201). Like their Neapolitan contemporaries, they sought to be understood by the public and to reform society in line with their vision of the common good. To understand this point, one must bear in mind that the Italian writers, from Serra to Beccaria, considered 'man', not gold, to be the real wealth of a nation. It was the industry of man that created wealth, and a synergy between human capital, civil society and economic development was central to the tradition. The 'more educated nations become', Verri, for example, argued, 'the more trade we see introduced' (P. Verri [1764] 1998a: 27–29; P. Verri 1771: 4–5; Porta and Scazzieri 2002: 84, 96). Education, however,

was not sufficient; one also needed the civil institutions of trust and cooperation for market forces to operate properly. History had shown that 'the cupidity of man' seldom aligned properly with the general good; it was thus the thankless task of the legislator to mediate between the needs of private and public. Said Verri, 'the private interest of each individual, when it coincides with the public interests, is always the safest guarantor of public happiness' (P. Verri 1771: 42). This connection was not, like in Adam Smith, automatic.

It was a tradition that sought to unify the civil and commercial elements of society, and considered the institutions of a civil society to be the fundamental prerequisites of a functioning market economy (Porta and Scazzieri 2002: 84). Liberty and competition brought entrepreneurship and economic development, but only if embedded in a fortuitous legislative infrastructure (Beccaria [1769] 1970: 15–16; Porta and Scazzieri 2002: 103–06). 'Liberty', Verri said, 'is born from the laws, not from license' (in Capra 2002: 283). Galiani, observing the Parisian riots in the heyday of Physiocracy, similarly commented, after a particularly bloody incident of civil disorder that resulted in the death of 113 people, that liberty had been preached to the point where the very foundations of society had been undermined:

> I accuse, Madame, the *economistes*. They have preached liberty so much, they have criticized the police, order, the rules so much; they have said so often that nature left to herself was so beautiful, worked so well, put herself in equilibrium, etc. that finally, convinced that they were proprietors of the pavement and that they had the liberty to walk, everyone wanted to profit from [these rights] (in Kaplan 1976: 606).

To be anachronistic, they were neither communists nor supporters of Ayn Rand, and Alessandro Verri summarized their sentiment in an article on 'The Spirit of Society' in *Il Caffè*. Stressing the importance of civil society as a basis for economic development, he argued that one should 'honour one's obligation to society' but not waste one's time in 'useless public offices' (A. Verri [1764] 1998: 402). There was here, as in all things argued by the reformers, a golden middle way between the needs of man and of society, between theory and practice.

Genovesi refined this idea in many of his works, culminating in a relational concept of rationality very different from the one explored in England and France – a civil economy where social institutions had to be in place for the market function to operate (Genovesi 1765: 27; Bruni and Sugden 2000; Bruni 2000: 288–89). Economic growth, Genovesi argued, could therefore not be expected overnight through contact and trade with a more developed country, as the material and institutional infrastructures might be too different (Venturi 1969: 575, 590). These early modern Italian writers were, in the nomenclature of modern economics, also *institutionalists*.

### Manufactures, Protectionism and Economic Development

The major Italians thus differed from the Physiocrats not only in considering the manufacturing sector as contributing more to the 'net product' than agriculture, but also in emphasizing the larger social and cultural forces it mobilized. Manufactures were more efficient at fuelling economic development because the increasing returns to scale resulting from the division of labour in manufactures fundamentally changed the socio-economic construct of a country (Galiani [1751] 1915: 37–39; Beccaria [1769] 1970: 181–82). The Neapolitans and the Milanese, both argued for a synergy rather than a fundamental opposition between industry and agriculture, and investments in them were vital to prepare for international commerce. Chevalier de Zinobi, the voice of anti-Physiocracy in Galiani's 1770 *Dialogues on the Corn Trade* – widely regarded as one of the starkest refutations of Physiocracy in the eighteenth century – argued that 'one has never seen, and one never will see, a city of manufactures where the surrounding areas are not fruitfully cultivated, even where the soil is sterile' (Galiani 1770: 113). Beyond mere economic growth, however, Galiani saw industry change society itself, observing that the moral as well as material culture of a diversified manufacturing economy was always more civilized than a purely agricultural one (Venturi 1960: 54). Likewise, Verri saw a clear correlation between the nature of a nation's economic activities and its moral make-up: 'industry' led the way from 'ferocity' and 'mortal lethargy' as it encourages citizens to 'work, invent, and perfect the arts and occupations that maintain the country' (P. Verri [1764] 1998c: 159).

One of the main tasks of government was therefore to nourish manufactures and to establish the institutional foundation, which individual interests would soon coincide with or fruitfully compete. The British Navigation Acts were considered the paradigmatic example of such legislation, and the British model of economic development was generally considered the ideal to follow (Beccaria [1769] 1970: 39; Salerni [1782] 1996: 113; Magnusson 1994: 200). English and French theories, as already noted, could not be adopted directly because the socio-economic conditions of the countries in question differed so greatly. Whereas, for example, the problem in Italy was to overcome the crisis that had destroyed Italian industry in the seventeenth century, France merely had to protect what Colbert and Louis XIV had already created (Beccaria [1769] 1970: 40–41; Venturi 1960: 55). The mechanisms of economic development were clear, but different policies had to take precedence in the different economies of Europe.

Most of the major Italian economists of the time were generally in favour of 'free trade' but, as Seligman has pointed out, the term had a very different connotation in the early modern period:

> Free trade . . . denoted in those days something very different from what it signifies today. It did not mean freedom to import goods without payment of duty, on the contrary, to . . . all the free traders of the day, free trade meant freedom to export goods as over against the companies which possessed a

monopoly of trade. . . . The freedom of trade meant freedom of competition, not freedom or exemption from taxation of duties. Almost all the 'Free Traders' were in fact what we should today call Protectionists. (Seligman 1920: ix)

They were opposed to monopolies and privileges, but were much more careful when it came to foreign commerce. In this sense, the Italian arguments were similar to the pre-Physiocratic liberal tradition in France represented by writers like François Véron de Forbonnais, a liberalism balanced by the state to ensure economic development (Kaplan 1976: 689; Minard 2000: 496). Verri and Beccaria were typical of this, and their axioms of international trade remained largely unchanged throughout their careers. Their first thoughts on economic issues appeared in 1764 in the aforementioned *Il Caffè*, where Pietro Verri published his *Elements of Commerce*, written, he tells us, 'in Vienna before reading the authors active in the field' (P. Verri 1763: 187). Even so, echoes of current cameralist and mercantilist dogma resound in Verri's four maxims of economic development, mitigated, of course, by the 'particular' context of the country (P. Verri [1764] 1998b: 37):[10]

1. Tariffs on exported manufactured goods are bad for commerce.
2. Tariffs on imported raw materials needed for domestic industry are bad for commerce.
3. Tariffs on exported raw materials needed for domestic industry are good for commerce.
4. Tariffs on imported manufactured goods are good for commerce.

Verri retained most of these dictums in his later works, consistently arguing that raw materials and, interestingly enough, books and scientific instruments should be imported free of customs, with finished goods exported likewise to invigorate domestic manufacture (P. Verri [1771] 1986: 104, 113; Verri in Capra 2002: 354). Beccaria would later teach the very same principles in his inaugural lecture at the University of Milan:

> It is not sufficient to know, that industry is enlivened, by easing the duties on the importation of the first materials, and on the exportation of them when manufactured; and by loading those which are imposed on imported manufactures, and exported materials: that every economical operation may be reduced to the means of procuring the greatest possible quantity of labour and action among the members of a state; and that in this alone consists true and primary riches, much rather than in the abundance of a precious metal, which, being nothing but a symbol, is always obedient to the call of industry and toil, and, in spite of every obstruction, flies from idleness and sloth. Along with these maxims we must attend to the particular situation of a country. (Beccaria [1769] 1970: 6–7)

The early articles in *Il Caffè* are interesting also for the emphasis they put on the uneven dynamics of economic development. The mechanics of international trade, Verri argued, were such that the existing differences between countries would often be amplified. Rich countries, increasing their population and improving their production and infrastructure, abounded with 'all the benefits that a happy commerce produces in the interior', while poor ones multiplied their misfortunes. 'Bad effects' become 'bad causes' in a vicious circle that brings a country to a state of 'perfect dependency on its neighbours . . . good for nothing more than a place to transplant colonies'. Countries stuck in this 'mediocrity' must seek to 'define their trade balance on their own terms' to escape (P. Verri [1764] 1998b: 31, 33) – an argument further refined by Sebastiano Franci in a later issue of the journal:

> A weak and poor people of little wealth, generally speaking, acts wrongly in passing its raw materials to the stronger and richer. These nations rich in industry will manufacture them, more than doubling their value and sustain with this fine art a large part of their populations, and profiting enormously they constantly maintain their superiority (Franci [1764] 1998: 148).

### From *Ben Comune* to *Felicita Pubblica*: The Cultural Continuity of Italian Political Economy from the Scholastics to the Enlightenment

Marco Polo describes a bridge, stone by stone.
'But which is the stone that supports the bridge?' Kublai Khan asks.
'The bridge is not supported by one stone or another', Marco answers, 'but by the line of the arch that they form.'
Kublai Khan remains silent, reflecting. Then he adds: 'Why do you speak to me of the stones? It is only the arch that matters to me.'
Polo answers: 'Without stones there is no arch.'

Italo Calvino, Invisible Cities

Italo Calvino here describes what seems to be a defining characteristic of Italian political economy in the eighteenth century. In dialectic with their scholastic heritage, Italians from Botero to Beccaria proposed a molecular, rather than an atomistic interpretation of economic life (Langholm 1998: 153 and *in passim*). The unique emphasis on man's role in the economy had roots in the undercurrents of neo-Platonism of late Renaissance culture, and was an integral part of Jacob Burckhardt's vision of the Renaissance as hailing the rediscovery of the individual (Burckhardt 1869; Kristeller 1979). The classical tradition of individualism in the Renaissance, however, was never divorced from the Christian ethos that saturated society. One could indeed argue that the two axioms of classical individualism and Christian communitarianism reinforced each other synergistically, and that the importance of collective individuality, seemingly a contradiction in terms, was integral to the Italian tradition of economic philosophy from the Middle Ages onwards.[11] It was a way of thought that favoured the organic coherence of the city-state – an anthropocentric doctrine whose legacy is clearly manifest throughout the entire trajectory of Italian political economy from the scholastics to the *Risorgimento*; Giovanni Botero (1544–1617), Tommaso Campanella (1568–1639), Antonio Serra (dates unknown), Antonio Genovesi

(1712–1769), Ferdinando Galiani (1728–1787), Pietro Verri (1728–1797), and Cesare Beccaria (1738–1794) were all touched by the communal conscience of what Werner Sombart called the *activist–idealist* socio-economic tradition.

Even Galiani's most caustic witticisms cannot obfuscate the deep concern for his fellowmen that saturates his writings, as well as the desire to act upon it; he admits, 'I would like to have the eloquence necessary to convey to everyone the passion I have for humanity, and it would be worthy of our century that men should begin to love each other.' Similarly, we find Verri complaining: 'Would that I could say something useful! Would that I could do something useful!' (Galiani 1750: 154; P. Verri [1771] 1986: 2). Eighteenth-century Italian economics was born where the medieval conception of the common good intersected with the Enlightenment ideal of social reform (Marino 1986: 126). This heritage was an overarching phenomenon that found expression in a variety of languages of representation; it was disseminated in sermons, in books and in art. Serra's *Breve Trattato* expressed, in written form, an ideology articulated visually in Ambrogio Lorenzetti's (c. 1290–1348) celebrated *Allegory of Good and Bad Government* in the Palazzo Pubblico in Siena.[12] Propagation of civic well-being was the essence of the reason of state doctrine, and economics, as it was codified, was embedded in this larger vision of society.

Man was consistently considered the real wealth of an economy, and the betterment of his mental and material faculties was thus at the centre of attention. Education, science and innovation were seen as investments in human capital by all the writers here discussed, and their policy proposals were remarkably uniform across the period. Observing that the basic mechanism of economic development, namely, that of state support for increasing return activities, remained unchanged across Europe from the thirteenth to the eighteenth century, they refused to let emerging theoretical models blind their common sense. 'The system used by the English to get rich', Carlo Salerni wrote at the end of the period, 'is not merely a hypothesis, but an evidently very certain thesis' (Salerni [1782] 1996: 82). Knowing the general rules of economic development, the challenge facing these economists lay in tailoring them to the peculiarities of the Italian situation. As economic historian P.H.H. de Vries has argued, 'to throw some light on the question of why some nations have become so rich and others stayed so poor, in the end one must focus on industrialization. So analysing the role of the state in the rise of the West in the end has to boil down to analysing the role of the state in industrialization' (Vries 2002: 126). This knowledge was clearly passed down from Serra to Salerni.

The Italian tradition, thus, seems to have approached the problem of economic development from the standpoint of state support for competitive individual initiative, rather than of unilateral state intervention or monopolistic privileges. Unless the sheer size of the industry made it suffer from barriers that were too high for entry by individual actors in the economy – in which case they adopted the approach of modern state capitalism – the state was, with few exceptions, seen as a stimulator and facilitator, rather than a proprietor (Costantini

1742: 103–04; Reinert 1999). Following Eli Heckscher, Jürgen Habermas argued that the economic dimension of the modern public sphere could only have developed under the auspicious supervision of a guiding central authority. Just as Calvino's Marco Polo would have no arch without stones, so the collective achievement of society rested on the communal laurels of individual entrepreneurs (Heckscher [1934] 1994: 273–85; Habermas 1965: 34–35).

Unlike the 'spontaneous order' and 'invisible hand' of Bernard de Mandeville (1670–1733), Quesnay and Adam Smith, this tradition stressed the importance of the state taking an active role in the planning and construction of society's arch (Mandeville 1714; Smith 1776: 477). England's penetration of world markets in the sixteenth and seventeenth centuries could never have occurred without the careful superintendence of royal charters granting certain privileges to entrepreneurs in specific sectors of the economy, but the after-the-fact nature of Mandeville's and Smith's writing enabled them to take certain fortuitous institutions for granted (Hintze 1975: 428). When, therefore, Beccaria and Verri wrote on the importance of entrepreneurs (Klang 1990), they concurrently emphasized the importance of a supporting legislature, of state mediation. Both the Neapolitan and Milanese schools believed that certain self-regulatory forces could enhance economic development when left to themselves, but, observing the historical trajectories of economic development, did not trust the mechanisms of the market when divorced from what they considered to be the basic institutions of a civil society, from the framework of the common good. Schumpeter noted that 'the "mercantilist" elements in Genovesi's teaching only prove the realism of his vision' (Schumpeter 1954: 177), and this devotion to real economic problems and the reality of underdevelopment indeed seems valid for all the major economic writers of the Italian Enlightenment.

### Notes

[1] This is the same mechanism – 'increasing the *per capita* income of a growing population despite the continued pressure of diminishing returns in agriculture' – identified by Douglass C. North and Robert Paul Thomas as taking place, 'perhaps for the first time', in seventeenth-century England and Holland. Later, they went on to argue 'the Netherlands . . . were the first areas of Western Europe to escape the Malthusian checks'. Interestingly enough, however, they also tell us 'the great cities of Milan and Venice each boasted a population of perhaps 2,00,000, and other Italian urban centres, such as Florence, Genoa, Naples, and Palermo, may have contained as many as 100,000. The giants of their times, these cities far exceeded in size their nearest rivals' (North and Thomas 1973: 47, 117, 131). Obviously, the Italians had stumbled upon something special.

[2] This was, it should be noted, not the first time that the English monarchy seriously damaged the Florentine economy. The most powerful bankers in Europe, the Bardi and Peruzzi companies, collapsed when Edward III defaulted on his sovereign loans during the period 1343–47. The tables have thus turned, as the great lenders of today were the great defaulters of earlier times (Hunt 2001; Sapori 1926).

[3] The use of the Potosi mines to highlight the importance of manufactures became a *leitmotif* in early modern political economy across Europe. The heretic Tommaso Campanella, best known for his utopia, *The City of the Sun*, argued for encouragement of national industries on the basis that they were 'more prolific than mines' (Campanella [1602] 1653). Similarly, in 1751, we find the Spaniard Geronymo de

Uztariz, one of the greatest influences on the Italian economists of the late eighteenth century, proclaiming that manufactures were 'a mine more fruitful of gain, riches, and plenty, than those of Potosi' (Uztariz 1751: 9). The great question of the sixteenth and seventeenth centuries was indeed why Spain, in spite of the fact that tens of thousands of tons of silver had reached Seville from the New World in the course of the period, was so economically underdeveloped. Cosimo Perrotta has argued that 'mercantilism was born in response to the failure of Spain', as it showed contemporaries that the true wealth of a kingdom was to be found in its productive apparatus, rather than in mere bullion. 'History', said US economic historian Hamilton, 'offers few instances both of such exact diagnosis of social ills and such terrible deafness to wise advice on the part of those in power' as the Spanish economists. While Hamilton spoke of the Spanish situation, Serra's was no different (Perrotta 1993: 19).

4 'Divested of nonessentials,' Schumpeter wrote, 'the "Malthusian" Principle of Population sprang fully developed from the brain of Botero in 1589' (Botero [1589] 1956; Schumpeter 1954: 254–55). The Venetian monk Giammaria Ortes, one of the more renowned pre-Smithian Italian economists, was also a real precursor of Malthus and the dismal science.

5 This idea grew to some prominence in the European intellectual tradition, and is widely evident in French, German, Italian, Spanish and Swedish literature of the early modern period.

6 Nietzsche began reading Galiani in 1884, and reread him every year until 1888 (Brobjer 1997: 679). Similarly, Schumpeter (1954: 292) referred to Galiani as 'one of the ablest minds that ever became active in our field'.

7 Galiani, writing on the problems of political arithmetic, commented that 'a miserable example' of this new field 'was the Englishman William Petty, who in his ingenious treatise on Political Arithmetic easily demonstrated, with his calculations, many things that were very far from any truths, as his ultimate goal was the glory of his nation' (Galiani 1750: 58).

8 This was also the hallmark of the German Historical School as it attempted, as Schumpeter said, to 'sail between the Scylla of liberalism and the Charybdis of communism' (Schumpeter 1954: 459).

9 The people of Gulliver's *Laputa* were 'perpetually conversant in lines and figures. If they would, for example, praise the beauty of a woman, or any other animal, they would describe it by rhombs, circles, parallelograms, ellipses, and other geometrical terms.' Their houses were ill-built and had no straight angles because of their contempt for practical applications of mathematics, but they were still 'perpetually enquiring into public affairs, giving their judgements in matters of state, and passionately disputing every inch of a party opinion' with predictable results (Swift [1726] 1994: 176–77).

10 This is essentially the scheme, reflecting centuries-old English policy, proposed by Charles King in 1723. Verri claimed to have read Forbonnais' works while stationed in Vienna in 1760, and commented positively on Forbonnais' translation of King's work in a 1766 letter to his brother (P. Verri [1771] 1986: xvii).

11 The medieval historian Caroline Walker Bynum has developed this argument for an earlier period, pointing out that the very first European autobiographies invented the 'self' within a communal context in the twelfth century. The Thatcherite 'there is no such thing as society' was still nine centuries away when Europe began its economic ascension.

12 Ambrogino Lorenzetti's fresco in Siena (Lorenzetti 1338–40) is discussed, among other places, in Skinner (1988). The concept of *ben comune* that it projects hails from at least as far back as Brunetto Latini ([1254] 1993) in the thirteenth century, and the relationship between the two is discussed in Henderson (1994: 16–20). For a discussion of Lorenzetti on modern public administration, see Drechsler (2001).

**References**

Abramowitz, Moses (1986), 'Catching Up, Forging Ahead and Falling Behind', *Journal of Economic History*, 46 (2): 385–406.

Adelson, Candace (1983), 'Cosimo I de' Medici and the Foundation of Tapestry Production in Florence', in *Firenze e la Toscana dei Medici dell' Europa del '500* ( Florence: Leo S. Olschki): 899–924.

Albertini, Rudolph von (1970), *Firenze Dalla Republica Al Principato* (Turin: Einaudi).

Beccaria, Cesare Bonesaria, Marquis of ([1764] 1998a), 'Tentativo Analitico Su i Contrabandi', in Francioni, Gianni and Sergio Romagnoli, eds, *Il Caffè 1764–1766* (Turin: Bollati Boringhieri): 173–75.

—— ([1764] 1998b), *A Discourse on Public Economy and Commerce* (New York: Burt Franklin).

—— ([1769] 1970) *Elementi di Economia Pubblica* in *Opere*, Vol. 2, Dei Classici Italiani (Milan: Societa Tipogr).

Besold, Christoph (1623), *Discursus politicus de incrementis imperiorum, eorumque amplitudine procuranda, Cvi inserta est dissertatio singularis, de novo orbe* (Argentorati: Impensis haeredum Lazari Zetzneri).

—— ([1589] 1956), *The Reason of State* (New Haven: Yale University Press).

Botero, Giovanni (1599), *Le Relationi Universali* (Venice: Appresso Giorgio Angelieri).

Brobjer, Thomas H. (1997), 'Nietzsche's Reading and Private Library, 1885–1889', *Journal of the History of Ideas*, (58) 4: 663–80.

Brown, Judith (1983), 'Concepts of Political Economy: Cosimo I de' Medici in a Comparative European Context', in *Firenze e la Toscana dei Medici dell' Europa del '500* (Florence: Leo S. Olschki).

Bruni, Luigino (2000), 'Ego Facing Alter: How Economists have Depicted Human Interactions', *Annals of Public and Cooperative Economics*, 71 (2): 285–313.

Bruni, Luigino and Robert Sugden (2000), 'Moral Canals: Trust and Social Capital in the Work of Hume, Smith and Genovesi', *Economics and Philosophy*, 16: 21–45.

Burckhardt, Jacob (1869), *Die Cultur der Renaissance in Italien: Ein Versuch* (Leipzig: E.A. Seemann).

Bynum, Caroline Walker (1980), 'Did the Twelfth Century Discover the Individual?', *Journal of Ecclesiastical History*, 31 (1): 1–17.

Calabria, Antonio (1991), *The Cost of Empire: The Finances of the Kingdom of Naples in the Time of Spanish Rule* (Cambridge: Cambridge University Press).

Campanella, Tommaso ([1602] 1653), *A Discourse Touching the Spanish Monarchy* (London: printed for Philemon Stephens and are to be sold at his shop at the Gilded Lion in Paul's Churchyard).

Capra, Carlo (2002), *I Progressi Della Ragione* (Bologna: Il Mulino).

Carli, Gian Rinaldo ([1765] 1998), 'Della patria degli italiani', in Francioni, Gianni and Sergio Romagnoli, eds, *Il Caffè 1764–1766* (Turin: Bollati Boringhieri): 421–27.

Cipolla, Carlo M. (1970), 'The Economic Decline of Italy', in Carlo M. Cipolla, ed., *The Economic Decline of Empires* (London: Methuen): 196–214.

[Costantini, Giuseppe Antonio] Sappetti, Giovanni (1742), *Elementi di commerzio* (Genoa: Giambatista Novelli).

Croce, Benedetto (1925), *Storia Del Regno Di Napoli* (Bari: Laterza).

Crosby, Alfred W. (1997), *The Measure of Reality: Quantification and Western Society, 1250–1600* (Cambridge: Cambridge University Press).

Custodi, Pietro (1803), *Scrittori Classici Italiani di Economia Politica* (Milan: G.G. Destefanis).

Darnton, Robert (1979), *The Business of Enlightenment: A Publishing History of the Encyclopedie* (Cambridge: Harvard University Press).

Defoe, Daniel ([1730] 1969), *A Plan for the English Commerce* (New York: Augustus M. Kelley).

Djiksterhuis, E.J. and C. Dikshoorn (1969), *The Mechanization of the World Picture* (Oxford: Oxford University Press).

Drechsler, Wolfgang (2001), *Good and Bad Government: Ambrogio Lorenzetti's Frescoes in the*

*Siena Town Hall as Mission Statement for Public Administration Today* (Budapest: Open Society Institute).

Ferrara, Francesco (1889), *Esame storico-critico di economisti e dottrine economiche del secolo xviii e prima metá del xix*, 2 volumes (Turin).

Franci, Sebastiano ([1764] 1998), 'Alcuni Pensieri Politici', in Francioni, Gianni and Sergio Romagnoli, eds, *Il Caffè 1764–1766* (Turin: Bollati Boringhieri): 143–50.

Galiani, Ferdinando (1750), *Della Moneta* (Naples: Giuseppe Raimondi).

—— ([1751] 1915), *Della Moneta*, edited by Fausto Nicolini (Bari: G. Laterza).

—— ([1752] 1977), *On Money* (Ann Arbor: published for Dept of Economics, University of Chicago by University Microfilms International).

—— (1770), *Dialogues Sur le Commerce des Bleds* (London).

—— (1979), *La Bagarre: Galiani's 'Lost' Dialogue*, edited by S.L. Kaplan (The Hague: M. Nijhoff).

Genovesi, Antonio ([1753] 1977), 'Discorso sopra il vero dine delle lettere e delle scienze' in *Scritti*, edited by Franco Venturi (Turin: Einaudi): 227–76.

—— (1757), *Storia del commercio della Gran Bretagna scritta da John Cary . . . Tradotta in nostra volgar lingua da Pietro Genovesi . . . con un ragionamento . . . di Antonio Genovesi* (Naples: Benedetto Casari).

—— (1765), *Lezioni di commercio o sia d'economia civile* (Naples: Remondini, Bassano).

—— (1772), *Lettere accademiche su la questione se sieno più felici gl'ignoranti, che gli scienzati . . .* (Venice: Giambattista Paquali).

—— (1977), *Scritti*, edited by Franco Venturi (Turin: Einaudi).

Gilbert, Allan H. (1968), *Machiavelli's Prince and Its Forerunners: The Prince as a Typical Book de Regimine Principum* (New York: Barnes & Noble).

Goldthwaite, Richard A. (1993), *Wealth and the Demand for Art in Italy, 1300–1600* (Baltimore: Johns Hopkins University Press).

Groenewegen, Peter (2002), *Eighteenth-Century Economics: Turgot, Beccaria and Smith and their Contemporaries* (London: Routledge).

Habermas, Jürgen (1965), *Strukturwandel der Öffentlichkeit: Untersuchungen zu einer Kategorie der Bürgerlichen Gesellschaft* (Neuwied am Rhein: Hermann Luchterhand Verlag).

Heckscher, Eli F. ([1934] 1994), *Mercantilism* (London: Routledge).

Henderson, John (1994), *Piety and Charity in Late Medieval Florence* (Oxford: Clarendon Press).

Hintze, Otto (1975), *The Historical Essays of Otto Hintze*, edited by Felix Gilbert (Oxford: Oxford University Press).

Hunt, Edwin S. (2001), *The Medieval Super-Companies* (Cambridge: Cambridge University Press).

Ilardi, Vincent (1993), 'Renaissance Florence: The Optical Capital of the World', *European Journal of Economic History*, 22 (3): 507–42.

Kaplan, S.L. (1976), *Bread, Politics, and Political Economy in the Reign of Luis XV* (The Hague: M. Nijhoff).

—— (1982), *The Famine Plot Persuasion in Eighteenth-Century France* (Philadelphia: American Philosophical Society).

Kauder, Emil (1953a), 'The Retarded Acceptance of Marginal Utility Theory', *Quarterly Journal of Economics*, 67 (4): 564–75.

—— (1953b), 'Genesis of the Marginal Utility Theory: From Aristotle to the End of the Eighteenth Century', *The Economic Journal*, 63 (251): 638–50.

Klang, Daniel M. (1990), 'Cesare Beccaria, Pietro Verri e l'idea dell'imprenditore nell'illuminismo milanese', in Sergio Romagnoli, Gian Domenico Pisapia, eds, *Cesare Beccaria tra Milano e l'Europa* (Rome-Bari: Cariplo-Laterza): 371–406.

Kristeller, Paul Oskar (1979), *Renaissance Thought and Its Sources*, edited by Michael Mooney (New York: Columbia University Press).

Krugman, Paul R. (1991), *Geography and Trade* (Cambridge: MIT Press).

Langholm, Odd Inge (1998), *The Legacy of Scholasticism in Economic Thought: Antecedents of Choice and Power* (Cambridge: Cambridge University Press).

Latini, Brunetto ([1254] 1993), *The Book of the Treasure = Li livres dou tresor* (New York: Garland Publishing).

Litchfield, R. Burr (1986), *Emergence of a Bureaucracy: The Florentine Patricians, 1530–1790* (Princeton: Princeton University Press).

List, Friedrich ([1841] 1959), *Das Nationale System der Politischen Ökonomie* (Basel: Kyklos Verlag).

Lorenzetti, Ambrogio (1338–40), *Allegory of Good and Bad Government* (Siena: Palazzo Pubblico).

Magnusson, Lars (1994), *Mercantilism: The Shaping of an Economic Language* (London: Routledge).

Malanima, Paolo (1982), *La decadenza di un'economia cittadina: l'industria di Firenze nei secoli xvi–xviii* (Bologna: Il Mulino).

—— (1983), 'L'industria fiorentina in declino fra '500 e '600', in *Firenze e la Toscana dei Medici dell' Europa del '500* (Florence: Leo S. Olschki): 295–308.

—— (1988), 'An Example of Industrial Reconversion: Tuscany in the Sixteenth and Seventeenth Centuries', in Herman van der Wee, ed., *The Rise and Decline of Urban Industries in Italy and the Low Countries* (Leuven: Leuven University Press): 63–74.

Mandeville, Bernard de (1714), *The Fable of the Bees: Or Private Vices, Publick Benefits* (London: J. Roberts).

Marino, John A. (1986), 'The State and the Shepherds in Pre-Enlightenment Naples', *The Journal of Modern History*, 58 (1): 125–42.

Mazzotti, Massimo (1998), 'The Geometers of God: Mathematics and Reaction in the Kingdom of Naples', *Isis*, 89 (4): 674–701.

McCray, Patrick W. (1999), *Glassmaking in Renaissance Venice: The Fragile Craft* (Aldershot: Ashgate).

Messbarger, Rebecca (1999), 'Reforming the Female Class: *Il Caffe's* Defence of Women', *Eighteenth-Century Studies*, 3 (3): 355–69.

Miller, Judith A. (2000), 'Economic Ideologies, 1750–1800: The Creation of the Modern Political Economy?', *French Historical Studies*, 23 (3): 497–511.

Minard, Philippe (2000), 'Colbertism Continued? The Inspectorate of Manufactures and Strategies of Exchange in Eighteenth-Century France', *French Historical Studies*, 23 (3): 477–96.

Molá, Luca, Reinhold C. Mueller and Claudio Zanier (2000), *La seta in Italia dal medioevo al seicento: Dal baco al drappo* (Venice: Marsilio).

Morelli, Roberta (1976), 'The Medici Silver Mines (1542–1592)', *Journal of European Economic History*, 5 (1): 121–40.

Myrdal, Gunnar (1956), *Development and Underdevelopment: A Note on the Mechanism of National and International Economic Inequality* (Cairo: National Bank of Egypt).

—— (1957), *Economic Theory and Underdeveloped Regions* (London: G. Duckworth & Co.).

Nietzsche, Friedrich ([1886] 2002), *Beyond Good and Evil* (Cambridge: Cambridge University Press).

Noether, Emiliana P. (1951), *Seeds of Italian Nationalism* (New York: Columbia University Press).

North, Douglass C. and Robert Paul Thomas (1973), *The Rise of the Western World: A New Economic History* (Cambridge: Cambridge University Press).

Olson, Richard (1993), *The Emergence of the Social Sciences, 1642–1792* (New York: Twayne).

Parigino, Giuseppe Vittorio (1999), *Il tesoro del principe: Funzione pubblica e privata del patrimonio della famiglia Medici nel cinquecento* (Florence: Leo S. Olschki).

Perrotta, Cosimo (1991), 'Is the Mercantilist Theory of the Favourable Balance of Trade Really Erroneous?', *History of Political Economy*, 23 (2): 301–36.

—— (1993), 'Early Spanish Mercantilism: The First Analysis of Underdevelopment', in Lars Magnusson, ed., *Mercantilist Economics* (Boston: Kluwer): 17–58.

Porta, Pier Luigi and Roberto Scazzieri (2002), 'Pietro Verri's Political Economy: Commercial Society, Civil Society, and the Science of the Legislator', *History of Political Economy*, 34 (1): 83–110.

Porter, Jeanne Chenault, ed. (2000), *Baroque Naples: A Documentary History, 1600–1800* (New York: Italica Press).

Quesnay, François [1758] (2003), 'Grani', in Paolo Casini, ed., *Enciclopedia o dizionario ragionato delle scienze, delle arti e dei mestieri ordinate da Diderot e d'Alembert* (Bari: Laterza): 470–77.

—— ([1759] 1968), *The Economical Table* (New York: Bergman).

Reinert, Erik S. (1995), 'Competitiveness and its Predecessors: A 500-Year Cross-National Perspective', *Structural Change and Economic Dynamics*, 6: 23–42.

—— (1999), 'The Role of the State in Economic Growth', *Journal of Economic Studies*, 26 (4/5): 268–326.

—— (2000), 'Full Circle: Economics from Scholasticism through Innovation and Back into Mathematical Scholasticism: Reflections on a 1769 Price Essay: "Why Is It That Economics So Far Has Gained So Few Advantages from Physics and Mathematics?"', *Journal of Economic Studies*, 27 (4): 364–76.

Reinert, Sophus A. and Erik S. Reinert (2004), 'An Early National Innovation System: The Case of Antonio Serra's 1613 *Breve Trattato*', in *Institutions and Economic Development* (forthcoming).

Ribton–Turner, C.J. (1887), *A History of Vagrants and Vagrancy and Beggars and Begging* (London: Chapmans and Hall).

Rolova, Alexandra (1983), 'La manifattura nell'industria tessile di Firenze del cinquecento', in *Firenze e la Toscana dei Medici dell' Europa del '500* (Florence: Leo S. Olschki): 309–26.

Roover, Raymond de (1963), *The Rise and Decline of the Medici Bank, 1397–1494* (Cambridge: Harvard University Press).

Ruffolo, Giorgio (2004), *Quando l'Italia era una superpotenza: Il ferro di Roma e l'oro dei mercanti* (Turin: Einaudi).

Salerni, Carlo ([1782] 1996), *Riflessioni sull'economia della provincia d'Otranto* (Lecce: Centro di studi salentini).

Sapori, Armando (1926), *La crisi delle compagnie mercantili dei Bardi e dei Peruzzi* (Florence).

Schmoller, Gustav ([1897] 1967), *The Mercantile System and its Historical Significance* (New York: Augustus M. Kelley).

Schumpeter, Joseph Alois (1954), *A History of Economic Analysis* (Oxford: Oxford University Press).

Seligman, E.R.A. (1920), *Curiosities of Early Economic Literature* (San Francisco: Privately Printed by John Henry Nash).

Serra, Antonio (1613), *Breve Trattato delle cause che possono far abbondare li regni d'oro & argento dove non sono miniere* (Naples: Lazzaro Scorriggio).

Skinner, Quentin (1988), 'Ambrogio Lorenzetti: The Artist as Political Philosopher', *Proceedings of the British Academy*: 1–56.

Smith, Adam (1776), *An Inquiry into the Nature and Causes of the Wealth of Nations* (London: Printed for W. Strahan and T. Cadell in the Strand).

Sombart, Werner (1902), *Der Moderne Kapitalismus* (Leipzig: Duncker & Humblot).

Spooner, F.C. (1956), 'The Principle of Utility: The Contribution of Ferdinando Galiani', *Cambridge Historical Journal*, 12 (1): 81–82.

Swift, Jonathan ([1726] 1994), *Gulliver's Travels* (London: Penguin).

Tron, Andrea ([1784] 1994), 'Serenissimo Principe', in Paolo Gaspari, ed., *Il testamento morale dell'aristocrazia veneziana* (Udine: Istituto editoriale Veneto friulano): 90–125.

Tubaro, Paola (2000), 'Un'esperienza peculiare del Settecento italiano: la 'scuola milanese' di economia matematica', *Studi settecenteschi*, 20: 193–223.

—— (2002), 'A Case Study in Early Mathematics Economics: Pietro Verri and Paolo Frisi, 1772', *Journal of the History of Economic Thought*, 24 (2): 195–214.

Uztariz, Geronymo de (1751), *The Theory and Practice of Commerce and Maritime Affairs* (2 Volumes), Vol. 1 (London: John and James Rivington).

Venturi, Franco (1960), 'Galiani tra enciclopedisti e fisiocrati', *Rivista storica italiana*, 72 (1): 45–61.

—— (1969), *Settecento riformatore* (Turin: Einaudi).

—— (1972), in Stuart Woold, ed., *Italy and the Enlightenment: Studies in a Cosmopolitan Century* (London: Longman).

Verri, Alessandro ([1764] 1998), 'Lo spirito di società', in Francioni, Gianni and Sergio Romagnoli, eds, *Il Caffè 1764–1766* (Turin: Bollati Boringhieri): 396–402.

—— (1998), 'Appendice V – Appunti di Alessandro Verri: idée per articoli', in Gianni Francioni and Sergio Romagnoli, eds, *Il Caffè 1764–1766* (Turin: Bollati Boringhieri): 811–13.

Verri, Pietro (no date), Undated Letter to Antonio Genovesi in the archives of the Mattioli Foundation, Milan, Classification number: Cart. 276: Correspondenza di Pietro Verri a vari destinatari 1763–1795 (ex CAR 083.01–11) Fasc. 7. Antonio Genovesi – Milano; 1 lett. s.d. (CAR 083.07) cc. 2.

—— (1763), 'Elementi di commercio', in 'Cose varie buone, mediocri, cattive del conte Pietro Verri fatti ne' tempi di sua gioventu, le quail con eroica clemenza ha transcritte di sua mano nell'anno 1763 ad uso soltanto proprio o degl'intimi amici suoi', manuscript in the archives of the Mattioli Foundation, Milan, Classification number: Cart. 373, Fasc. 1, carte: 187.

—— ([1764] 1998a), 'Il tempio dell'ignoranzia', in Francioni, Gianni and Sergio Romagnoli, eds, *Il Caffè 1764–1766* (Turin: Bollati Boringhieri): 27–29.

—— ([1764] 1998b), 'Elementi del commercio', in Francioni, Gianni and Sergio Romagnoli, eds, *Il Caffè 1764–1766* (Turin: Bollati Boringhieri): 30–38.

—— ([1764] 1998c), 'Considerazioni sul lusso', in Francioni, Gianni and Sergio Romagnoli, eds, *Il Caffè 1764–1766* (Turin: Bollati Boringhieri): 155–62.

—— ([1764] 1998d), 'Gi studi utili', in Francioni, Gianni and Sergio Romagnoli, eds, *Il Caffè 1764–1766* (Turin: Bollati Boringhieri): 311–18.

—— ([1771] 1986), *Meditazioni sulla economia politica*, edited by Peter Groenewegen, (Fairfield: Augustus M. Kelley).

Vries, Jan de (1984), *European Urbanization 1500–1800* (Cambridge: Harvard University Press).

Vries, P.H.H. de (2002), 'Governing Growth: A Comparative Analysis of the Role of the State in the Rise of the West', *Journal of World History*, 13 (1): 67–138.

Wallerstein, Immanuel (1974), *The Modern World System I: Capitalist Agriculture and the Origins of the European World Economy in the Sixteenth Century* (San Diego: Academic Press).

—— (1980), *The Modern World System II: Mercantilism and the Consolidation of the European World Economy, 1600–1750* (Boston: Academic Press).

Will, Georg Andreas (1782), *Versuch über die Physiokratie, deren Geschichte, Literatur, Inhalt und Wert* (Nürnberg).

Zanden, Jan Luiten van (2001), 'Early Modern Economic Growth: A Survey of the European Economy, 1500–1800', in Maarten Prak, ed., *Early Modern Capitalism: Economic and Social Change in Europe 1400–1800* (London: Routledge): 69–87.

# German Economics as Development Economics

## From the Thirty Years' War to World War II

*Erik S. Reinert*

Three main elements make a study of the German economic tradition[1] particularly rewarding for development economists. First of all, German economics was born late and at a time when the nation was particularly backward, poor and ravaged by the Thirty Years' War (1618–48), which had cost the lives of up to 70 per cent of the civilian population in some areas. Therefore, from its very inception, German economics was that of a backward nation attempting to catch up with its wealthier neighbours. As opposed to English and American economics, whose philosophical base changed radically when the nations attained world economic power, the analytical base of German economics was not modified as the nation grew wealthier. Second, German economics has consistently, through the centuries, seen the economy from a different vantage point with different metaphors: essentially from the point of view of production rather than trade, and operating at a much lower level of abstraction than today's mainstream economics and its predecessors. Third, the scope of economics in the German tradition has been much wider than in the Anglo-Saxon mainstream. Factors such as geography and history, technology and technical change, government and governance, and social problems and their remedies, have all been central to the approach since its very inception.

A frequent theme in German historical writing is the idea of the country as a *verspätete* nation, a laggard nation, as compared to the rest of Europe. In such a situation, the state plays a very different role than in the more developed nations.[2] As Keynes said, 'the worse the situation, the less laissez-faire works.' It was therefore only natural that other latecomers – in particular, the United States and Japan – built their economic theories and policies on the German model.[3] During the nineteenth century, united in a common position against English economics, economics in Germany and the United States strongly influenced and fertilized each other. These catching-up nations formed a common theoretical front against England, a nation that not only made it politically clear that she saw it as a primary goal to prevent other nations from following the path of industrialization, but also – for the first time in the history of economics – possessed an economic theory that made this goal a legitimate one. From a policy perspective, the novelty of the economics of Smith and Ricardo was that they made colonialism morally defensible.[4]

The nineteenth century produced important German–American economic exchanges and alliances against English classical economics. Friedrich List, a German political refugee in the United States, was inspired by the vision and arguments of US economists: publications by Daniel Raymond and Mathew Carey in 1820 and 1821 provided List with new ammunition and inspiration. Later in the century, another German–American pair of economists, Henry Carey and Eugen Dühring, supported and defended each other. During the nineteenth century, both US and Japanese economists were trained in German economics: US economists through their graduate studies at German universities, and Japanese economists through their training under not only German economics professors in Japan but also a large number of German-trained US professors teaching in Japan (see Sugiyama and Mizuta 1988). There were no graduate schools in economics in the United States at that time, and most US economists received their Ph.D.s at German universities, as did all the founders of the American Economic Association. Reading knowledge of German was mandatory for a Ph.D. in economics in the United States until World War II.

We should not, however, exaggerate the differences between the German economic tradition and that of the rest of continental Europe. In the long term, the most important dividing line was between the English economic tradition and the continental European traditions seen as a whole. The works available in English on the German economic tradition tend to be seen from an Anglo-Saxon viewpoint, where German economics is seen in contrast to the English tradition without recognizing its similarities to the rest of the continental tradition. To most historians of economic thought, cameralism – the particular German form of economics – is solely a German phenomenon. Many are not aware that both the term 'cameralism' itself and the works of the cameralist authors spread from Sweden and Russia to Spain and Italy.[5] The textbook written by the first professor of economics outside Germany, Anders Berch in Uppsala (Berch 1747), used the term 'cameralism' in its title. The first professor of economics in northern Italy in the 1760s, Cesare Beccaria, was one of 'cameral sciences'.

The only two German-language economists broadly studied in the rest of the world – Karl Marx and Joseph Alois Schumpeter – are, in fact, much less original in the context of the German tradition than they appear in the standard historiography of economic thought. Marx and Schumpeter indeed shared a typical 'German' view of productive forces bringing about change in society. In his Foreword to the Japanese edition of *The Theory of Economic Development* (reproduced in Clemence 1951: 158–63), Schumpeter stressed the similarities between Marx' approach and his own, contrasting their approach with Walrasian and Marshallian economics. In the German production-based tradition, capital *per se* has no value, and this is reflected both in Schumpeter and in Marx. As a result, the interest rate under perfect equilibrium in Schumpeter's system would be zero. This finds its parallel in Marx's proposition that constant capital does not produce any surplus value. However, these similarities, according to Schumpeter, are 'obliterated by a very wide difference in general outlook' (in Clemence 1951: 161).

Seen from the perspective of German economics, the part of Marx's work alien to this tradition was his use of Ricardo's labour theory of value. Marx's contemporaries among German economists, starting with Eugen Dühring who was the first to comment on his work, therefore tended to be sympathetic towards Marx's economic analysis but not to his turning the social pyramid upside down as the solution to society's ills. Still, Marx's influence on the German economists who followed him is clear. In fact, in his book review of Werner Sombart's main work, *Der moderne Kapitalismus,* Gustav Schmoller, the oldest of the giants of the New Historical School, chided his younger colleague for being too greatly influenced by Marx.

### Permanent Characteristics of the German Economic Tradition

It is possible to distinguish an economic tradition in Germany from after the end of the Thirty Years' War in 1648. Prior to this date, in the tradition of Xenophon, a literary tradition generally labeled *Hausvaterliteratur* gave advice on how to run estates, small and large. *Fürstenspiegel* ('Kings' Mirror'), of which the best known is *Sachsenspiegel* from the twelfth century, were books that collected the laws and customs of the German states. During the three hundred years from 1648 until the German economics tradition dissolved after World War II in 1945, a continuity of principles and approaches can be observed that clearly distinguished this type of economics, both from English economics after 1776 and from today's mainstream economics. In the chapter on 'Mercantilism and Economic Development' in this volume, we point to the similarities between English economics before 1776 and the German tradition.

Different types of economics tend to be influenced by the professions from which the economists are recruited. English economists were, to a large extent, merchants and traders who brought their professional perspective with them. Adam Smith spent many years as a customs inspector, adding to the commercial bias of English economic theory. Indeed, a common German criticism of English classical economics has been that it reduced the science of economics to *catalectics*, to a science limited to the study of barter, trade and exchange. German economists, by contrast, were involved in the management of the many small German states. The term cameralism itself originates in the *camera principis* or *Kammer,* that is, treasury. The perspective of the cameralists was that of public management, of taxes and institutions, laws and regulations. Their view of economic development was, therefore, very practical, and led them to a consideration of production – rather than trade alone – and the balance between different economic activities. For example, the need for creating a healthy base for taxation led them to favour the promotion of mechanized manufacturing, whose employees would gain a taxable income and whose owners were much better tax subjects than farmers or small artisans. German economists were, almost to a man,[6] in ardent opposition to the French Physiocrats, who established agriculture as the only producer of 'net wealth' (see also the chapter on 'The Italian Tradition of Political Economy' in this volume).

The German economic tradition focuses on the state as an important economic facilitator and occasionally also as an entrepreneur of last resort in difficult situations (Reinert 1999). Probably also as a legacy of the chaos of the Thirty Years' War, a chaos similar to that of any 'failing state' today, pragmatism called for an orderly environment, with the state as a necessary facilitator in order to create individual opportunity and happiness. The state is seen as something through which, rather than against which, individual liberty and progress are gained within the framework of a *common weal*.[7] Through this tradition, German economics provides key insights for contemporary economies where the 'natural order' is non-productive rent-seeking involving raw materials and/or cheap labour, and where the 'natural order', at times, is utter chaos.

German economics is above all an *Erfahrungswissenschaft* – a science based on experience. There is little metaphysical speculation and high abstractions; many considered the economic theories of David Ricardo to be an example of 'metaphysical speculation'.[8] *Strukturzusammenhänge* – structural coherence and connections – among economic factors, and between the economy and the rest of society, are not only obvious, understanding such connections is also most important for both economic theory and policy. Synergies would be one example of this. Compared to Anglo-Saxon economics, the German approach has therefore always been holistic. Economics was to become an umbrella science of the social sciences. There was only one criterion for what was to be included under the heading of 'economics': relevance. To the degree that nutrition might be important to the economy at one point in time, it would be a part of economics.

*Praxisnähe* – closeness to reality – and relevance have been key criteria for academic quality in this tradition. There is also a fundamental understanding that important economic factors are irreducible to mere figures and symbols. A frequent criticism is that standard economics often produces *qualitätslose Grössen*, quantities that are devoid of any qualitative understanding. Even the most accurate and comprehensive description of a human being by all his or her quantifiable aspects – height, weight, percentage of water and trace minerals – would leave out the key factor in economic development, what Friedrich Nietzsche called *Geist und Willenskapital:* the wit and will of mankind.

As it developed, German economics came to be solidly based on the philosophical foundation of Gottfried Wilhelm von Leibniz (1646–1716) and Christian Wolff (1679–1754),[9] arising from the legal tradition of *Naturrecht* or natural law. The devastation of the Thirty Years' War created a need for a common basis of law regardless of creed. In the natural 'uncivilized state', the natural law tradition maintains that man still has moral obligations, the origins of which are to be found in nature. Modern state theory also emerged in the same period. At the core of the system of Christian Wolff, who came to be the basis of

German economics starting around 1750, rests the presupposition that man is essentially a social, peaceful and rational being. Related to this is a fundamental belief in man's common sense: *der gesunden Menschenverstand.*

Schumpeterian elements are deeply embedded in the German economics tradition. A focus on learning and progress, very clear in Leibniz and Wolff, is based on the *Gottesähnlichkeit* of man: man's near-God-like quality of being able to create new things. Being born in the image of God meant that it was man's pleasurable duty to invent. At its most fundamental level, the contrast between English and German economics lies in the view of the human mind. To John Locke, man's mind is a blank slate – a *tabula rasa* – with which he is born, and which passively receives impressions throughout life. To Leibniz, man has an active mind that constantly compares experiences with established schemata, a mind both noble and creative.

Of Adam Smith's ideas, the one most repudiated by German economists was that man is essentially an animal that has learned to barter. In the tradition that followed Smith, ideas and inventions have been produced outside the economic system. Karl Menger, the founder of the Austrian School of Economics, dedicated a whole chapter in his *Grundrisse* to refute Smith's view on this point. In the German tradition, including Marx and Schumpeter, the view is that man is an animal who has learned to invent. Nietzsche later added the point that man is the only animal that can keep promises, and therefore creates laws and institutions. Putting these elements together, we have an impressionistic picture of what differentiates English from German economics – barter and 'metaphysical speculation', on the one hand, and production and institutions, on the other.

To sum up, the following are the main characteristics that distinguish the German economic tradition – from Gottfried Leibniz and Christian Wolff, via Johann Gottlob von Justi and Friedrich List, to the *Verein für Sozialpolitik* and the Historical Schools:

- Centre of theory: man and his needs: *Der Mensch und seine Bedürfnisse.*
- A non-mechanical understanding of the world: qualitative *'verstehen'*, as opposed to purely quantifiable *'begreifen'* (Drechsler 2004).
- An *activist–idealist* approach to economic policy based on morality and ethics, as opposed to a *passive–materialistic* attitude to economic policy (these are Werner Sombart's terms).
- 'History matters': theory and policy must be based on the context and should understand the cumulative mechanisms in economics.
- Technology and new knowledge are the driving forces of the economy.
- Focus on production, rather than trade.
- Economic activities are seen as qualitatively different as carriers of economic growth.
- Economic harmony is man-made, not natural. Passivity is more likely to create 'spontaneous disorder' than 'spontaneous order'.

### Cameralist Economic Policy: From Veit von Seckendorff (1626–1692) to Wilhelm von Hörnigk (1640–1714)

Veit Ludwig von Seckendorff (1626–1692) has been called the 'Adam Smith of Cameralism' (Small 1909), and justifiably so. His times were violent and extremely difficult for Germany. The Thirty Years' War (1618–48) was a religious war, initially intra-German, which gradually came to involve several European powers at the time, including Spain, France, Denmark and Sweden. The war had no winner, but it became obvious to a number of German intellectuals of the next generation that the real loser was civilized society as such. When Seckendorff was 16 years old, his father, a German in the service of the Swedish army, was executed as an alleged spy. By the time Seckendorff died at the age of 66, the armies of Louis the XIV of France had recently utterly destroyed one German state, the Palatinate (*Pfalz*). In between, there were wars with the Turks and two more wars with France that led to the loss of Strasbourg, where Seckendorff had studied. Cameralism, in our view, cannot be properly understood outside this context of a simultaneous reconstruction of a civilized society and of what would today be called 'failed states': states where economic life and basic institutions had to be built, virtually, from scratch. The 'natural order' of the day was barbarism.

Seckendorff entered the service of a former official in the Swedish army, Duke Ernst of Sachsen–Gotha, called Ernst *der Fromme* or Ernst the Pious. Seckendorff loyally identified himself with the *common weal* of the state he served, but was also patriotic about greater Germany. He is referred to as one of the most learned men of his times; he corresponded with Leibniz, among others, and his high ethical standards made him a prototype for later German bureaucrats.

In 1656, at the age of 30, Seckendorff finished his most important work and the first book in the cameralist literature, *Der Teutsche Fürstenstaat* (*The German Principality*). The book became the standard handbook for economic policy in Germany and went through a number of editions over the next 98 years. The *Fürstenstaat* is a kind of 'owner's manual' for a small state. There are accurate descriptions of history, population, economic conditions, administration, school system, law and justice. The principles followed in the very successful reconstruction of the state of Sachsen–Gotha and its institutions after the Thirty Years' War are described. Seckendorff's approach was clearly a holistic and organic one, where the state is an organism and its *common weal* can only be understood in its totality (*Ganzheit*). His views were similar to those of the Italian economists of the Renaissance. The emphasis on the totality, on *Ganzheit*, was to be a hallmark of German economics and German philosophy for the next 300 years.[10]

Seckendorff travelled to the Netherlands, accompanying Count Ernst. The wealth and religious tolerance he observed there made a huge impression on him (Stolleis 1995:158). Early economic policy in Europe was frequently based on benchmarking against the successful states – the Netherlands (Reinert, ed. 2004c) and Venice being the obvious cases – and against Spain, with its inflow of gold accompanied by deindustrialization and increasing poverty, as the case to avoid. To Seckendorff, the Dutch appeared as 'examples of the wisest and in production and trade (*in Gewerb*) the most experienced people' (Seckendorff 1665). From the Netherlands, Seckendorff understood the crucial need for manufactures and also the need to cluster economic activities, both arguments that Antonio Serra had already raised at a theoretical level in 1613. Seckendorff's economic measures included promotion of manufactures and resettlement of artisans from the countryside in the cities, where they were likely to make a much better living. He promoted the extension of agriculture and of activities adding value to the produce of the land. He also eased the mobility of labour by eliminating fees required for settlement and resettlement. With him, we find the origins of the welfare state, of care for the poor and of government responsibility for the elderly. In his wish to limit the powers of the guilds, he showed liberal tendencies well ahead of his times.

Seckendorff's policies were, to a large extent, reflected in von Hörnigk's principles published eighteen years later, which we shall discuss in detail below. Seckendorff established in the eighteenth century what Albert Hirschman calls 'a multi-level conspiracy for development'. He was an early proponent of a school of economists and political writers that was to dominate Europe in the next century: writers who convinced the kings and rulers that their *right to rule* a state or country also entailed a *duty to develop* that state. The thirteenth-century idea of a common good, originating in Italian humanism, was slowly being transformed into an idea of public happiness, and the ruler was put in charge of the project. Wilhelm Roscher coined the descriptive term 'enlightened despotism' for this kind of rule (Roscher 1868: 77).

The enlightened ruler – the 'philosopher–king' in Christian Wolff's terms – was in charge of this 'developmental dictatorship', and the job taken up by the cameralists following Seckendorff was to advise, assist, guide, correct, flatter and cajole the ruler into doing his job properly. The logic that emerged was, the better the ruler, the wealthier the people. Instead of judging his success by his own wealth, the ruler's success would be based on the wealth and happiness of his people.[11]

Of the cameralists, the first true economist was Johann Joachim Becher (1635–1682), whose varied career matched that of the 'economist adventurers' of the next century. Here, however, we concentrate on Becher's university companion and brother-in-law, Philipp Wilhelm von Hörnigk (1640–1714), who delivered economic policy measures in the most succinct way. Like Johann Heinrich Gottlob von Justi in the next century, Hörnigk was a German-born economist in the service of Austria. His book *Österreich über alles, wann es nur will* (*Austria above everyone else, if only she had the will to*) was published anonymously in 1684, and was the most successful German-language economics book of the period. Like Seckendorff, Hörnigk corresponded with Leibniz, the famous and practically inclined philosopher of the time. Hörnigk's economics was 'reality economics', based on intensive studies of the actual situation in the country. His 1684 book reached at least sixteen editions and remained in print for a full hundred years (Carpenter 1977: 10). The centenary edition was published in 1784 under the title *Bemerkungen über die österreichische Staatsökonomie (Remarks on the Economy of the State of Austria)*. In this edition, it was claimed that Austria could thank Hörnigk's book for most of her wealth.

As in the case of Seckendorff, understanding Hörnigk requires an understanding of the setting. Civilization, as it was known then, was under threat. Just two years before Hörnigk's book was published, the Turks had ended one of several unsuccessful sieges of Vienna. Austria suffered great famines during 1648–50, 1692–94, 1698–1702 and 1712–13, and devastating epidemics in the 1630s, 1650s and 1680s. To the north, the once powerful Hanseatic League had long been in decline, and to the south, neighbouring Venice and Italy had started on a similar downward path. These were challenging times for Austria.

Hörnigk distrusted merchants and complained that wealthy people who had the funds to invest did not do so. He recommended a different kind of shock therapy from that of today's economists and the Washington Consensus: complete prohibition of luxury goods from abroad that would prompt the rich to invest in national manufacturing. Like William Petty in England at that time, Hörnigk was an early proponent of 'political arithmetic'. Among other things, he calculated the income from artisans in a successful Dutch city.

We shall summarize below Hörnigk's 'Nine Points of Economic Policy' from his 1684 book, and briefly comment on the circumstances in which such policies, most unusual today, would be appropriate and efficient. Hörnigk's recommendations were representative not only of German economic policy, both then and later, but also of principles that, to varying degrees, were typical of Europe's way out of underdevelopment.[12]

Hörnigk's *first* point was 'to inspect the country's soil with the greatest care, and not to leave the agricultural possibilities of a single corner or clod of earth unconsidered. Every useful form of *plant* under the sun should be experimented with, to see whether it is adapted to the country.' In this type of economic theory that was famous for its bias towards manufacturing, it is most interesting that the first reference should be to agriculture. Agricultural productivity advanced extremely slowly for centuries; so, typically, the economists of the day saw that the only way to raise production was by extending the arable area through the draining of marshes, etc. Most interesting was the 'Schumpeterian' element of introducing new crops.

*Second*, 'all commodities found in a country, which cannot be used in their natural state, should be worked up within the country, since the payment for *manufacturing* generally exceeds the value of the raw material by two, three, ten, twenty, and even a hundred fold'. Unemployment and underemployment represented huge problems at the time, and this 'multiplier effect' of manufacturing was commonly found, both in terms of value added and employment. The first instance was probably Fernando Ortiz's memorandum to the king of Spain in 1558 (see the chapter titled 'Mercantilism and Economic Development' in this volume for a further discussion).

*Third*:

> For carrying out the above two rules, there will be need of people, both for producing and cultivating the raw materials and for working them up. Therefore, attention should be given to the population, that it may be as large as the country can support, this being a well-ordered state's most important concern, but, unfortunately, one that is often neglected. And the people should be turned by all possible means from idleness to remunerative *professions*; instructed and encouraged in all kinds of *inventions*, arts, and trades; and, if necessary, instructors should be brought in from foreign countries for this.

*Fourth*, once in the country, gold and silver,

> whether from its own mines or obtained by *industry* from foreign countries, are, under no circumstances to be taken out for any purpose, so far as possible, or be allowed to be buried in chests or coffers, but must always remain in *circulation*; nor should much be permitted in uses where they are at once *destroyed* and cannot be utilized again. For under these conditions, it will be impossible for a country that has once acquired a considerable supply of cash, especially one that possesses gold and silver mines, ever to sink into poverty; indeed, it is impossible that it should not continually increase in wealthy and property.

The emphasis on gold and silver was what the mainstream history of thought told us to expect, an emphasis supposedly exposing the 'primitiveness' of these theories. However, see Perrotta (1991) for an alternative view.

Therefore, *fifth*, 'the inhabitants of the country should make every effort to get along with their domestic products, to confine their luxury to these alone, and to do without foreign products as far as possible.' As Perrotta (1993) argues, import substitution was a key aspect of mercantilism. The first, and hugely successful, such import substitution strategy was the English 'Tudor plan' from 1485–1603 (see Reinert 1995; and the chapter on 'The Italian Tradition of Political Economy' in this volume).

*Sixth*: 'In case the said purchases were indispensable because of necessity or *irremediable* abuse, they should be obtained from these foreigners at first hand, so far as possible, and not for gold or silver, but in exchange for other domestic wares.' This was the clearing system that was operating also in Europe in the years after World War II, in order to avoid balance of payments deficits.

*Seventh*: 'Such foreign commodities should in this case be imported in unfinished form, and worked up within the country, thus earning the wages of *manufacturing there*.' The multiplier mechanism of manufacturing applied both to the value added effect and the employment effect, and, additionally, solved the balance of payments problem.

*Eighth*: 'Opportunities should be sought night and day for selling the country's superfluous goods to these foreigners in manufactured form, so far as this is necessary, and for gold and silver; and to this end, *consumption*, so to speak, must be sought in the farthest ends of the earth, and developed in every possible way.' The 'cult of export' was not invented by the Washington Consensus. This was another way of improving balance of payments deficits endemic to poor countries, where Keynesian measures alone may only suck in imports.

*Ninth*:

> Except for important considerations, no importation should be allowed under any circumstances of commodities of which there is a sufficient supply of suitable quality at home; and in this matter neither sympathy nor compassion should be shown to foreigners, be they friends, kinsfolk, *allies,* or enemies. For all friendship ceases, when it involves my own weakness and ruin. And this holds good, even if the domestic commodities are of poorer quality, or even higher priced. For it would be better to pay for an article two dollars which remain in the country than only one which goes out, however strange this may seem to the ill-informed.

This sums up the value added, employment and balance of payments arguments, arguments that may also be presented in a neoclassical production possibility frontier-type analysis.

### The Eighteenth Century: The Birth of Academic Economics and of Specialization in the Field

The eighteenth century, the Age of Enlightenment, was characterized by a very considerable literary production, including of the cameralist sciences. *Bibliografie der Kameralwissenschaften*, the main bibliographical source, lists 14,040 items – with some duplication – over 1,184 pages (Humpert 1937), the majority of the publications. Johann Heinrich Gottlob von Justi (1717–1771), the most influential German economist of the century, was also the most prolific writer among the economists, with a total of 67 published books (Reinert 2004a). Thirteen different contemporary translations were made of eight of Justi's books, into five different languages.

This was also the century of the first economics journals, mixing practical advice, theory and news on the whereabouts of economists, in typical cameralist style. The best known German economists of the time – Justi, Georg Heinrich Zincke (1692–1769) and Johann Beckmann (1739–1811) – published their own journals. Practical works on agriculture, arts, inventions and manufacturing also abounded all across Europe at the time. In addition to being an age of discoveries, the eighteenth century was an age of science and scientific academies, with the founding of large museums in Europe.

The world's first two professorships in economics (and cameralism) were established in Germany in 1727, about a century before the first such professorship in England. The first professorship in economics outside Germany was in Uppsala in Sweden, starting some time in the 1830s. The countries to follow suit were Finland (then part of Sweden), at the Åbo (Turku) Academy; then Austria, with Justi being named professor in the cameral sciences in 1752 in Vienna; and Italy, where Antonio Genovesi was appointed professor of political economy, University of Naples, in 1754.

Since the early 1970s, Kenneth Carpenter, a librarian at Harvard University, has collected large amounts of material documenting the translations of economics books in Europe before 1850. He describes a pattern of frequent translations between continental European languages but less frequent translations to and from English.[13] The material is not yet fully systematized, but the section on Sweden, which is finished but remains unpublished, shows that out of 207 economics publications translated into Swedish before 1850, 84 were from German, 55 from French and 51 from English. The rest were from Danish and multilingual sources. The widespread myth, of English origin, that German economics has been the 'odd man out' in the history of economic thought, seems to be thoroughly unfounded.[14]

Johann Heinrich Gottlob von Justi was probably the most representative German economist of the period. He was both a synthesizer and a modernizer of the German tradition, absorbing the important novelties of the 1700s into the consensus of the late 1600s. One example of a new institution was fire insurance. Perhaps the most important novelty of the century was the discovery of important synergies between manufacturing and agriculture: by promoting manufacturing, one would not be punishing agriculture, but quite the contrary. The segmentation of the field of cameralism into subfields, with their own publications and textbooks, was a sign of a maturing science. Justi himself wrote a book on the theory of finance, and his 1754 inaugural lecture as professor of the cameral sciences in Vienna was about the relationship between science and economic welfare, a theme that was to be the subject of a book by Johann Gottfried von Herder (1744–1803) some twenty years later.

Geography had been an important element in continental European economics since the books by Giovanni Botero (1588) and Antonio Serra (1619). From the eighteenth century, it became fashionable to describe economics in stages: from hunting and gathering, to herding, agriculture and, finally, agriculture and manufacturing (Reinert 2000). Justi placed these historical stages on a geographical plane using concentric circles, placing the urban increasing returns sector at the centre. This is the tool normally attributed to Johan Heinrich von Thünen (1783–1850). Both Justi and von Thünen thoroughly understood the importance of nurturing and protecting the manufacturing area, both geographically and economically the core of any nation-state (Reinert 2004a). When a German economist stated, 'It is known that a primitive people do not improve their customs and institutions later to find useful industries, but the other way around' (Meyen 1770: 11), he was expressing something that could be considered the common sense of the time.

Also, technology had always been an integral part of cameralism; in the 1770s, from the economics professor Johann Beckmann at the University of

Göttingen, the world got its first economics textbook focusing on technology. Beckmann built on Justi's foundations, publishing a third edition of Justi's two-volume book, *Factories and Manufacturers*.

Johann Friedrich von Pfeiffer (1718–1787) wrote a successful cameralist textbook (Pfeiffer 1764–65, 1777–78), as well as a very early history of economic thought covering about thirty authors – German, French, English and Italian – in six volumes (Pfeiffer 1781–84). As previously mentioned, virtually all the German economists were opposed to Physiocracy, and Pfeiffer provided a systematic theoretical refusal of Physiocratic doctrines in a book entitled *The Anti-Physiocrat* (Pfeiffer 1780).

Joseph Schumpeter compared German mercantilism with English classical economics succinctly:

> He (Justi) saw the practical argument for laissez-faire not less clearly than did A. Smith, and his bureaucracy, while guiding and helping when necessary, was always ready to efface itself when no guidance or help seemed needed. (Schumpeter's footnote here: 'This was not merely a dream. It will be pointed out below that the bureaucracy in the typical German principality actually tried to behave like this.') Only he saw much more clearly than did the latter all the obstacles that stood in the way of its working according to design. Also, he was much more concerned than A. Smith with the practical problems of government action in the short-run vicissitudes of his time and country, and with particular difficulties in which private initiative fails or would have failed under the conditions of German industry of his time. His laissez-faire was a laissez-faire plus watchfulness, his private-enterprise economy a machine that was logically automated but exposed to breakdowns and hitches which his government was ready to mend. For instance, he accepted as a matter of course that the introduction of labour-saving machinery would cause unemployment: but this was no argument against the mechanization of production because, also as a matter of course, *his* government would find equally good employment for the unemployed. This, however, is not inconsistency, but sense. And to us who are apt to agree with him much more than we do with A. Smith, his (Justi's) vision of economic policy might look like laissez-faire with the nonsense left out. (Schumpeter 1954: 172)

### The 'Historical Schools' of the Nineteenth and Twentieth Centuries

After an initial period of resistance to the ideas of David Ricardo and English economics, the 1830s and, particularly, the 1840s saw the growth of a very strong belief in the merits of laissez-faire capitalism. This period has a lot in common with the triumphalist period following the fall of the Berlin wall that came to mark the 1990s. This first period culminated in the repeal of the corn laws in England in 1846, when the English, for a while, extremely skilfully managed to convince the rest of the world to no longer protect its manufacturing industry by no longer protecting their own agriculture. There are many parallels between the 1840s and the period in which we now live: never since, until now, has such blind faith in the virtues of free markets dominated academia and policy-making to such an extent. The route from the overwhelming social problems of the mid-nineteenth century to the national welfare states that were to follow decades later, therefore, contains clues on how contemporary problems, this time on a global rather than a national scale, can be handled.

Perhaps the most essential feature of mercantilist economic policy was to diversify the economy away from agricultural monoculture into diversified manufacturing. Protecting agriculture would mean protecting the old feudal order that one wished to get rid of. The English bluff – withdrawing the protection of agriculture to convince the rest of the world to stop protecting manufacturing industry – would easily have been called by the great continental economists of the eighteenth century – by a Montesquieu in France, by a Galiani or a Genovesi in Italy, by a Justi in Germany. The same would have been true for the economists of the preceding seventeenth century, to whom the proposal would have appeared even more ridiculous. From 1820 onwards, however, resistance to Ricardian economics was to come not from Europe but from the United States, with important policy-focused publications by Daniel Raymond and Mathew Carey in that year, and important theoretical work against Smithian economics by John Rae in 1834. In Europe, during this period, there was mainly one lonely voice speaking out against the economic policy of liberalism and peripheral deindustrialization: Friedrich List (1789–1846). Once an American citizen, List was clearly inspired by the arguments forwarded by Daniel Raymond, a Baltimore lawyer.

List himself was converted from a free trader to one who saw the need to protect agriculture after he saw the devastating results of deindustrialization in France following the fall of Napoleon. Most of what Friedrich List wrote has never been translated from German into other languages, so the very strong opinion many mainstream economists have of List is narrowly based. List tells us the way things work, but does not generally tell us why. He convincingly argues that the cultivation and protection of agriculture will not yield the same results as the protection of manufacturing (Reinert 1998). He tells us that the producers of olive oil will be poor in the absence of manufacturing, but not really why. With some justification, therefore, he may be criticized as a theorist. List's policy recommendations were fine, and his feel for the right historical sequencing of policy measures was probably unique, but, as compared to Antonio Serra, he failed to explain their underlying mechanisms. List's theoretical concepts were vague, or, as Werner Sombart said about him: 'His concepts levitate like undelivered souls on the banks of Hades' (Sombart 1928: 929). However, his holistic vision of the synergies of economic development and national wealth creation, products of increasing return activities and of heavy investments in infrastructure, as the driving forces behind national wealth, was almost unprecedented.

From the perspective of German economics, Friedrich List was the great free trader who forged the German customs union, the *Zollverein*. The rest of the world sees him as the great protectionist. List was also the first to have a vision of a European common market. Most economists today fail to understand how one can be protectionist in one context and a free trader in a different context. In List's vision, global free trade was desirable only after every nation had achieved a comparative advantage in increasing return activities. Only when the asymmetries of colonial and neocolonial trade had been eliminated would all parties benefit from free trade. List's vision was fully compatible with the European mercantilist mainstream of the preceding 300 years, and with Serra's theoretical explanation.

Historically based and context-specific economic theories were to dominate German economic theory from around 1850 to the hundred years that followed. This period is normally divided in three – into the 'older', 'younger' and 'youngest' historical schools. As has also been suggested by others, it is convenient to treat List as representing a 'proto-historical school'. He raised the Italian arguments – from Botero and Serra to Galiani – that the cities and their manufacturing activities are the keys to personal freedom, to the arts, to the division of labour and, indeed, to civilization itself. A point made by German economists as early as Leibniz, and so masterfully restated by Galiani, was repeated by List, who insisted that manufacturing was also the key to creating wealth in agriculture, 'the only way to liberate agriculture from its chains'.

The first shot in the long fight between the German historical schools and English classical economics was fired in the year 1848, by a book by Bruno Hildebrand (1812–1878). A few years later, Karl Knies (1821–1898), perhaps the most under-rated of these economists, presented his theoretical work on the historical method in economics. Knies inspired the most prominent and influential economist in the United States at the turn of the nineteenth century, Richard Ely (1854–1943), founder and then president of the American Economic Association from 1899 to 1902, at that time classified as a 'Christian socialist'.

In 1886, another influential US economist inspired by German economics, Edwin Seligman (1861–1939), outlined the programme of the German Historical School as follows. For Seligman, the School:

1. Discards the exclusive use of the deductive method, and stresses the necessity of historical and statistical treatment.
2. Denies the existence of immutable natural laws in economics, calling attention to the interdependence of theories and institutions, and showing that different epochs or countries require different systems.
3. Disclaims belief in the beneficence of the absolute laissez-faire system.
4. Maintains the close inter-relations of law, ethics and economics, and refuses to acknowledge the adequacy of the presumption of self-interest as the sole regulator of economic action.

Key members of the 'older' Historical School were Hildebrand, Knies and Wilhelm Roscher (1817–1894). Key members of the 'younger' Historical School were Gustav von Schmoller (1838–1917), Adolph Wagner (1835–1917) and Lujo Brentano (1844–1931). The 'youngest' Historical School was represented by Werner Sombart (1863–1941) and Max Weber (1864–1920). In the next section, we discuss the policies emanating from this school of economics.[15]

The foundations of Schumpeterian economics were also laid by the Historical School. Schumpeter's best known concept in economics, 'creative destruction', was first used by Werner Sombart, who was heavily influenced by Friedrich Nietzsche (see Reinert and Reinert (2004).

### The Social Problem and the *Verein für Sozialpolitik*

Ricardo, and still more those who popularized him, may stand as an example for all time of the extreme danger which may arise from the unscientific use of hypothesis in social speculations, from the failure to appreciate the limited applications to actual affairs of a highly artificial and arbitrary analysis. His ingenious, though perhaps over-elaborated reasonings became positively mischievous and misleading when they were unhesitatingly applied to determine grave practical issues without the smallest sense of the thoroughly abstract and unreal character of the assumptions on which they were founded. (H.S. Foxwell, professor of economics, Cambridge University, 1899)

1848, also the year of publication of *The Communist Manifesto*, saw a 'backlash' against Ricardian and laissez-faire economics. In all the European languages, 'the social problem', which had lingered under the surface ever since the end of the Napoleonic Wars, suddenly surfaced with incredible vigour, and produced both revolutions across Europe and a lot of literature on the subject. But, as Galiani had so eloquently pointed out 70 years before, mankind is a great connoisseur of effects but a poor judge of causes. In our view, Professor Foxwell's comments about Ricardo anticipate what Schumpeter was later to call the Ricardian vice of economics.

The reaction of German economists to this challenge is slightly confused by frequent mention of three overlapping categories or groups of economists: the German Historical School; the *Kathedersozialisten* ('Socialists of the Professorial Chair'); and the Association for Social Policy, *Verein für Sozialpolitik*. This requires some clarification.

The German Historical School is a term later introduced to refer to these generations of German mainstream economists. *Kathedersozialist* is a somewhat unfortunate term imposed on a group of economists by a contemporary journalist; in the same year the majority of them founded the *Verein für Sozialpolitik*. The first term used by the journalist was 'freshwater sailors', a derogatory reference made by European sailors to colleagues who thought they were sailors but had never experienced 'the real thing', that is, the reality and perils of the ocean (Oppenheim 1872). The intent was the same: to accuse these economists of trying to improve the real world without having much experience of it themselves. Unlike Ricardian economics, however, these economists were much closer to analysing 'the real thing', the context and reality of economics. Compared to English classical economics, Ricardo was the 'freshwater sailor' in a sea of arbitrary assumptions, while the *Kathedersozialisten* were attempting – successfully, in the long term – to tackle the world as it really was.

Probably a quotation from Gustav Schmoller's opening speech at the founding meeting of the *Verein für Sozialpolitik*, in a private home in Eisenach on Sunday, 6 October 1872, best explains the background for its creation:

> The deep cleavage in our society separating entrepreneurs and workers, owning and not owning classes, represents a threat of a social revolution. This threat has drawn closer. In wide circles there have been serious doubts whether the economic doctrines which dominate on today's market – and which were expressed at the Economic Congress – forever will keep their dominance. Will the introduction of the free right to carry on business (*Gewerbefreiheit*) and the elimination of all mediaeval legislation on guilds really create the perfect economic conditions that the hotheads (*Heißsporne*) of that tradition predict?

It was the original *Verein für Sozialpolitik,* active from 1872 to 1932, that built the theoretical and practical foundations of twentieth-century European welfare states. The Scandinavian welfare states, which were to become the most prominent, took over not only many German institutions, but often also their names in literal translation. Significantly, the *Verein* ceased to exist the year Hitler came to power, but its work had largely been completed by then.

The creators of the welfare state then were economists whose common trait was that they were anti-Ricardian, people who disliked communism just as much as they disliked liberalism. However, when these economists, their theories and political opinions are carefully studied, they come across as a very diverse group. The question that arises is, how a group with these differences managed to be so productive, and to create so many new institutions and social reforms. The *Verein* continued a tradition that started with Seckendorff and Leibniz, producing what to modern economists would look like microscopic analyses of economies and economic history. From the accumulation of such micro-data, context-dependent policy conclusions were drawn at a high level of abstraction. The method of the Historical School can be compared with the case-study method of the Harvard Business School at a national, rather than a company, level. The case-study method was established by the Harvard School's first dean, an enthusiastic student of Schmoller, Edwin Gay (1867–1946), whose own studies of economics and economic history in German-speaking Europe lasted more than twelve years.

An important element that kept the *Verein* together was a common research agenda, around which facts were gathered from all regions of German-speaking Europe, with papers written and presented at annual meetings. One year they would discuss problems caused by the lack of health insurance, another year how to create a system protecting workers from unemployment, and the next year the consequences of 'Fordist' mass production. A fascinating issue of the time was how to address the poverty of areas that specialized in economic activities that had not been mechanized and/or remained highly intensive in unskilled labour. The 'home workers', *Heimarbeiter,* were mostly paid by piece.

Such specialization in 'unmechanizable' production bereft of scale effects and untouched by the ruling techno-economic paradigm clearly parallels today's *maquilas* (low-tech assembly plants). However, unlike the Mexican *maquila* workers of today, these workers were theoretically free to move to other, more industrialized areas of Germany at the time.

It has been argued that the *Verein für Sozialpolitik* rarely disagreed with the imperial economic policy of Bismarck, implying that they were uninfluential or 'puppets' of the regime. In our view, causality runs the other way: Bismarck's economic policy rarely disagreed fundamentally with the views of the *Verein*. Bismarck understood social reality and problems, and also that the liberals had no cure; he therefore relied heavily on the recommendations of the *Verein*, which, as noted earlier, covered an unusually wide political spectrum.

As we saw, the scholarly output of cameralism was enormous, as was the scholarly production of the next century of German economics, particularly following 1848. The papers and reports of the *Verein für Sozialpolitik* conferences fill 188 volumes and occupy five metres of shelf space. The first century of *Schmoller's Jahrbuch* (1871–1971), the most influential journal of the same group of economists, fills almost seven metres of shelf space. In addition, there are literally dozens of other journals and an enormous number of books and monographs. We do not have to accept the neoliberal claim that 'there is no alternative'; here lie the bases for a full-fledged alternative to neoclassical economics, unfortunately locked in a language that was once the lingua franca of economics but which today is relatively inaccessible.[16]

The famous *Methodenstreit* between German and Austrian economists, a kind of civil war inside German-language economics, started in the 1880s between Gustav Schmoller and Carl Menger (see Reinert 2003a). Viewed from today's vantage point, this occasionally vitriolic academic discussion was essentially a quibble over details. Carl Menger, the academic who supposedly argued against the use of history in economics, stated: 'A highly developed theory of economic phenomena is inconceivable without the study of economic history'; 'No reasonable person conceals the importance of historical studies for research in the field of political economy'; and 'History is indispensable for theoretical economics.' Schmoller and Menger, both agreed that both induction and deduction were needed, and the *Methodenstreit* was apparently about who was to be in the driver's seat – over which of the two was going to be the 'main science' and which would be the 'auxiliary science'.

In spite of the *Methodenstreit* civil war, German economics probably reached its highest point of influence around 1900. Both in the United States and in Japan, economic theory and policy were heavily influenced by German economics. Much to the satisfaction of German economists, John Stuart Mill had recanted on two key features of English classical economics relating to economic development: the wage funds doctrine (which limited the resources available for wages and salaries) and the free trade doctrine (Mill admitted the usefulness of industrial tariffs). It was generally agreed that Ricardo's abstract system had produced social disasters. A symptom of the loss of influence was Cambridge economist W. Cunningham's book, *The Rise and Decline of the Free Trade Movement* (London: Clay/Cambridge University Press), 1904. It was, therefore, with a certain justification that Gustav Schmoller, in his inaugural lecture as *Rektor* of the University of Berlin in 1897 (Schmoller 1897), celebrated the victory of empirically oriented economics over dogmatic economics, both left and right.

### 1945–47: The Morgenthau Plan Validates the German Economics Tradition

German economics, with an unbroken tradition from about 1650 to 1950, is uniquely valuable as a full-fledged alternative to today's mainstream economics. This tradition represents the most consistent bulwark against mechanistic and simplistic economic solutions of all political shades. We have attempted to build on this theoretical tradition in constructing the Other Canon of economics (www.othercanon.org). Creating, motivating, directing and controlling market forces in order to enhance human welfare has been the *leitmotiv* of German economic theory since its inception after the Thirty Years' War. After World War II, German-type economics continued to dominate German economic policy in its 'social market economy'.

The economic integration of Europe, at least until the 2004 extension, followed Friedrich List's prescriptions of symmetrical integration. In Europe, German pragmatism ruled at home, recently with a huge emphasis on innovation, while neoclassical economics became an export article ruling Europe's relationship with the rest of the world. As a theoretical tradition, the German tradition of economics was essentially thrown out – in our view, totally unjustifiably – with the bath water of Nazism. Policies based on this theoretical tradition developed not only Europe, but also the United States and Japan; indeed, such policies have been a mandatory passage point for all successful national transitions out of poverty.

After World War II, the core idea of cameralism as development economics – the idea that national development needs an increasing returns manufacturing sector – was vindicated through a large-scale experiment, the Morgenthau Plan. The purpose of this plan, named after Henry Morgenthau, the US Secretary of the Treasury during 1934–45, was to prevent Germany from ever starting a war again (Morgenthau 1945). This was to be achieved by deindustrializing Germany, making it a pastoral economy by closing factories, taking the industrial machinery out of the country, and filling the mines with water. The plan was approved in an Allied meeting in 1943, and carried out after the German capitulation in May 1945.

The Morgenthau Plan was abruptly stopped in 1947 when ex-President Herbert Hoover of the United States, on a fact-finding mission, reported back from Germany: 'There is the illusion that the New Germany left after the annexations can be reduced to a "pastoral state". It cannot be done unless we exterminate or move 25,000,000 out of it.' Hoover had rediscovered the wisdom of the cameralist and mercantilist population theorists: an industrialized nation has a much larger carrying capacity in terms of population than an agricultural state. The deindustrialization process had also led to a sharp fall in agricultural yields and to institutional collapse, providing evidence of the importance of the linkages between the industrial and agricultural sectors that were a hallmark of cameralist economics. Less than four months after Hoover's alarming report from Germany, the US government announced the Marshall Plan, which aimed to achieve exactly the opposite of the Morgenthau Plan: Germany's industrial capacity was to be brought back to its 1938 level at all costs. It cannot be emphasized enough that the Marshall Plan was not just a financial plan but, principally, a *reindustrialization plan*.

After years of neglect, the Morgenthau Plan was resurrected *de facto* by the Washington Consensus, starting in the 1980s and, even more strongly, after the end of the Cold War in 1991. This new *de facto* plan came with the label of 'structural adjustment', which often had the effect of deindustrializing third world nations (Reinert 2004b). These two ideal types of economic policy – the Marshall Plan and the Morgenthau Plan – embodied the 'virtuous' and 'vicious' circles that were fashionable, but not well explained, in the heyday of development economics during the 1950s and 1960s (Reinert 2003b).

In 1947, the United States understood the destructive forces that had been put in motion with the Morgenthau Plan. In his Harvard speech in June 1947, announcing what came to be called the Marshall Plan, US Secretary of State George Marshall stressed that 'the farmer has always produced the foodstuffs to exchange with the city-dweller for the other necessities of life'. This division of labour, that is, between increasing return activities in the cities and the countryside, was 'at the present time . . . threatened with breakdown'. George Marshall then made a remarkable recognition of cameralist and mercantilist economic policy: 'This division of labor is the basis of modern civilization.' Civilization requires increasing return areas, something that people from Antonio Serra to Abraham Lincoln and Friedrich List had been saying for a long time. However, this core of five centuries of economic theory has always eluded the trade-based English economics and its successor, today's mainstream economics. Its conceptual and instrumental tools fail to grasp this factor – a blind spot in mainstream economics that causes untold human suffering today. Herein lies the key to understanding the growing number of 'failed states' that have followed in the wake of the Washington Consensus. In 1953, George Marshall was awarded the Nobel peace Prize.

I am indebted to Wolfgang Drechsler, Rainer Kattel and the editor for helpful comments on this chapter. The usual disclaimer applies.

### Notes

[1] In this chapter, the term 'German economics' will be used to cover all economics originally written in the German language.

[2] For a discussion of the role of the state in the German economic tradition, see Reinert (1999).

[3] For a discussion of the choice of the German model in Japan, both after the Meiji Restoration and after 1945, and in the United States, see Reinert (1995).

[4] This is documented in Reinert, ed. (2004c).

[5] This is also the case of Tribe (1988, 1995).

[6] The exceptions are August Schlettwein (1731–1802) and Theodor Schmalz (1760–1831), both marginal figures in the history of German economic thought.

[7] I am indebted to Wolfgang Drechsler for assistance in formulating this paragraph.

[8] A very useful discussion of different ways of understanding economic phenomena in German versus mainstream economics is found in Drechsler (2004).

[9] For a discussion, see Reinert and Daastøl (1997).

[10] Othmar Spann (1878–1950) represented an extreme case of 'holistic economics'.

[11] An example of an English translation of a German book on this subject is Wolff (1750).

[12] This part of Hörnigk's book was translated by Arthur Monroe (1930).

[13] The preliminary results are published in Carpenter (1977).

[14] This point is also forcefully made by the Spanish historian of economic thought, Ernest Lluch (1996: 163–75).

[15] For a discussion of the Historical School, see Shionoya, ed. (2001).

[16] Prof. Jürgen Backhaus, now of Erfurt University, has, for almost two decades, organized the Heilbronn Symposia, the main purpose of which is to render important German economic analyses accessible in the English language.

### References

Berch, Anders (1747), *Inledning til Almänna Hushålningen, innefattande Grunden til Politie, Oeconomie och Cameralwetenskaperna* (Stockholm: Lars Salvius).

Carpenter, Kenneth (1977), *Dialogue in Political Economy: Translations from and into German in the 18th Century*, Kress Library Publications No. 23 (Boston: Harvard Business School).

Clemence, Richard V. (1951), *Essays of J.A. Schumpeter* (Cambridge, Massachusetts: Addison-Wesley).

Drechsler, Wolfgang (2004), 'Natural versus Social Sciences: On Understanding in Economics', in Erik S. Reinert, ed. (2004c).

Humpert, Magdalene (1937), *Bibliografie der Kameralwissenschaften* (Cologne: Schroeder).

Lluch, Ernest (1996), 'El Cameralismo mas allá del mundo germánico', in *Revista de Economía Aplicada*, 4 (10): 163–75.

Meyen, Johan Jacob (1770), *Wie kommt es, dass die Oekonomie bisher so wenig Vortheile von der Physik und Mathematik gewonnen hat; und wie kann man diese Wissenschaften zum gemeinen Nutzen in die Oekonomie einführen, und von dieser Verbindung auf Grundsätze kommen, die in die Ausübung brauchbar sind?* (Berlin: Haude & Spener).

Monroe, Arthur (1930), *Early Economic Thought: Selections from Economic Literature prior to Adam Smith* (Cambridge, Massachusetts: Harvard University Press).

Morgenthau, Henry, Jr. (1945), *Germany is Our Problem: A Plan for Germany* (New York: Harper).

Oppenheim, H.B. (1872), *Der Katheder-Sozialismus* (Berlin: Oppenheim).

Perrotta, Cosimo (1991), 'Is Mercantilist Theory of the Favourable Balance of Trade Really Erroneous?' *History of Political Economy*, 23 (2): 301–36.

—— (1993), 'Early Spanish Mercantilism: The First Analysis of Underdevelopment', in Lars Magnusson, *Mercantilist Economics* (Boston: Kluwer): 17–58.

Pfeiffer, Johann Friedrich von (1764–65; 1777–78), *Lehrbegriff sämtlicher oeconomischer und Cameralwissenschaften*, 6 volumes (Stuttgart und Mannheim: Johann Christoph Erhard und C.F. Schwan).

—— (1780), *Der Antiphysiocrat, oder umständliche Untersuchung des sogenannten Physiocratischen Systems* (Frankfurt: Esslingersche Buchhandlung).

—— (1781–84), *Berichtigungen berühmter Staats- Finanz- Policei- Cameral- Commerz- und ökonomischer Schriften dieses Jahrhunderts, von dem Verfasser des Lehrbegriffs sämtlicher Ökonomischen und Cameralwissenschaften*, 6 volumes (Frankfurt: Esslingersche Buchhandlung).

Reinert, Erik S. (1995), 'Competitiveness and Its Predecessors: A 500-year Cross-National Perspective', *Structural Change and Economic Dynamics*, 6: 23–42.

—— (1998), 'Raw Materials in the History of Economic Policy; or, Why List (the Protectionist) and Cobden (the Free Trader) Both Agreed on Free Trade in Corn', in G. Parry, ed., *Freedom and Trade: 1846–1996* (London: Routledge).

—— (1999), 'The Role of the State in Economic Growth', *Journal of Economic Studies*, 26 (4/5).

—— (2000), 'Karl Bücher and the Geographical Dimensions of Techno-Economic Change', in Jürgen Backhaus, ed., *Karl Bücher: Theory, History, Anthropology, Non-Market Economies* (Marburg: Metropolis Verlag).

—— (2003a), 'The Austrians and the Other Canon', in Jürgen Backhaus, ed., *Evolutionary Economic Thought: European Contributions and Concepts* (Cheltenham: Edward Elgar).

—— (2003b), 'Increasing Poverty in a Globalized World: Marshall Plans and Morgenthau Plans as Mechanisms of Polarization of World Incomes', in Ha-Joon Chang, ed., *Rethinking Economic Development* (London: Anthem Press).

—— (2004a), 'Johann Heinrich Gottlob von Justi (1717–1771): The Life and Times of an Economist Adventurer', in Jürgen Backhaus, ed., *Johann Heinrich Gottlob von Justi: The Beginning of Political Economy* (Boston: Kluwer).

—— (2004b), 'The Dutch Republic 1500–1750: Economic Strategy and Economic Performance in the Views of Contemporary European Economists', in Oscar Gelderblom, ed., *The Political Economy of the Dutch Republic*.

——, ed. (2004c), *Globalization, Economic Development and Inequality: An Alternative Perspective* (Cheltenham: Edward Elgar).

Reinert, Erik S. and Arno Daastøl (1997), 'Exploring the Genesis of Economic Innovations: The Religious Gestalt-Switch and the *Duty to Invent* as Preconditions for Economic Growth', *European Journal of Law and Economics*, 4 (2/3): 233–83.

Reinert, Erik S. and Hugo Reinert (forthcoming 2004), 'Creative Destruction in Economics: Nietzsche, Sombart, Schumpeter', in Jürgen Backhaus and Wolfgang Drechsler, eds, *Friedrich Nietzsche 1844–2000: Economy and Society* (Boston: Kluwer).

Roscher, Wilhelm (1868), 'Der Sächsische Nationalökonom Johann Heinrich Gottlob von Justi', in *Archiv für die Sächsische Geschichte*: 76–106.

Schmoller, Gustav (1897), *Wechselnde Theorien und Feststehende Wahrheiten im Gebiete der Staats- und Socialwissenschaftlichen und die Heutige Deutsche Volkswirtschaftslehre, Rede bei Antritt des Rectorats* (Berlin: W. Büxenstein).

Schumpeter, Joseph (1954), *History of Economic Analysis* (New York: Oxford University Press).

Seckendorff, Veit Ludwig von (1665), *Additiones oder Zugaben und Erleuterungen zu dem Tractat des Teutschen Fürstenstaats* (Frankfurt: Gotzen).

Shionoya, Yuichi, ed. (2001), *The German Historical School: The Historical and Ethical Approach to Economics* (London: Routledge).

Small, Albion W. (1909), *The Cameralists: The Pioneers of German Social Polity* (New York: Burt Franklin).

Sombart, Werner (1928), *Der Moderne Kapitalismus*, Vol. 2: *Das Europäische Wirtschaftsleben im Zeitalter des Frühkapitalismus* (München und Leipzig: Duncker & Humblot); 2-volume edition 1902, 4-volume edition 1919, 6-volume edition 1928.

Stolleis, Michael, ed. (1995), *Staatsdenker in der Frühen Neuzeit* (Munich: Beck).

Sugiyama, Chuhei and Hiroshi Mizuta (1988), *Enlightenment and Beyond: Political Economy Comes to Japan* (Tokyo: University of Tokyo Press).

Tribe, Keith (1988), *Governing Economy: The Reformation of German Economic Discourse 1750–1840* (Cambridge: Cambridge University Press).

—— (1995), *Strategies of Economic Order. German Economic Discourse (1750–1950)* (Cambridge: Cambridge University Press).

Wolff, Christian (1750), *The Real Happiness of a People under a Philosophical King Demonstrated; Not only from the Nature of Things, but from the Undoubted Experience of the Chinese under their first Founder Fohi, and his Illustrious Successors, Hoam Ti, and Xin Num* (London: M. Cooper).

# The Capitalist Transformation

*Mushtaq Husain Khan*

The transition of a small number of developing countries to high living standards over the last four decades has brought to the fore debates on the content and conditions of the capitalist transformation. What are the necessary and sufficient conditions for the sustained and rapid improvements in living standards that have historically been achieved in countries going through successful capitalist transformation? The capitalist late developers were different in many respects from the early developers, although they were recognizably capitalist, given the important role of private-sector capitalists in these transitions. In late developers, the state played a bigger role in ensuring and maintaining high rates of investment and the shift to higher productivity technologies.

Beyond these very general observations, there is little agreement about the institutional preconditions, economic policies and state capacities that are needed to achieve this transformation. Earlier debates about the definition of capitalism – about the key features that made it significantly more dynamic in generating productivity growth as compared to previous systems, and the preconditions for the transition to capitalism – connect, in interesting ways, with the more recent controversies about the conditions for late development.

For non-Marxist neoclassical institutional economists, capitalism is defined by the private ownership of assets and market coordination of all activities not organized within firms (Williamson 1985). For Marxists, capitalism is much more than this: it is a specific relationship between classes of owners and non-owners of the means of production, such that, not only do capitalists own the means of production, but workers are systematically separated from the ownership of these means of production and are forced to work for capitalists in order to survive. Both non-Marxist and Marxist definitions of capitalism try to capture the key institutional features that can explain the much higher productivity and productivity growth of the capitalist system, as compared to all previous (or, in the non-Marxist view, all alternative) systems. An important problem with the neoclassical definition of capitalism is that many pre-capitalist systems also had extensive private property ownership as well as extensive markets. Here, the Marxist definition does identify something distinctive about the new capitalist system that began to emerge in England from the sixteenth century onwards, because the separation of the working people from the means of production *was* something new.

Another merit of the Marxist approach to capitalism is that while Williamson and the new institutional economics can explain why any private property system can be *efficient* in terms of reducing transaction costs, the Marxist definition aims to explain why successful capitalist economies enjoyed historically unprecedented rates of productivity *growth*. The neoclassical definition of capitalism derives from the analytical argument that well-defined private property rights reduce transaction costs and allow markets to reach their full efficiency potential. The Marxist definition focuses, instead, on capitalism as a system of compulsion. Thus, Wood (2002) argues that capitalism is characterized not only by the presence of market *opportunities*, which have always been present in societies with markets, but also by hitherto unknown market *compulsions*, which ensure that both capitalists and workers have to continuously strive to improve their performance just in order to survive.

The distinction between these two views is relevant for understanding the limitations of the dominant view in contemporary economics – that a necessary and sufficient condition for constructing dynamic economies in developing countries is to create conditions for markets to work well. This perspective has venerable precedents going back to long before its current neoclassical incarnation. It is supported by part of the classical economic tradition of Adam Smith. Some versions of the Marxist argument, while they strongly distinguish capitalism from the market as such, nevertheless also support the claim that removing restrictions on markets was a critical feature of the transition to capitalism.

On the other hand, there are powerful challenges to these views within Marxism itself, including some of the most interesting work done by Marx himself. These arguments point out that not only is capitalism a fundamentally different system of property rights and class relationships, but that its dynamism has to be understood as brought about by a *change* in the market logic to one of compulsion, rather than an *extension* of the pre-existing role of the market as a provider of profit opportunities. They points to the institutional and property rights changes required for the emergence of this compulsion in what we know as early capitalism. If these changes are not equivalent to market-enhancing reforms, then, identifying what they are, and the class and political constraints preventing their emergence, is of paramount importance.

Doing this, however, may not necessarily tell us much about the conditions for capitalist transformation in contemporary developing countries. There are important differences between early and late capitalism. The historical evidence, coming mostly from East Asia over the last four decades, suggests that there are important institutional differences between early and late developers, particularly as regards a much bigger role for the state in providing part of the compulsion for productivity growth among late developers. Why was the system of compulsion that was sufficient to drive productivity growth among early developers apparently inadequate for late developers? If there are, indeed, significant differences between early and late developers, capitalist transformation raises yet another question that we have to answer. First, we have to decide whether the market-enhancing view of capitalism is appropriate, or whether the distinctive feature of capitalism is a set of institutional, property rights and class relationships that create capitalists and workers, and compel rapid productivity growth. Second, if capitalism is a productive system that is more than just a market economy, we have the equally important challenge of explaining why the property rights and institutional structures that have been necessary for compelling productivity growth in late capitalism are different from those in early capitalism, and identifying what these differences may be.

These issues are critically important, regardless of whether or not we believe that a capitalist transformation is in the interest of poorly performing developing countries. There is a strong position within Marxism which argues that meaningful socialism cannot be constructed in poor countries that have not gone through a period of capitalist growth. But, even if we believe that a non-capitalist path to development is possible and desirable in poor countries, very similar questions arise about identifying the institutional and property rights structures that can accelerate productivity growth in such a non-capitalist or socialist economy, as well as the process of transformation through which these rights can come about. The worst situation is arguably one where the conventional wisdom about how to create 'market economies' in developing countries persists, despite having produced remarkably poor results in countries most in need of transformation.

We will look, first, at the debate between the claim that removing restrictions on the market created capitalism, and the claim that the emergence of capitalism was a social transformation involving fundamental changes in property rights and class relationships. Second, we will look at the reasons as to why late development may require significantly different institutions and rights from early capitalist development. We will conclude by examining the implications for current debates within development economics about reforms to accelerate development in developing countries.

The conditions determining the transition to capitalism in western Europe have been debated for a long time by historians, both Marxist and non-Marxist. This is an important question, because capitalism as a new and radically more dynamic economic system first emerged in England and then in some parts of western Europe. Yet, for a long time, these areas had been relatively technologically and commercially backward as compared to other parts of Europe, such as Florence or the Dutch Republic, and indeed compared to many areas in Asia and the Middle East. Two sorts of explanations have been put forward, and the divide between them is still relevant for understanding contemporary debates on the determinants of, and obstacles to, the transition to high-productivity economies in developing countries today.

The first type of explanation argues that capitalism emerged through the freeing up of further market opportunities. According to this position, the transition to capitalism happened in those countries where the obstacles to the market were first removed. These obstacles included political obstacles set up by feudalism, which included barriers to the movement of labour and capital, and barriers that prevented land being freely sold; and ideological or religious obstacles that prevented markets from becoming the main regulator of resource allocation in society. The obstacles were first overcome in England and then in some parts of western Europe because internal and external factors weakened feudal restrictions and ideologies, and allowed the market to grow. The group of historians and economists making this case often differ on which obstacles were more important and the mechanisms through which they were overcome, but agree that capitalism emerged because of the *removal of obstacles to the market*. Despite many important differences between them on other critical issues, Marxist historians like Maurice Dobb (1946) and Paul Sweezy (1950) share the view that the distinctive feature of capitalism is that it removed many of the fetters that had constrained the market economy under feudalism.

This strand of Marxist thinking argue that in the absence of specific constraints, there were powerful forces operating in the form of technical progress, accumulation and profit-seeking activities in the pre-capitalist market economy that created systemic pressures towards capitalist production. The difference between Dobb and Sweezy in this debate is about the process that weakened feudalism and reduced its ability to restrict the market so that capitalism could emerge. For Dobb, the process that began to remove obstacles to the market was a class struggle between lords and peasants *internal* to the feudal economy. This weakened the political ability of feudalism to restrict markets and allowed the growth of petty commodity production, which, in turn, grew into capitalism. Sweezy's debate with Dobb is essentially about whether these internal forces were sufficient to dissolve the feudal fetters.

Sweezy is not convinced, and argues that the growth of long-distance trade played a key role in weakening feudalism and allowing capitalism to grow. For him, the removal of fetters constraining the growth of internal markets depended on the incorporation of the feudal society into systems of external markets. Thus, not only is capitalism the removal of fetters in the internal market, but, moreover, the removal of these internal fetters was assisted by the growth of long-distance trade, which created a market logic that the political power of feudalism could not constrain. The growth of long-distance trade, in turn, weakened the ability of feudalism to restrict internal markets.

The Dobb–Sweezy debate is very sophisticated and has many aspects (for a fuller discussion, see Hilton 1976), but it does not address some critical questions. If Dobb is right, why did not class struggles of different types in other pre-capitalist societies sufficiently weaken internal restraints within those societies for petty commodity production to expand to the point when modern capitalism began to emerge? After all, feudalism was quite weak in many parts of the world that were fairly commercialized, including non-European areas like India, but capitalism did not emerge there. On the other hand, if Sweezy is right, why did commercialization and long-distance trade not act as a solvent that allowed capitalism to emerge in other trading areas, including China, India, Italian city-states like Florence and the Dutch Republic?

Without many of its subtleties, the modern neoclassical position is similar to this early debate within Marxism in so far as it also believes that the economic take-off of developing countries depends on removing, or at least reducing, restrictions on markets. From a very different analytical perspective, non-Marxist economic historians like Douglass North (1990) argue that capitalism emerged in western Europe through changes in property rights that allowed the market economy to work more efficiently. They conclude that if obstacles to the operation of markets can be removed, productivity growth and rising living standards will follow. In earlier versions of the neoclassical position, the emphasis was simply on liberalization of markets and reduction of state restrictions.

More recently, the neoclassical position has been enriched by inputs from the New Institutional Economics, which argues that, for markets to work efficiently, transaction costs in the market have to be reduced, requiring a number of institutional changes. It adds a number of other requirements for the take-off to take place, including the stabilization of property rights, which requires lowering expropriation risk and reducing corruption (North 1990). It also suggests the necessity of democratization, to reduce the ability of states to engage in *ex post* expropriation (Olson 1997, 2000).

All these reforms are essentially motivated by the desire to make markets work better. Implicitly, the neoclassical position argues that the main difference between advanced capitalist countries and poorly performing developing countries is that markets do not work effectively in the latter. If restrictions on the proper working of markets can be removed, these countries too will rapidly begin to resemble the advanced capitalist countries. In other words, they will, in fact, become capitalist.

In contrast to all these, the conventional Marxist position is not only to distinguish the market from capitalism, but also to point out that removing market restrictions is not *sufficient* for the transition. (Later, we will discuss a number of reasons why removing restrictions on the market may not even be *necessary* for the transition to capitalism.) After all, markets had existed for thousands of years without leading to capitalism. Moreover, areas that were relatively more commercialized, such as Florence or the Dutch Republic, did not make the first transition to capitalism. Nor was there any sign of capitalism in India or China despite the presence of widespread long-distance trade within these empires, and between them and the rest of the world. Since differences in the degree of marketization did not correlate with the degree of capitalist development in the pre-capitalist era, it is more consistent to argue that capitalism is not just about extending market opportunities but, rather, about the imposition of a completely new structure of property rights and institutions that introduces radically new compulsions for productivity growth.

Marx pointed out that capitalism is indeed a unique system of property rights where, for the first time, the market operates in such a way that productivity is rapidly enhanced and technological progress happens in a sustained manner. The reason is that the property rights and class relationships of capitalism are such that both capitalists and workers are *compelled* to continuously improve their productivity, simply in order to survive. This market compulsion had never existed before, and was a sharp break from the role of the market in earlier societies, where it had provided *opportunities* for greater profit. Robert Brenner (1976, 1985) and Ellen Meiskins Wood (2002) powerfully represent this position, and it can be argued that this is much closer to the position of Marx himself in his detailed analysis of how class structures change in the run-up to capitalist transformation, including through processes of primitive accumulation.

The transition to these specific structures happens largely through political and social processes, rather than through extensions of the market. The internal configuration of class and state power was most conducive for this transformation in England, and this is why the transition to capitalism first occurred in English agriculture. The processes through which this happened included the forced transfer of land to an emerging class of agrarian capitalists, which was essential for the creation of capitalism in England. Market opportunities were important and, indeed, the new large landlords needed to have markets to sell their products, but the presence of markets alone did not lead to similar transitions in other countries where the class configuration between landlords, tenant farmers and the state was different (Brenner 1976, 1985).

This analysis says that the reason why capitalism emerged in England did indeed have a lot to do with internal class struggles and state strategies (as Dobb has suggested). But these struggles were important *not* because they led to the weakening of feudal restrictions on the market, but because they led directly to changes in property rights and class relationships that were necessary for a capitalist economy to emerge. The historical evidence can be read as being strongly in favour of this second interpretation of the conditions under which capitalism emerged in the west (Brenner 1976, 1985; Wood 2002).

If this view is correct, it has enormous significance for current debates on the institutional conditions for rapid productivity growth in developing countries. Dynamic capitalist economies are unlikely to emerge simply by removing obstacles to the market and trying to make their markets more efficient. Rather, we have to ask what rights and institutions are necessary in the context of the contemporary world economy for rapid productivity growth, and how these can be introduced. This perspective suggests that the construction of capitalist societies in developing countries where capitalism is not fully developed may require a *social transformation,* and this may require or be held up by specific balances of power between internal classes and the state (Khan 2002). Moreover, this social transformation may involve substantial internal conflicts between different sections of existing propertied classes, as property rights and class relationships are altered.

The huge social transition from pre-capitalist or largely pre-capitalist societies, where markets created opportunities but not an over-riding set of social compulsions, to capitalist societies, where markets operated to *compel* the maximization of profit and continuous productivity growth, is described by Polanyi (1957) as the *great transformation*. However, Polanyi, like Dobb, argues that the transition was driven largely by technological developments within pre-capitalist society, which necessitated the development of large-scale production. This, combined with the weakness of internal constraints within feudalism in western Europe, allowed the great transformation to happen in Europe.

If we ignore, for a moment, the debate about the process through which capitalism is set up, Polanyi makes the important observation that once capitalism has emerged, the *retention* of some market restrictions could be necessary for political purposes, to make it politically palatable. If markets become completely unfettered society may disintegrate, given the very powerful forces of social dissolution set in train by the capitalist market logic. This was the first time that the political necessity of the state mediating capitalist markets and easing some of the pain of continuous market restructuring was pointed out. Polanyi's argument suggests that once capitalism has been set up, fully unrestricted markets may be damaging for it and may indeed result in its political collapse. Thus, some degree of market restriction, paradoxically, may be politically *necessary* for the survival of capitalism.

A more powerful set of reasons as to why some specific types of market restrictions may be necessary for capitalism emerges when we look at late capitalism. In early developers, the creation of a propertyless class of workers and a class of asset owners who were competing amongst themselves to survive was sufficient to ensure relatively rapid productivity growth through market competition. It is not clear that a similar structure of rights in contemporary developing countries would have the same effect, given that now developing countries have to *catch up* with advanced countries who already have higher productivity and better technologies than they do. A catching-up country that has free trade would very likely be stuck with low-technology production.

In theory, if a market exists and a country has cheaper labour than another, capital should flow to the cheap labour country. But this theory ignores that competitiveness and productivity are high in some countries only because their social structures impose compulsions for high productivity. If productivity is low and does not grow, low wages by themselves will not attract investment. This is simply a matter of arithmetic. Even if wages in the developing country are one-twentieth that in an advanced country, if productivity is one-fortieth, unit labour costs will be *twice* as high in the developing country.

Productivity differentials between advanced and developing countries are likely to be particularly high in high-technology industries, and less so in low-technology industries. Given the wage differential, this would make it profitable for capitalist owners to shift the location of some low-technology industries to developing countries, but not to necessarily shift high-technology industries. This, rather than the relative costs of labour and capital, is a more powerful explanation of why only low-productivity industries are likely to migrate to developing countries that rely simply on markets, with no internal strategy of social transformation. But we are now referring to a social transformation towards property rights, institutional and class structures that can enforce productivity growth in a context of catching up.

The literature on the developmental state (Aoki, Kim and Okuno–Fujiwara 1997; Woo–Cumings 1999; and many others) and case studies of catching-up countries like South Korea (Amsden 1989) and Taiwan (Wade 1990) show that successful catching up requires a range of institutions and interventions that are quite different from those in classical capitalism. It is important to understand in outline why this might be so.

A critical problem with establishing high-productivity industries in developing countries is that learning how to use sophisticated processes, and setting up the internal and external systems required to achieve the potential productivity of high-technology industries *takes time*. This very simple point was made a long time ago by Kenneth Arrow, who introduced the term '*learning-by-doing*' to describe the fact that productivity is always initially low when workers (and managers) have to work with new machines, and gradually improves only as workers learn how to use them. This means that unless there is some institutional system that both allows this learning to take place and *ensures* that resources are not wasted if learning fails, successful investment in high-productivity sectors is unlikely to happen.

The conventional answer to this in developing countries has been to support infant industries through conditional subsidization policies. But conditional subsidization requires not just appropriate intentions on the part of the state, but also, and critically, a power structure that allows the state to withdraw support when performance is poor, and to restructure and reallocate assets rapidly when required (Khan 2000a). Thus, in late developers, the social transformation does not only have to create a working class with the imperative to work and a capitalist class that owns property. There has also to be a distribution of power between the state and capital that allows different strategies of catching up to be organized and implemented, because market competition between capitalists will no longer suffice to ensure rapid productivity growth. In short, specific systems of state-led compulsion are required to complement market compulsion among late developers.

This approach can help to explain why different systems of state support of technology acquisition have played a key role in late developers. Although outright infant industry subsidization was not always used, in all the successful late developers, the state evolved some system of carrots and sticks to attract high-technology industries while retaining the ability to withdraw this support or otherwise sanction non-performers if the performance in bringing in high-productivity technologies was poor. Not all late developer states were equally good in achieving these goals but they were all substantially successful, and this explains their relative success as compared to the vast majority of developing countries that performed rather poorly. Because very different institutional and property rights structures can be used to create incentives and compulsions for technical progress, the internal power structures required to implement and police these strategies differ quite significantly. This means that the internal power structures and class conflicts that may allow a viable capitalist economy to emerge are not very narrowly defined, and more variants of capitalist transition may emerge in the future. On the other hand, this does not mean that every developing country has an internal power structure that is suitable for rapid implementation of the new institutional and property right structures that would be appropriate for capitalist catching-up strategies. In many poorly performing developing countries, there may indeed be internal conflicts that block social transformation to economies which are more productive (Khan 2002).

This analysis helps us to evaluate the mainstream consensus that a perfectly working market *is* capitalism, and that bringing about the conditions for a well-working and efficient market *is* creating the conditions for a capitalist transition. What is required (in the conventional wisdom) for such a market-driven transition?

First, we require stable property rights, defined by low expropriation risk. Note that we do not require any specific *structure* of property rights, all we need is that *all* existing rights should be well-defined and non-expropriable. It does not matter if existing rights are peasant rights over land or the land rights of large unproductive landlords, or anything else. The assumption is that as soon as we have property rights with low expropriation risk, transaction costs will fall and efficient allocations will follow. The point made by Brenner and Wood that markets did not lead to the emergence of capitalism for thousands of years till forced changes in rights created capitalism in England in the sixteenth and seventeenth centuries has to be answered by these theorists.

Second, it is argued that well-working markets require no intervention by states, so a well-working capitalism requires the virtual absence of state intervention. Intervention creates rents (incomes above opportunity incomes) and this impedes the operation of competitive markets. This claim contradicts the role of the state as an agency of social classes pushing the social transformation that creates versions of capitalism. It also ignores the role of the state in managing the politics of capitalism, in the way Polanyi has pointed out.

Third, the mainstream view argues that well-working markets require the absence of rent-seeking and corruption since these processes create rents and destabilize property rights. So, it is argued that creating the conditions necessary for a take-off involves fighting corruption and rent-seeking as well.

Finally, it is assumed that since rent-seeking benefits a minority, the majority will use democracy to ensure that rent-seeking does not happen. The majority will also ensure that the state does not expropriate resources from investors *ex post*. Therefore, it is argued, we need to have democracy to make a market economy work. These reforms add up to the so-called good governance agenda, now recognized as a set of preconditions for market-led (capitalist) growth.

But what is the evidence that good governance is necessary for generating economic dynamism in any developing country? While a lot of cross-sectional evidence is presented in support of the conventional models, the regression exercises do not actually support the claims that are made (see Khan 2002 for a critique). Figure 1 plots Knack and Keefer's Property Rights Stability Index (incorporating corruption, rule of law, bureaucratic quality, government contract repudiation and expropriation risk) for 1984, the earliest available year, against GDP growth rates for the decade 1980–90. We can treat 1984 as the index for the beginning of the period in question. The interesting observation is that while the regression line has the positive slope expected by the mainstream approach to development (although the statistical fit is very poor), the countries in our sample separate into three quite separate groups. Most countries belong to either group 1 (low-growth developing countries, defined by a growth rate below the advanced country average) or group 3 (advanced industrialized countries, defined by high per capita incomes).

The first group has low growth (by definition) and poor governance characteristics, while the second has higher growth and the best governance characteristics. The (weak) slope of the regression line depends on most countries being in one or the other of these two groups. But the most interesting group is group 2 (developing countries that are catching up, by virtue of having higher growth rates than the advanced countries). This group is interesting because, though the countries in it are not numerous enough to make a difference to the slope of the regression line, they are the only ones actually catching up. A visual examination of the data shows that while their growth is significant, their property rights and other governance characteristics are *not* significantly different from the developing country average.

FIGURE 1   *Relationship between Stable Property Rights and Growth*

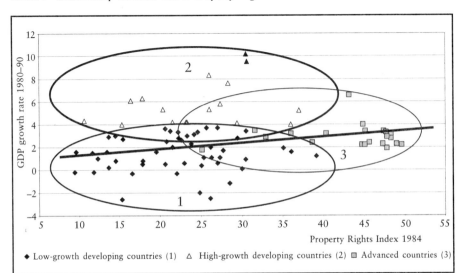

This evidence raises a very important question for catching-up policies in developing countries. Do group 1 countries try to reach group 3 by *first* emulating the market and governance characteristics of group 3 countries? Or do they look at history and try to attain the governance characteristics of group 2 countries, as these are the only ones that are actually catching up? The route to group 3 may be through group 2, in which case, the required institutional, market and class characteristics of group 1 countries should be sought in group 2, rather than group 3. The first route can be described as an attempt to create capitalism through creating the conditions for efficient markets. The second route is the route of constructing a capitalist transformation that, in late developers, involves not just the transformation of property rights to create a capitalist and a working class, but also the development of different types of state capacities to push technological progress through systems of conditional incentives and compulsion.

The debate on how the capitalist transformation of poorly performing developing countries is to be organized has acquired very significant implications. The marketization strategy, with its focus on stable property rights and the creation of a well-working market, is clearly the dominant strategy. But while stable property rights and well-working markets are important characteristics of an advanced capitalist economy, creating a capitalist economy always requires substantial restructuring of pre-existing property rights and incentives for emerging capitalists to rapidly acquire new technologies. During this transition, the condition of stable property rights is therefore an odd one to aim for, particularly since the existing structure of rights and production systems are, by definition, generating low productivity and productivity growth. The real question is whether or not we can ensure that the economic and social restructuring that is taking place in every developing country is taking the country in the direction of a viable capitalist economy. The danger is that the good governance approach allows us to bypass difficult questions about the social transformation and instead focus on reforms that would, at best, work if the aim is to make an already existing capitalist market economy work better. This assumes that a capitalist market economy exists in the first place when, in most developing countries, the problem is to organize the capitalist transformation itself.

**References**

Amsden, Alice (1989), *Asia's Next Giant: South Korea and Late Industrialization* (Oxford: Oxford University Press).

Aoki, Masahiko, Hyung-Ki Kim and Masahiro Okuno–Fujiwara, eds (1997), *The Role of Government in East Asian Economic Development: Comparative Institutional Analysis* (Oxford: Clarendon Press).

Brenner, Robert (1976), 'Agrarian Class Structure and Economic Development in Pre-Industrial Europe', *Past and Present*, 70: 30–75.

—— (1985), 'The Agrarian Roots of European Capitalism', in T.H. Aston and C.H.E. Philpin, eds, *The Brenner Debate: Agrarian Class Structure and Economic Development in Pre-Industrial Europe* (Cambridge: Cambridge University Press).

Dobb, Maurice (1946), *Studies in the Development of Capitalism* (London: Routledge).

Hilton, Rodney H., ed. (1976), *The Transition from Feudalism to Capitalism* (London: Verso).

Jomo K.S. and C.B. Edwards (1993), 'Malaysian Industrialization in Historical Perspective', in Jomo K.S., ed., *Industrializing Malaysia: Policy, Performance, Prospects* (London: Routledge).

Khan, Mushtaq H. (2000a), 'Rents, Efficiency and Growth', in Mushtaq H. Khan and K.S. Jomo, eds, *Rents, Rent-Seeking and Economic Development: Theory and Evidence in Asia* (Cambridge: Cambridge University Press).

—— (2000b), 'Rent-Seeking as Process', in Mushtaq H. Khan and K.S. Jomo, eds, *Rents, Rent-Seeking and Economic Development: Theory and Evidence in Asia* (Cambridge: Cambridge University Press).

—— (2002), 'State Failure in Developing Countries and Strategies of Institutional Reform', in Bertil Tungodden, Nick Stern and Ivar Kolstad, eds, *Towards Pro-Poor Policies: Aid Institutions and Globalization* (Oxford: Oxford University Press for World Bank).

North, Douglass C. (1990), *Institutions, Institutional Change, and Economic Performance* (Cambridge: Cambridge University Press).

Olson, Mancur (1997), 'The New Institutional Economics: The Collective Choice Approach to Economic Development', in Christopher Clague, ed., *Institutions and Economic Development* (Baltimore: Johns Hopkins University Press).

—— (2000), 'Dictatorship, Democracy, and Development', in Mancur Olson and Satu Kähkönen, eds, *A Not-So-Dismal Science: A Broader View of Economies and Societies* (Oxford: Oxford University Press).

Polanyi, Karl (1957), *The Great Transformation* (Boston: Beacon Press).

Sweezy, Paul M. (1950), 'The Transition from Feudalism to Capitalism', *Science and Society*, 14 (2): 134–57.

Wade, Robert (1990), *Governing the Market: Economic Theory and the Role of Government in East Asian Industrialization* (Princeton, N.J.: Princeton University Press).

Williamson, Oliver E. (1985), *The Economic Institutions of Capitalism* (New York: The Free Press).

Woo–Cumings, Meredith, ed. (1999), *The Developmental State* (Ithaca: Cornell University Press).

Wood, Ellen Meiskins (2002), *The Origins of Capitalism: A Longer View* (London: Verso).

# The Pioneers of Development Economics and Modern Growth Theory

*Jaime Ros*

> Launching a country into self-sustaining growth is a little like getting an airplane off the ground. There is a critical ground speed which must be passed before the craft can become airborne. (Rosenstein–Rodan 1961, quoting from MIT 1957: 70)

> Proceeding 'bit by bit' will not add up in its effects to the sum total of the single bits. A minimum quantum of investment is a necessary, though not sufficient, condition for success. This, in a nutshell, is the contention of the theory of the big push. (Rosenstein–Rodan 1961: 57)

After two decades of near-inactivity, economic growth has again become the subject of intense theoretical and empirical research. The enormous efforts in the last decade and a half attempt to explain the process of economic growth in both developed and developing countries with a unified analytical framework. Big questions such as why some nations are poorer than others and why the economies of some countries grow so much faster than others, have now become central to the research agenda of mainstream growth theory.

Some fifty years ago, a new field of economic theory emerged, aiming to answer similar questions, to address issues about the persistence of underdevelopment and to search for remedies to overcome poverty. As Taylor and Arida (1988) put it in their survey of development thinking, the nature of these questions meant that the new field had to rely on a paradigm built upon notions of imperfect competition, increasing returns and labour surpluses not properly integrated into and, in some cases, altogether alien to established economic theory. Yet, even though the contributions of this early period have been the object of renewed interest in recent years (see, in particular, Murphy, Shleifer and Vishny 1989) – Paul Krugman (1992) has called them 'high development theory' – they have generally been ignored in the recent wave of theoretical and empirical research on economic growth.[1]

The purpose of this chapter is to look at the contributions of classical economic development theory, especially the writings of Paul Rosenstein–Rodan, Ragnar Nurkse and Arthur Lewis, from the perspective of modern growth theory.[2]

The chapter shows the significance of these contributions by the pioneers of development economics to modern economic growth theory, and their current relevance for both theoretical and empirical reasons. The first argument developed here can be summarized as follows. Old ('exogenous') growth theory relies on two assumptions. The first is the assumption of diminishing returns to capital not offset by high elasticity of factor substitution. The second assumption is that there is no surplus labour, so that the elasticity of labour supply cannot offset the effects on growth of diminishing returns to capital. Recent 'endogenous' growth models have abandoned the first assumption but keep the second. Early development theory abandoned the second and combined it with the assumption of increasing returns to scale. This chapter attempts to show that the key contributions of early development economics consequently provide a more general approach to the problem of economic development than the recent endogenous growth literature. A second argument is that these early approaches to development are also more empirically promising than either old or new growth theory. Though the second argument is not fully developed, some suggestive empirical evidence is provided to support its claim. The corollary of these arguments is that it may well be desirable to draw much more heavily on the very rich past of development theory.

### Growth Theory: Old and New

The old growth theory of the 1950s and 1960s or, more precisely, what has survived in mainstream economic theory from those years, is the neoclassical growth model formalized by Robert Solow (1956) and others in the mid-1950s. The Solow model refers to a competitive capitalist economy in which production is carried out by means of physical capital and labour under conditions of constant returns to scale and diminishing returns to each factor of production. The economy operates at full employment, with inelastic labour supply

FIGURE 1   *An 'Exogenous' Growth Model*

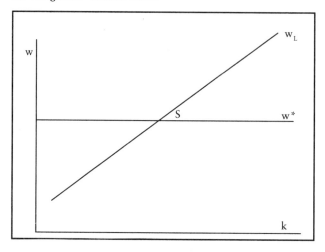

that grows at a constant and exogenous rate. Technology is a public good that improves at an exogenously given rate.

Figure 1 presents a simple version of the Solow model which assumes no technical progress and population growth, a Cobb–Douglas technology and an exogenous savings rate. In the figure, $w$ and $k$ are the logs of the real wage and the capital stock, or (with appropriate normalization) the capital–labour ratio (on this real wage diagram, see Ros 2000). The $w_L$ curve is a locus of labour market equilibrium showing the equilibrium real wage as a positive function of the economy-wide capital–labour endowment: as the capital–labour ratio increases, the marginal product of labour at full employment rises and, thus, the equilibrium real wage as well.[3] The $w^*$ curve is a locus of stationary capital endowments, showing the real wage required to generate a rate of return on capital that yields a rate of capital accumulation equal to the rate of depreciation of capital stock. Below (above) this locus, the real wage is lower (higher) than the required value and, thus, the rate of return and rate of capital accumulation are higher (lower) than in the stationary state. Under our present assumptions, this locus is a horizontal line: there is a unique value of the real wage (independent of the capital–labour ratio) that generates a rate of capital accumulation equal to the depreciation rate.[4]

Two well-known results follow from this framework. First, the economy converges to an equilibrium (shown as $S$ in Figure 1) in which output and capital are stationary. With Harrod-neutral technical progress and labour force growth, output and capital grow at the same rate, equal to the rate of growth of the labour force plus the rate of technical progress.[5] The second result refers to what happens when the economy is off the equilibrium path due, for example, to the fact that the capital–labour ratio is below its steady state value. The economy's growth rate will then be higher than in the steady state – the excess being a function of the gap between the $w^*$ and $w_L$ curves – and the economy's growth will be so much faster, the lower the initial value of the capital endowment per worker. Thus, starting from a relatively low capital–labour ratio, the economy converges to the equilibrium path at a diminishing rate of growth.

Diminishing returns to capital in the production function have a major influence in generating both these results.[6] It will be useful later to think of the role of diminishing returns to capital as follows. In the economy considered, output will eventually stagnate since its equilibrium path is a stationary state in which the economy generates a gross investment rate just equal to the capital stock depreciation rate. If, starting from this equilibrium, net investment became positive, the influence of diminishing returns to capital would set in motion forces that hinder the persistence of this positive net investment rate. The larger capital stock, as a result of positive net investment, can be seen as having two consequences:

(i) Output per worker is now higher since each worker has greater capital stock at his/her disposal.

(ii) This larger capital stock implies that labour demand is now greater at the initial real wage; in the face of an inelastic labour supply, the equilibrium real wage has to be higher.

Diminishing returns to capital imply that the effect of the larger capital stock on labour productivity is not strong enough to offset the effect of the higher equilibrium real wage on the rate of profit. As a result, the market equilibrium wage rises above the required wage ($w^*$). The rate of return on capital falls below its stationary state value and positive net investment cannot be sustained. The capital stock will contract and eventually return to its stationary state value. In this equilibrium state, there is not, and cannot be, an endogenous process of capital accumulation. This helps us understand the crucial role played by technological progress and labour force growth in this theory: these are the only forces capable of neutralizing the influence of diminishing returns to capital. Steady state growth is the *outcome* of these forces, simply because no other force is capable of sustaining growth.

All this is, of course, in the equilibrium path. If initial conditions are such that capital stock per worker is smaller than in the steady state, there is an additional force that drives growth: the fact that the rate of return on capital is higher than the one prevailing in the steady state under these conditions (the equilibrium wage is lower than the required wage). This is what makes the rate of capital accumulation higher than the depreciation rate. The second result of the model follows: off the steady state – starting from a low capital–labour ratio – the economy converges to the equilibrium path with a decreasing rate of growth. Diminishing returns to capital again provide the mechanism involved: as the capital stock per worker increases, the productivity effects of capital accumulation are unable to compensate for the negative effects that higher real wages have on the rate of return on capital. The rate of return and, with it, the rate of capital accumulation thus tend to fall.

From the perspective of endogenous growth theory, these properties of the Solow model raise theoretical and empirical objections. The first result appears to leave the theory in a rather unsatisfactory state: in the long run, economic growth is attributed to exogenous forces that the theory leaves unexplained. The second result has the implication that incomes per capita across countries should have a strong tendency to converge.[7] That is, the economies of poor countries with small capital endowments per worker should grow at higher rates than those of richer nations. The problem here is that we do not observe the convergence suggested by the theory or, at least, by the theory without further extensions. While there have been processes of convergence among today's developed economies (the United States, western Europe and Japan), the disparities between rich and poor countries have generally tended to persist. In many cases, the gaps have widened, and only in a few has convergence proceeded at a rapid pace. The degree of convergence has been less than the theory suggests, as differences in rates of return on capital have been less than one would expect on the basis of disparities in capital–labour ratios, and capital has not flowed internationally to the poorest countries.

Taken together, the theoretical and empirical shortcomings of the old neoclassical growth model have generated the perception that they may well have a common source in the specification of technology in the model, which gives too prominent a role to diminishing returns to capital. If technology can be respecified in such a way as to counteract the influence of diminishing returns, this could, in principle, overcome the two perceived weaknesses of the old framework. It could endogenously generate growth without having to rely exogenously on technical progress, thus enhancing the explanatory power of the theory. At the same time, such endogenous growth could weaken the strong convergence properties of the traditional model, making the theory more consistent with observed historical experience. How should technology be respecified to meet these two objectives? Several departures can be found in the recent literature, some more revisionist than others, depending on the emphasis given to each of the two objectives. I shall mostly focus on the original articles that triggered the new wave of endogenous growth models.

A first option is to abandon the assumption of constant returns to scale. Bringing in increasing returns to scale would strengthen the positive effects of capital accumulation on labour productivity, as the effects of a higher capital–labour ratio on output per worker is now enhanced by the positive effect of a larger capital stock and scale of production. This opens up the possibility, in the model presented above, that the positive productivity effects of capital accumulation offset the negative effects on the rate of return to capital of higher real wages. If increasing returns are strong enough, capital accumulation could then continue indefinitely even in the absence of exogenous technical progress or labour supply growth.

This road was taken by Paul Romer's (1986) article that triggered the recent wave of contributions to growth theory. Romer identified the externalities generated by R & D investments as the source of increasing returns. Because the return to investments in new technologies can only be partially appropriated privately, the social rate of return can be well above the private rate of return. Thus, even if the returns to capital are diminishing for an individual firm, returns may be increasing for the economy as a whole if account is taken of the externalities. When this is so, capital accumulation feeds itself, generating a self-sustained expansion, in fact, with a growth rate increasing over time. The basic insight of the Romer model can also be presented using our $w_L$–$w^*$ diagram (see Figure 2a). The key departure from the Solow model is that the technological parameter in the production function is now a positive function of the aggregate capital stock, thus generating increasing returns to capital.

The dependence of technology on the size of the capital stock modifies the shapes of the two curves in the diagram. In particular, the $w^*$ locus is no longer horizontal but positively sloped, since, with increasing returns, there is no longer a unique real wage but rather a locus of (w, k) combinations that generates the same rate of return to capital. Moreover, if externalities from the capital stock are sufficiently strong as to generate increasing returns to capital in the

FIGURE 2   *Endogenous Growth Models*

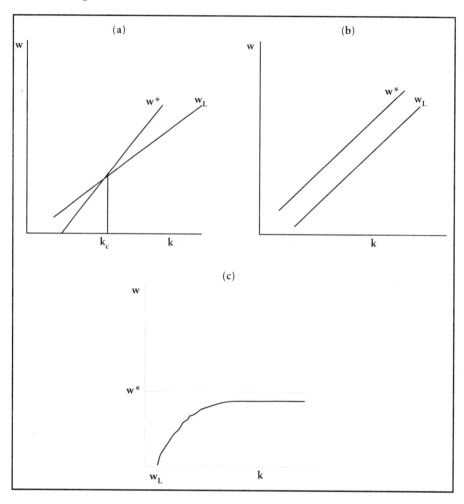

economy as a whole, it is easily shown that the slope of the $w^*$ curve will be higher than the slope of the $w_L$ curve, making the equilibrium at the intersection of the two curves unstable. An economy with a capital–labour endowment greater than $k_c$ in the figure will generate a growth path of self-sustained expansion with increasing real wages along the $w_L$ locus and increasing rates of return, and of capital accumulation (both functions of the gap between the two loci). For this to happen, returns to capital, and not only to scale, must indeed increase. If the slope of the $w^*$ locus is less than the slope of the $w_L$ locus, the properties of the model will not be different from those of the neoclassical model. A special case is when the coefficient of the capital stock in the aggregate production function is equal to 1, and technology displays constant returns to capital. In such an AK model, the slopes of the two curves are the same, and the economy grows without bounds at a constant rate of growth (Figure 2b).

A sufficiently high elasticity of factor substitution can also counteract the role of diminishing returns to capital and can generate sustained growth over time. In this case, the real wage effects on the profit rate are offset, not by productivity gains from increasing returns but, rather, by the high elasticity of substitution that more than proportionately reduces the demand for labour, decreasing the share of wages in total output. It is then possible that, even with constant returns to scale, a high elasticity of factor substitution will make persistent growth possible (see Solow 1956: 70–71; Jones and Manuelli 1990). The slope of the $w_L$ curve now falls as $k$ increases and approaches the same slope as the $w^*$ line when $k$ goes to infinity. As illustrated in Figure 2c, if $w^*$ is higher than $w$ when $k$ tends to infinity, the two curves will not intersect and growth will proceed at a diminishing rate, converging to a constant rate as $k$ tends to infinity. The rate of accumulation does not converge to Harrod's natural rate, as in the Solow model, because, with an elasticity of substitution of more than unity, the profit share increases as $k$ rises and tends to unity when $k$ tends to infinity. Then, as in the AK model, returns to capital become constant.

This model thus blends features of the AK model with the Solow model. Two economies with identical technology and savings rates, but which differ in their initial capital–labour ratios, will not converge to identical levels of output per worker. They tend to converge to the same growth rate and, for this reason, the initial income gap will not fully disappear. As in the AK model, the strength of convergence is weaker compared to the Solow model. However, the transitional dynamics are similar to those of the neoclassical model since the economy with the lower capital–labour ratio grows at a faster rate.

Another road was taken by Robert Lucas (1988). Although Lucas brought in externalities and increasing returns, his model does not require the assumption of increasing returns to generate self-sustained growth (see Rebelo 1991; Romer 1991). The distinctive feature of his model – in terms of the specification of technology – is the existence of a reproducible factor that can be produced without the use of non-reproducible factors.

The mechanics of economic growth in these conditions may be illustrated by the following example of a two-sector economy. In one sector, goods and services are produced by means of physical and human capital under constant returns to scale. The other is a knowledge-producing sector that only uses human capital to increase the quantity of human capital that can be used in each of the two sectors. In the absence of non-reproducible factors in the production of human capital, the model generates a steady state path in which the rate of physical capital accumulation is equal to, and determined by, the rate of human capital accumulation. The latter is proportional to the investment effort that society realizes in the human capital-producing sector, that is, to the share of its human resources that society devotes to the generation and transmission of knowledge. In this equilibrium path, income per capita increases continuously – in the absence of exogenous technological change and with a constant rate of return to human capital – as a result of the ever-increasing endowment of human capital per capita. Physical capital accumulation is endogenous and persistent, not a result of the productivity effects of increasing returns, as in the Romer model, but because continuous accumulation of human capital increases the productivity of physical capital and neutralizes the influence of diminishing returns.

This account of the Lucas model can be similarly represented as the Solow model (see Figure 1), although, of course, with a different interpretation: $w$ is now the return to human capital and $k$ the ratio of physical to human capital. In the steady state path these two variables remain constant but, because human capital is growing at a constant rate, physical capital grows at the very same rate. If not on the steady state, with a relatively high endowment of human capital, the economy will converge to the steady state with a growth rate initially above the equilibrium rate. And, vice versa, the economy will converge to a steady state with an initially low growth rate if initial conditions are such that the ratio of physical to human capital is relatively high. After a war or an earthquake has destroyed mostly physical capital, for example, the economy will recover faster than after an epidemic that has mainly destroyed human capital.

This Lucas-type model is thus one in which physical capital accumulation and output growth are driven by the accumulation of human capital, analogous to the way capital accumulation is driven by technical progress and labour force growth in the Solow model. It is not surprising, therefore, that one implication of the model that has attracted most attention is also analogous to an implication of the Solow model: starting with a relatively low ratio of physical to human capital (as in a developing country well endowed with human resources) off the steady state, the economy's growth rate will be relatively high compared to that on the equilibrium path. The mechanics of economic growth are similar to those in the Solow model, although the engine of growth is different.[8]

### Growth and Development: Classical Development Theory

None of the objections to the old neoclassical growth model is new. Attempts to endogenize technical progress – such as Kaldor's technical progress function and Arrow's model of 'learning by doing' – were not absent in the old growth theory literature. The economics of technical change is a discipline that produced a vast literature well before endogenous growth theory took off. Less well recognized is that the same applies to the weak degree of convergence in income levels across countries as an empirical objection to the neoclassical model. One could even claim that this observation was the starting point from which development economics took off. The discipline emerged precisely to explain the sluggishness of economic progress and the persistence of poverty in underdeveloped countries. Interestingly, the issue to which Ragnar Nurkse devoted most attention in the early 1950s – why capital does not flow internationally to the poorest countries[9] – is one that has attracted much attention in the new growth literature (see, in particular, Lucas 1990).

The relevance of the early development theory of the 1940s and 1950s for the current state of growth theory is that it offers a more general and, I shall try to argue, more promising path away from the neoclassical model of growth.

What one may call the growth model of early development theory can indeed be seen as a departure from the neoclassical growth model[10] that involves two basic ingredients. The first refers to increasing returns to scale associated with:

(i) pecuniary external economies at the aggregate level, generated by internal economies of scale in modern industrial production – dramatized by Rosenstein–Rodan's (1943) example of the shoe factory which would have to employ no less than 20,000 workers to operate profitably with modern technologies – and by economies of scale due to indivisibilities and technical discontinuities in infrastructure provision or, as he put it, 'social overhead capital', that 'require a minimum high quantum of investment which would serve, say, fifty factories but would cost far too much for one' (Rosenstein–Rodan 1984: 208);

(ii) technological externalities associated with industrial training and arising from the incomplete appropriation of its social returns.

Rosenstein–Rodan (1943) was probably the economist who most vehemently departed from traditional theory in this respect.

The second ingredient refers to an elastic labour supply arising from the presence of surplus labour. It is not my purpose here to even try to briefly summarize the vast literature on the subject. I shall simply point out that the early views on underdevelopment as a situation characterized by a small capital endowment in relation to available labour supplies led to the conclusion that the elasticity of the labour supply in these conditions was likely to be higher than in developed economies with a much higher capital–labour ratio. The reason was that with a low aggregate capital–labour ratio, the marginal product of labour at full employment in the capital-using sector would be so low that a fraction of the labour force would remain employed in a non-capitalist or subsistence sector, using technologies with negligible capital intensity. It is worth quoting Lewis (1954: 47) at length here:

> The capitalist sector is that part of the economy which uses reproducible capital, and pays capitalists for the use thereof. (This coincides with Smith's definition of the productive workers, who are those who work with capital and whose product can therefore be sold at a price above their wages.) We can think, if we like, of capitalists hiring out their capital to peasants; in which case, there being by definition an unlimited number of peasants, only some will get capital, and these will have to pay for its use a price which leaves them only with subsistence earnings. More usually, however, the use of capital is controlled by capitalists, who hire the services of labour. . . . The subsistence sector is by difference all that part of the economy that is not using reproducible capital. Output per head is lower in this sector than in the capitalist sector, because it is not fructified by capital. . . . As more capital becomes available more workers can be drawn into the capitalist from the subsistence sector, and their output per head rises as they move from one sector to the other.

The key necessary condition for the coexistence of these two sectors is that the average product of labour in the non-capitalist sector is higher than the marginal product of labour that would prevail if the whole labour force was employed in the capitalist sector.[11] And this is what usually happens when the economy-wide average capital endowment per worker is low. As long as the two sectors coexist, the labour supply to the capitalist sector is bound to be more elastic than in a developed economy where the higher capital endowment per worker makes the use of subsistence technologies unprofitable. How much more elastic this labour supply is depends on the size of the subsistence sector (and thus, on the economy-wide capital–labour ratio), the elasticity of substitution in demand between the goods produced by the two sectors and the nature of returns to labour in the subsistence sector.[12] Under some specific conditions (infinite elasticity of substitution between the goods produced in the two sectors and constant returns to labour in the subsistence sector), the supply of labour to the capitalist sector will be perfectly elastic, as in Lewis's well-known model. But whether the labour supply is perfectly elastic or only imperfectly so is of no importance, as we shall now argue, to the growth model of early development theory.

Lewis was the economist who developed and emphasized the surplus labour assumption. Drawing on Smith, Young and Rosenstein–Rodan, Nurkse stressed the role of income effects associated with increasing returns. The two ingredients – increasing returns and surplus labour – were present from the 'beginning' in Rosenstein–Rodan (1943), as he rightly claimed four decades later (Rosenstein–Rodan 1984). I believe that only Rosenstein–Rodan fully perceived the general equilibrium implications of these two assumptions taken together.[13]

As some recent contributions have made clear, bringing these two ingredients – increasing returns and an elastic labour supply – together can generate a model with multiple equilibria in which, depending on initial conditions, the economy can be stuck in a poverty trap that can only be overcome through a 'big push'.[14] Such a model is illustrated in the $w_L$–$w^*$ diagram. The diagram refers to a simple version of the argument that relies exclusively on 'technological externalities' as a source of increasing returns. The presence of increasing returns to scale makes the $w^*$ locus slope upwards, as in the Romer model, and for the same reasons (the productivity effects of capital accumulation), although the source of increasing returns is rather different. The presence of a non-capitalist sector flattens the shape of the $w_L$ locus, provided the elasticity of substitution in demand between goods is high enough (greater than unity). The slope of this locus increases with the size of capital stock, reflecting a decline in labour supply elasticity as an increasing share of the labour force is employed in the capitalist sector and the size of the subsistence sector shrinks. With this shape of the $w_L$ locus and provided that increasing returns to scale are not so high as to generate an increasing rate of return on capital indefinitely, the $w^*$ locus will intersect the $w_L$ locus twice: one intersection (at point R in Figure 3) with a low level of real wages and a small capital stock, similar to the unstable equilibrium in the Romer-type model presented above, and another with high real wages and a large capital stock (point S) and which is stable, as in the Solow model.

FIGURE 3   *An Early Development Theory Model*

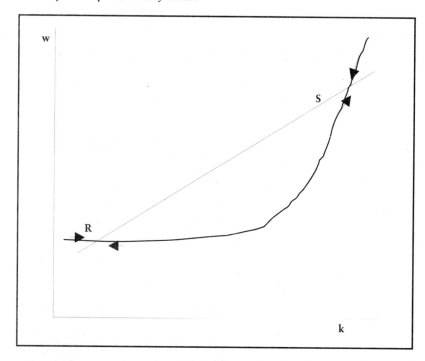

Below the low level intersection, there is a poverty trap. The elastic supply of labour and increasing returns interact negatively to hinder the expansion of the capitalist sector: the elastic labour supply sets a floor for the real wages that the capitalist sector has to pay and, together with the initial conditions of low productivity and small market size, prevents the profitable use of capital-intensive technologies with increasing returns. The inducement to invest is adversely affected so that the initial conditions of low productivity, capital scarcity and small market size persist.

Beyond the low level intersection, there is, in contrast, a virtuous circle (on which more below) between productivity increases and the inducement to invest. This virtuous circle may converge to the high level equilibrium in which labour surpluses have been largely absorbed into the capitalist sector, and the economy, with a large capital endowment, is able to generate high real wages. Lewis (1954), and then Fei and Ranis (1964), viewed this high equilibrium as the end of the development process or the final stage of the transition phase towards a mature economy in which the growth rate would depend exclusively, as in the Solow equilibrium path, on technical progress and labour force growth. In between the vicious and virtuous circles, there is a low level and unstable equilibrium associated with Rosenstein–Rodan. For, it corresponds to that critical mass of investments which generates the externalities and scale economies required for a big push towards sustained economic development.

Early development theory, with the exception of Lewis, focused on the vicious circle of poverty and the conditions for the big push, since those were the issues of greatest practical relevance in those days. These aspects have also received most attention in recent formalizations of these early insights (Murphy, Shleifer and Vishny 1989; Krugman 1992). I want to highlight what happens beyond the unstable equilibrium (associated with the big push) in the transition to a mature economy. One finds that Nurkse's references to a virtuous circle were correct: in this phase, the interactions between increasing returns to scale and an elastic supply of labour become positive and counteract the influence of diminishing returns to capital. The reason is that the productivity effects of capital accumulation are strengthened by the presence of increasing returns to scale, while an elastic supply of labour exerts a moderating effect on the real wage effects of capital accumulation. Growth can then proceed with a constant or even increasing rate of return on capital.

As the economy-wide endowment of capital per worker increases and the size of the non-capitalist sector shrinks, the supply of labour will become increasingly inelastic. In the absence of Romer-type dramatically increasing returns to scale, or of a very high elasticity of factor substitution, the influence of diminishing returns to capital will reappear. The economy will then converge to a high level mature economy equilibrium. In this case, the model does not fully endogenize growth, for when the economy has reached maturity, it does not offer a growth theory different from traditional or newer ones. It offers, however, a theory of endogenous accumulation during the transition to a mature economy with different and, in my view, more convincing implications than those that can be derived from either the old or new vintages of growth theory.

### Assessment and Concluding Comments

The growth model of early development theory has implications for cross-country growth performance that overcome the shortcomings of the Solow model. This model does not expect strong and straightforward convergence: given an elastic labour supply, increasing returns tend to generate divergence and only generate convergence when the elasticity of labour supply falls as the capital–labour ratio increases. The implication is that we should expect the highest rates of growth in the intermediate stages of the transition, when increasing returns interact with a still high elasticity of the labour supply. This implies convergence among middle- and high-income countries simultaneously with divergence across middle- and low-income countries.

This big picture is quite consistent with the broad trends of the last five decades: convergence among OECD economies and a number of middle-income developing economies, together with increasing heterogeneity among developing countries. The model also accommodates two striking features of post-war development trends. First, the highest growth rates were to be found among developing countries and a number of industrial countries that were initially relatively less developed. For example, in the period 1965–85, the economies in the highest growth quintile in the World Bank data reported by Barro and Lee

(1993) were all developing economies, plus Malta, Japan, Portugal, Norway, Greece, Italy and Finland. Second, the lowest growth rates were typically found among the low-income countries.[15] Again, according to the World Bank data reported in Barro and Lee (1993), most of the economies in the lowest growth quintile for 1965–85 (sixteen out of twenty-two economies) were low-income countries in Sub-Saharan Africa and Asia. Similar conclusions were reached by Ros (2000) for the period 1965–92.

This is surely an incomplete picture, but if unrealized convergence is the reason for abandoning the Solow model, the model of early development theory seems to offer an attractive and worth exploring alternative. In particular, it offers a better answer to the question of why the lowest growth rates are typically found among the initially poorest countries. It thus provides a more attractive framework than the extension of the Solow model suggested by Mankiw, Romer and Weil (1992), which involves bringing human capital into the Solow model along with labour and physical capital, or Barro's analytical framework, which incorporates human capital and political risk, in particular (Barro 1991, 1997).

The implications also seem more consistent with the broad trends of the post-war period than those one may derive from endogenous growth models. I say this with some hesitation, for most recent empirical research has focused on testing the traditional model, with revisions and extensions, rather than on empirically testing endogenous growth models, as if rejection of the traditional model provides support for the new growth theory. However, the new growth models appear to imply an excessive degree of divergence, much greater than suggested by historical experience.

As already discussed, recent growth models that rely on increasing returns to scale to sustain growth, assume that externalities deriving from the process of capital accumulation are so large as to generate non-diminishing returns to capital in the aggregate production function. Taking a very long-term perspective, Romer (1991) finds this assumption attractive because it is consistent with the fact that the productivity growth rates of technological leaders have been increasing over the centuries. But this analytical framework does not explain cross-country differences in growth rates. Just as diminishing returns to capital in the neoclassical model tend to generate too much convergence, the assumption of increasing returns to capital tends to generate too much divergence: not only should gaps in per capita income widen over time, differences in growth rates should also become larger, for which there is no empirical support.

This implication is avoided in endogenous growth models that restrict the coefficient on capital in aggregate production to unity (the AK model). With constant returns to capital, these models generate sustained growth at a constant, rather than increasing rate. But they do so at the cost of more restrictive assumptions about technology with no empirical support.[16] To go back to my main point, this difficulty is not present in the growth model of early development theory. This model can generate constant or even increasing growth rates over a long transition period without having to rely on restrictive assumptions about technology. The reason is simply that the forces generating constant or increasing growth rates are not exclusively technological. They are rooted in the interaction between some increasing returns to scale and a sufficiently elastic supply of labour.

The approach in which endogenous growth is driven by human capital accumulation is promising for explaining differences in growth rates across developing countries and, in particular, the extraordinarily high growth rates of the East Asian miracles. Yet, these models also imply an excessive degree of divergence. Differences in growth rates tend to persist indefinitely, thus generating increasing gaps in per capita income levels. If one adds the assumption that the share of resources invested in human capital is likely to increase with per capita income, then, widening gaps in growth rates should also be observed.

Moreover, as Pack (1994) and Rodrik (1994) have convincingly argued, the comparative performance of East Asia is difficult to reconcile with a human capital-based explanation of economic growth. Many other poor countries with similar or higher levels of education were not able to quickly grow. Birdsall, Ross and Sabot (1995) suggest that South Korea's growth would have been less (close to 5 per cent per year instead of close to 6 per cent), but still much faster than the developing country average, if its initial level of education had been similar to the developing country average.

While the East Asian countries made substantial investments in education while experiencing rapid economic growth, the same happened in many other countries that were unable to grow fast. The commitment to improving educational standards was almost universal across the developing world. The results of these human capital investments were often very different, but differences in growth rates may have had a major part in this. This endogeneity problem is illustrated by the comparison between Korea and Mexico (see Birdsall, Ross and Sabot 1995). In 1970, Korea's public expenditure in basic education per eligible child was only slightly higher than Mexico's. Two decades later, Mexico's expenditure on education was only 25 per cent of the Korean level; secondary enrolment rates were twice as high in Korea than in Mexico, and the gap in tertiary enrolment rates had become even higher (39 per cent versus 15 per cent). This divergence cannot be explained by public expenditure policy alone: in fact, by the mid-1970s, after the expansion of the first half of that decade, expenditure in basic education as a percentage of GDP temporarily reached higher levels in Mexico than in Korea. The explanation for these increasing gaps has to be found in the fact that Korea's GDP grew at annual rates of 9.6 per cent, compared to Mexico's 3.5 per cent per year, which meant that with the same percentage of GDP invested in education, the resources that Korea was able to invest in this sector expanded at a vastly superior rate.[17]

Pack also reminds us that, unlike today, investments in R & D were of little significance in the developing economies of East Asia before the mid-1980s. Yet, by then, these countries had been able to sustain extraordinarily high growth rates for almost three decades. Ranis (1995) tells an interesting and significant story. In the 1960s (from 1960 to 1967), around 15 per cent of Taiwan's college graduates went to the United States to undertake postgraduate studies. This is a good indicator of the very high rate of human capital formation for a country with the income level of Taiwan in the 1960s, especially since two-thirds of those students went into science and engineering. Yet, and this is the most revealing part of the story, only 4.5 per cent of them returned each year. By contrast, in the second half of the 1980s, when Taiwan's industrialization was no longer based on labour-intensive manufactures and was becoming increasingly science- and technology-intensive, more than 90 per cent of such highly trained graduates were returning. Thus, human capital reserves, created over the years, were a necessary condition for technology-intensive industrialization to take off, but did not represent a sufficient condition.

It is not easy to reconcile these facts with the notion that differences in the rate of economic growth across countries are to be primarily explained by differences in the rate of human capital formation. More generally, it is hard to reconcile them with a view of the development process in which physical capital accumulation and output growth are essentially driven by human capital formation. This assertion is not meant to downplay the importance of human capital formation in economic development. Nor does it mean that early development theory did not neglect the role of human capital. In fact, it did, although perhaps less than is sometimes asserted.

This role can be incorporated into the analytical framework of early development theory. The resulting insights turn out to be quite useful for their implications[18] of what pattern of production and trade specialization will influence how much returns increase. This will preserve the attention that early development theory gave to industrialization and the accumulation of physical capital. It is, at the same time, a model that points to new research areas and difficult questions; that leads to enquiries, for example, about income distribution and demographic factors that may be behind the accumulation of human capital. Such a research programme strikes me as a most promising avenue to enhance our understanding of different growth performances across developing countries and of the very process of economic development.

I am indebted for comments on a previous version of this chapter to Amitava Dutt, Peter Skott and Lance Taylor. The usual caveat applies.

### Notes

1. An example is the book by Barro and Sala-i-Martin (1995), where the only reference to early development theory is to Lewis's (1954) classic article that, strangely, is regarded as a big push model.
2. This chapter draws on Ros (2000), in particular, the analysis of the contributions of the pioneers of development economics presented there.
3. As shown in Ros (2000), the equation of the $w_L$ curve is obtained by substituting an inelastic labour supply into the labour demand function and solving for $w$ as a function of $k$.
4. The equation of the $w^*$ locus is obtained by substituting the expression for the profit

rate ($r$) as a function of the real wage into the condition for stationarity of the capital stock (the equality between the rate of capital accumulation and the depreciation rate) (see Ros 2000).

5  In this case, $k$ should be interpreted as the capital–labour ratio, with labour measured in efficiency units. The required real wage will then be growing at a rate equal to the rate of technical progress.

6  Another is the elasticity of substitution between capital and labour that is set at unity in our assumed Cobb–Douglas production function. Yet another, as argued below, is the assumption of an inelastic labour supply.

7  Except, of course, for differences across countries in determinants of the steady state level of income, that is, savings rates, labour supply growth and rates of depreciation of capital stock. At the same time, the convergence properties of the model should be strengthened by the high degree of international capital mobility, since the influence of diminishing returns to capital should make capital flow from rich to poor countries with lower capital–labour ratios and higher rates of return on capital investment.

8  A perhaps more relevant comparison would be the two-sector models of Mahalanobis (1955) and Feldman (1928) as described in Domar (1957), as pointed out by Srinivasan (1994). The sector producing physical capital goods uses only reproducible factors (physical capital goods). The model generates endogenous growth without having to appeal to increasing returns to scale, and the equilibrium growth rate is determined by the share of investment devoted to capital accumulation in the capital goods-producing sector.

9  In Nurkse (1952) and his classic book on the problems of capital formation in underdeveloped countries (Nurkse 1953).

10  *Avant la lettre*, one might add, since most of these writings preceded the neoclassical model of growth, at least as formalized by Solow in the mid-1950s.

11  Strictly this is so in a model in which the two sectors produce the same goods, like the one Lewis seems to have in mind in the quotation above.

12  A full formal treatment of this proposition and others below is presented in Ros (2000, Chapter 3).

13  Expanding on this topic would take us far beyond the scope of this chapter. The basic point is that Nurkse's description of the vicious circle is frequently 'too Smithian', overemphasizing the circularity between the size of the market and the level of productivity (division of labour). This has led to misunderstanding of the 'big push' argument (and to its incorrect assimilation with Nurkse's balanced growth doctrine).

14  Cf. Murphy, Shleifer and Vishny (1989), and Krugman (1992, 1995). Despite these useful contributions to a clarification of the difficult analytical issues involved in Rosenstein–Rodan's argument, the forces accounting for the trap below the low level interior equilibrium are often incorrectly interpreted. For example, after illuminating discussions of the sources of multiple equilibria in terms of increasing returns *and* the elasticity of factor supplies, when he comes to describe in words and summarize the arguments, Krugman (1992, 1995) refers to 'the circular relationship in which the decision to invest in large-scale production depended on the size of the market, and the size of the market depended on the decision to invest. Whatever the practical relevance of this theory, it made perfectly good logical sense' (Krugman 1995: 23). If this was all, Rosenstein–Rodan would have little to add to Adam Smith and Young. This incorrect interpretation seems widespread; see, for example, Stiglitz's (1992) comment on Krugman (1992).

15  On the subject, cf. also Sen (1993). Of the sixteen countries with the lowest growth rates reported by Sen, twelve were low-income countries in Sub-Saharan Africa.

16  As Solow (1994: 51) has observed: 'If (this branch of the new growth theory) found strong support in empirical material, one would have to reconsider and perhaps try to find some convincing reason why Nature has no choice but to present us with constant returns to capital. On the whole, however, the empirical evidence appears to be less than not strong; if anything, it goes the other way.'

17  Another factor was the fact that Korea started its demographic transition earlier than

Mexico. This explains why the number of school-age children increased by 60 per cent in Mexico but fell by 2 per cent in Korea in those two decades.

[18] For a model along these lines, see Ros (2000, Chapter 6).

### References

Arrow, K.J. (1962), 'The Economic Implications of Learning by Doing', *Review of Economic Studies*, 29: 155–73.

Barro, R.J. (1991), 'Economic Growth in a Cross-Section of Countries', *Quarterly Journal of Economics*, 106: 407–44.

—— (1997), *Determinants of Economic Growth* (Cambridge, Massachusetts: MIT Press).

Barro, R.J. and J. Lee (1993), 'Losers and Winners in Economic Growth', in *Proceedings of the World Bank Annual Conference on Development Economics 1993* (Washington DC: World Bank.

Barro, R.J. and Xavier Sala-i-Martin (1995), *Economic Growth* (New York: McGraw-Hill).

Birdsall, Nancy, D. Ross and R. Sabot (1995), 'Inequality and Growth Reconsidered: Lessons from East Asia', *World Bank Economic Review*, 9 (3), September: 477–508.

Domar, Evsey (1957), *Essays in the Theory of Economic Growth* (London: Oxford University Press).

Fei, John and Gustav Ranis (1964), *Development of the Labour Surplus Economy* (Homewood, Illinois: Irwin).

Feldman, G.A. (1928), 'K Teorii Tempov Narodnogo Dokhoda', *Planovoe Khoziaistvo*, 11: 146–70.

Jones, L.E. and R.E. Manuelli (1990), 'A Convex Model of Equilibrium Growth: Theory and Policy Implications', *Journal of Political Economy*, 98: 1008–28.

Krugman, Paul (1992), 'Towards a Counter-Counterrevolution in Development Theory', in *Proceedings of the World Bank Annual Conference on Development Economics 1992*, Supplement to the *World Bank Economic Review* and the *World Bank Research Observer*.

—— (1995), *Development, Geography and Economic Theory* (Cambridge, Massachusetts: MIT Press).

Lewis, W.A. (1954), 'Economic Development with Unlimited Supplies of Labour', *Manchester School of Economic and Social Studies*, May.

Lucas, R.E., Jr. (1988), 'On the Mechanics of Economic Development', *Journal of Monetary Economics*, 22(1), July: 3–42.

—— (1990), 'Why Doesn't Capital Flow from Rich to Poor Countries?' *American Economic Review*, 80, May: 92–96.

Mahalanobis, C. (1955), 'The Approach to Operational Research to Planning in India', *Sankhya: The Indian Journal of Statistics*, 16.

Mankiw, Greg, D. Romer and D. Weil (1992), 'A Contribution to the Empirics of Economic Growth', *Quarterly Journal of Economics*, 152, May: 407–37.

MIT (1957), *The Objectives of United States Economic Assistance Programs* (Washington DC: Center for International Studies, Massachusetts Institute of Technology.

Murphy, Kevin, Andrei Shleifer and Robert Vishny (1989), 'Industrialization and the Big Push', *Journal of Political Economy*, October.

Nurkse, Ragnar (1952), 'Some International Aspects of the Problem of Economic Development', *American Economic Review*, May.

—— (1953), *Problems of Capital Formation in Underdeveloped Countries* (New York: Oxford University Press).

Pack, Howard (1994), 'Endogenous Growth Theory: Intellectual Appeal and Empirical Shortcomings', *Journal of Economic Perspectives*, 8 (1), Winter.

Ranis, Gustav (1995), 'Another Look at the East Asian Miracle', *World Bank Economic Review*, 9 (3), September: 509–34.

Rebelo, Sergio (1991), 'Long Run Policy Analysis and Long Run Growth', *Journal of Political Economy*, 99 (3), June: 500–21.

Rodrik, Dani (1994), 'Getting Interventions Right: How South Korea and Taiwan Grew Rich',

NBER Working Paper No. 4964, National Bureau of Economic Research, Washing-ton DC.

Romer, P.M. (1986), 'Increasing Returns and Long-Run Growth', *Journal of Political Economy*, 94 (5), October: 1002–37.

—— (1991), 'Increasing Returns and New Developments in the Theory of Growth', in W. Barnett, ed., *Equilibrium Theory and Applications: Proceedings of the 6th International Symposium in Economic Theory and Econometrics* (Cambridge: Cambridge University Press).

—— (1994), 'The Origins of Endogenous Growth', *Journal of Economic Perspectives*, 8 (1), Winter.

Ros, Jaime (2000), *Development Theory and the Economics of Growth* (Ann Arbor: University of Michigan Press).

Ros, Jaime and P. Skott (1998), 'Dynamic Effects of Trade Liberalization and Currency Over-valuation under Conditions of Increasing Returns', *Manchester School of Economic and Social Studies* 66 (4), September.

Rosenstein–Rodan, Paul (1943), 'Problems of Industrialization of Eastern and South-Eastern Europe', *Economic Journal*, June–September.

—— (1961), 'Notes on the Theory of the Big Push', in H. Ellis, ed., *Economic Development for Latin America, Proceedings of a Conference held by the International Economic Association* (New York: St. Martin's Press).

—— (1984), 'Natura Facit Saltum: Analysis of the Disequilibrium Growth Process', in Gerald Meier and Dudley Seers, eds, *Pioneers in Development* (New York: Oxford University Press).

Sen, Amartya (1993), 'Economic Regress: Concepts and Features', *Proceedings of the World Bank Annual Conference on Development Economics 1993* (Washington DC: World Bank).

Solow, Robert M. (1956), 'A Contribution to the Theory of Economic Growth', *Quarterly Journal of Economics*, 70, February: 65–94.

—— (1988), *Growth Theory: An Exposition* (New York: Oxford University Press).

—— (1994), 'Perspectives on Growth Theory', *Journal of Economic Perspectives*, 8 (1), Winter.

Srinivasan, T.N. (1994), 'Long Run Growth Theories and Empirics: Anything New?'; Paper presented at the Endogenous Growth and Development Conference, International School of Economic Research, University of Siena, Certosa di Pontignano, Siena, Italy, 3–9 July.

Stiglitz, J.E. (1992), 'Comment on "Towards a Counter-Counterrevolution in Development Theory" by Krugman', in *Proceedings of the World Bank Annual Conference on Development Economics*, Supplement to the *World Bank Economic Review* and the *World Bank Research Observer*.

Taylor, Lance and Persio Arida (1988), 'Long-Run Income Distribution and Growth', in Hollis Chenery and T.N. Srinivisan, eds, *Handbook of Development Economics*, Vol. 1 (Amsterdam: North-Holland).

# International Trade in Early Development Economics

*Amitava K. Dutt*

Early development economics is often characterized as advocating dirigiste and autarkic policies, and as being suspicious of markets and international interactions through trade and factor movements. Early development economists are often blamed for providing the intellectual underpinning of state-led, inward-looking development policies, which led to economic stagnation in many less developed countries (LDCs). This criticism proceeds to say that it was only after these problems were recognized, with the rise to dominance of neoclassical economics in development economics, and after free market as well as outward-oriented policies were adopted, that some LDCs began to perform better.[1]

The purpose of this chapter is to examine how the early development economists dealt with international economic issues and to evaluate the subsequent indictment of them. After examining the contributions of economists who may be called the precursors of early development economics, the chapter discusses the work of the early development economists under four heads. First, it examines some of the early major contributions to development economics in general (which did not aim to discuss international issues in particular) and what they had to say about international themes. Second, it turns to a major contribution of early development economics that focused on international issues, the work of Myrdal, who wrote extensively on the global economy and the role of LDCs in it. Third, applications of standard international trade theory to development issues are discussed. Fourth, the distinctive aspects of the treatment of international issues in early development economics, which distinguish it from standard international trade theory, are examined. Finally, the conclusion summarizes the main ideas about international issues, specifically international trade, in early development economics, and briefly evaluates the validity of these ideas in light of subsequent events and contributions.

This chapter will confine its attention to early contributions in development economics, interpreted to mean work published before 1960. It will also not discuss two lines of work in early development economics that have a great deal to say on international issues, that is, the structuralist (see, for instance, Prebisch 1950), and the early radical and dependency approaches (see, for instance, Baran 1957), which are covered in other chapters in this volume and which flowered after the 1950s. It will, for the most part, discuss international trade issues and, occasionally, issues relating to capital flows, and not give much attention to labour mobility and technology transfers.

### The Precursors

Although development economics is a relatively new sub-discipline of economics, in the sense that it emerged after World War II due to the coincidence of certain forces including the independence of a number of poor countries, ideas of relevance to LDCs have been discussed throughout the long history of economics. The discussion of international issues is certainly no exception to this. Though the problems of countries that are poor today were not the main concern of economists of the past, who were mainly concerned with their own economies which are now advanced, they often commented on them and wrote on the problems of the now-rich countries in their earlier stages of development.[2]

International issues were a central concern of the mercantilists who were, by and large, in favour of the accumulation of precious metals for the purpose of augmenting the power of their countries, and therefore tried to increase the trade surplus. For this, they supported various kinds of import restriction and export promotion policies. Even in Britain, the world's first industrial nation, such so-called mercantilist policies led to high tariffs on manufactured imports as late as the 1820s, well after the onset of the Industrial Revolution. Restrictions and, sometimes, bans were imposed on imports of superior products from other countries, such as India, which, in the early part of the eighteenth century, had a thriving cotton industry (see, for instance, Chang 2002).

Adam Smith criticized the mercantilist approach to international trade by arguing that the main benefit of trade lay not in generating a trade surplus but in mutually beneficial exchange. He was therefore extremely critical of government interference in trade, and the granting of trading monopolies and trade protection. In modern international trade theory, Smith is generally credited with the development of the theory of absolute advantage, according to which countries export goods in which they enjoy an absolute cost advantage – due to technological factors – over their trading partners. He also took the view that such trade between two trading countries benefits both, even under conditions of balanced trade.

It is somewhat surprising that this essentially static theory of international trade should have captured the attention of modern trade theorists, because Smith's vision of the economy was essentially a dynamic one, in which growth occurred with the expansion of the market and the increasing division of labour. Myint (1958) has argued that Smith's dynamic theory of trade, what he calls the productivity theory, is his more important contribution to trade theory. According to this theory, trade allows countries to expand their markets for some of their goods, increase the division of labour in them and raise productivity over time, in an irreversible manner. Myint (1958) has also pointed out that Smith had a third theory of trade, the vent for surplus theory, according to which an economy produces some goods for which there is no domestic demand when it is able to export it, and therefore uses previously unutilized factors specific to these products. It thereby gains from putting to use previously unemployed resources.

David Ricardo is normally credited with extending Smith's absolute advantage theory to the case where a country may not enjoy an absolute advantage in any line but may nevertheless trade, and gain from trade, in lines in which it has a comparative advantage. In the textbook Ricardian model of trade, this is demonstrated by assuming that labour is the only factor of production, that labour-output ratios are fixed (implying constant returns to scale), that perfect competition prevails everywhere and that there are no international factor movements. Though Ricardo clearly uses this approach to show static gains from trade in his famous England–Portugal and textiles–wine example, the popularity of it is again somewhat surprising, since it is not integrated with his dynamic theory of growth and income distribution.

In this theory, the economy produces two goods – a manufactured good, produced under conditions of constant returns and an agricultural good, produced under conditions of diminishing returns due to the fact that the marginal product of labour falls as cultivation is extended to land which is progressively less fertile. The number of workers – who, for simplicity, can be assumed to receive a fixed subsistence wage – is determined by the previously accumulated wages fund allocated between the two sectors to equalize profits across sectors, and the amount of land under agricultural cultivation is therefore determined. The amount of cultivated land is determined to yield a zero rent on the least fertile land under cultivation. Savings and investment are the sole province of the profit-receiving capitalists. Capital accumulation, which leads to an expansion of the wages fund over time, brings less and less fertile land under cultivation in agriculture, increasing rent and squeezing profit. When profit is squeezed to the extent that capitalists no longer have an incentive to invest, accumulation stops and the economy reaches a stationary state. The possibility of trade in this framework implies that if the country is allowed to import the agricultural product, less land needs to be brought under cultivation, rent falls, profits rise and the economy expands beyond its autarkic stationary state. In this sense, by allowing accumulation to occur beyond the autarkic steady state, free trade is advantageous, and this was the reason behind Ricardo's support for the repeal of England's corn law. However, what of the country exporting food and importing manufactures? Its stationary state level of the wage fund, or capital, is pushed below what it is in autarky. So, the gain to the agriculture-importing country is associated with a loss to the agriculture-exporting country.

Ricardo's comparative advantage theory of trade became part of the standard corpus of classical theory as crystallized by John Stuart Mill and others. However, trade policy did not follow its dictates, other than in Britain, then the world's most industrialized nation. In the United States, after independence from Britain, southern agrarian interests supported free trade, while northern manufacturing interests advocated industrial protection. In this, they had the support of the first US Secretary of Treasury, Alexander Hamilton, who argued, in his *Reports of the Secretary of the Treasury on the Subject on Manufactures* (1791), that foreign competition and 'forces of habit' would prevent the establishment of manufacturing unless their initial losses were covered by government assistance in the form of tariffs or bans on imports. With such protection, 'infant industries' could become internationally competitive (see Chang 2002: 25). In the nineteenth century, American tariffs were among the highest in the world, and it was only after World War II that the US significantly liberalized its trade and took up the cause of free trade. In his 1841 book, *The National System of Political Economy*, Friedrich List argued that backward countries needed tariff protection against the products of advanced countries in order to develop new manufacturing industries, and he reviewed the experiences of countries, including the UK and the US, which had successfully industrialized under trade protection, to make his point (see ibid.).

By the time development economics emerged as a separate subdiscipline, there were two conflicting intellectual currents at work. On the one hand, trade theory came to be dominated by what was called the classical theory of trade, which built on the theory of comparative advantage and was developed primarily by the Swedish economists, Eli Heckscher and Bertil Ohlin. Ohlin's formalizations stressed differences in factor endowments as explaining differences in comparative advantage, shifting the focus away from technological differences, which were emphasized in earlier approaches to comparative advantage. This approach saw rich countries as having a comparative advantage in manufacturing because of technological advantages (as stressed in the earlier approaches) and also because they used capital more intensively (as stressed by Ohlin), and poor countries as having a comparative advantage in primary products (and, perhaps, simple, labour-intensive manufactures). Moreover, this approach saw free trade as being advantageous to all countries.

On the other hand, there were strong intellectual currents at play that supported government intervention in the economy. These flowed from the experiences of the Great Depression and the rise of Keynesian interventionism, wartime controls, the influence of Soviet planning, and the aspirations of the leaders of newly independent LDCs to shape the fortunes of their backward economies, veering them away from their colonial role as hewers of wood and drawers of water. Which trend would dominate in development economics?

### Early Development Economics

This section reviews some early key contributions to the new subdiscipline of development economics as it emerged after World War II, and discusses how international issues were related to them. We select four influential contributions of this early phase of development economics, namely, Rosenstein–Rodan's theory of the big push, Nurkse's theory of the vicious circle and balanced growth, Lewis's theory of economic development with unlimited supplies of labour and Hirschman's theory of unbalanced growth through linkage effects.

One of the earliest important contributions to development economics was that of P.N. Rosenstein–Rodan (1943), who advocated the idea of balanced expansion with a big push in poor countries. He argued that industrialization required the simultaneous expansion of a number of sectors, which would generate incomes that would create markets for each other and therefore make each kind of investment profitable. If just one industry expanded, only a part of the income generated by it would be spent on its product, so that the industry would not be profitable in the first place. Rosenstein–Rodan emphasized the importance of what may be called horizontal demand linkages with his example of the shoe factory, but he also discussed other linkage effects that involved the expansion of sectors supplying inputs to other sectors, such as hydroelectric power stations and railroads, and the development of labour skills in manufacturing.

In this discussion, Rosenstein–Rodan explicitly noted that he was not arguing for autarkic development in which an LDC produces all goods and withdraws from international interactions. In fact, he argued that such autarkic development was problematic because it requires capital accumulation to take place out of domestic savings without the use of foreign savings, implying reductions in the standard of living, and because it prevents the country from participating in the beneficial international division of labour, making it produce goods (such as capital goods) that it can produce only at high cost (Rosenstein–Rodan 1943: 203). Thus, he was in support of industrialization making use of the externalities that individual firms will ignore in their decision-making but which can be internalized by social planners – for mainly producing consumer goods, which will lead to the development of skills, public utilities with large externalities and some capital goods, and not for autarkic development.

Nurkse (1953), another major early contributor to the new sub-discipline, emphasized the role of capital formation in economic development, and focused on both investment incentives and savings capacity, couching his arguments in terms of the vicious cycle of poverty. On the investment side, poor countries with low productivity had small markets for manufactured goods, which kept returns to investment low, which implied low levels of investment, and which kept productivity low. On the savings side, low productivity implied low incomes, low capacity to save, low capital accumulation and hence levels of capital stock, and, therefore, low productivity. For Nurkse, economic development required that these two vicious circles had to be overcome. The investment incentives obstacle was relatively easy to overcome, since it could be done through appropriate organization of investment in a balanced manner along lines advocated by Rosenstein–Rodan, but this required a large amount of capital. The more difficult problem was overcoming the savings problem. Nurkse distinguished between densely populated and sparsely populated regions in analysing the problem. The former were characterized by labour that was disguisedly employed, so that they consumed without contributing anything to production in the food-producing sector, which produced mainly for self-consumption than for sale. They could therefore be moved to the industrial sector without requiring additional food, if those remaining in the subsistence sector could be prevented from increasing their consumption; they could continue consuming what they consumed when they were in the subsistence sector. This made the problem of industrialization easier in these countries. For countries with a sparse population, however, industrialization required an increase in the productivity of labour in agriculture to supply the growing demand for food.

So far, this summary of Nurkse's (1953) contributions does not refer to international issues at all. However, he wrote extensively on international themes (also discussed in Nurkse 1952). He stated in his introduction (Nurkse 1953: 1) that '[a]mong the topics selected for review are some international aspects of the problem of capital formation in the less developed countries. In fact, I may be criticized for devoting more attention to the international aspects than is warranted by their true relative importance.' International issues entered his argument at numerous points.

First, he took up the possibility that exports can provide investment incentives, making balanced growth unnecessary. He argued that for poor countries, exports according to comparative advantage imply exporting primary products that face declining terms of trade unless the markets for these products are expanding, as was apparently not the case during the period (Nurkse 1953: 21–22; see also Nurkse 1952). He argued that the simultaneous increase in production of manufactured goods, over a range of sectors, for domestic markets would eventually enable poor countries to develop their comparative advantage in these products and further increase investment incentives in these lines. Thus, he was not in favour of autarky but wished to expand exports by first developing manufacturing industry.

Second, he asked if foreign capital could be a source of savings that could help LDCs to escape from their vicious cycle of poverty. The problem here was that foreign direct investment faced the same lack of investment incentives in these countries as did domestic producers, and shied away from manufacturing in LDCs. To the extent that they brought in capital to primary producing and extracting sectors, they exacerbated the terms of trade problem of these countries, worsening the problem of capital formation. Foreign aid could help, but it was difficult to channel such inflows to savings and investment, rather than to finance an increase in consumption.

Third, he argued that international interactions exacerbated the problem of low savings for LDCs. Saving in these countries was, according to Nurkse, not just a function of their own income but of their income relative to that of rich countries, as in Duesenberry's theory of consumption. When income and consumption increased in rich countries, international demonstration effects, let loose by closer integration of the world 'thanks to education and mass media of communication' (Nurkse 1953: 63), led to increases in consumption in poor countries, reducing their savings below what it would be without international influences. Overall savings were reduced not only by such effects, but also by increasing the demand for imported consumer goods; there was also an adverse effect on the foreign exchange position of the poor countries and their ability to import invest-ment goods.

Finally, Nurkse pointed to the problems that could result from restric-tions on luxury imports, which could make the domestic production of such luxury goods more profitable and lead to no increase in savings rates, which, according to him, was essential for growth. Thus, he recognized some of the problems with import restrictions and recommended measures that increase sav-ings by reducing overall luxury consumption.

Lewis's (1954) contribution on development with surplus labour has also had an enormous influence on development economics. Lewis characterized poor countries as dual economies, with a subsistence sector with disguised unemploy-ment or surplus labour and pre-capitalist modes of production, and a modern sector using capital and producing under capitalist conditions with hired labour. Production in the capitalist sector is limited by the stock of capital, which req-uires savings and investment to expand, and savings take place from capitalist profits, as in the classical approach to growth. For Lewis, the existence of surplus labour in the subsistence sector made the process of development of the capitalist sector easier. This was because labour is available to the sector cheaply, at (per-haps slightly higher than) the average income (and product) of peasant workers in the subsistence sector. Low wages mean high profits, so that capital accumula-tion proceeds apace in the modern sector. Profit-maximizing capitalists in the modern sector employ workers up to when the marginal product of labour is equal to the wage in that sector. With capital accumulation and the outward movement of the marginal product curve of labour, workers move from the subsis-tence to the modern sector.

This process occurs as long as the wage, in terms of the product of the modern sector, does not rise. Its rise is prevented by two main features of the economy: first, the existence of surplus labour, which implies that earnings in the subsistence sector remain low; second, because the withdrawal of labour from the subsistence sector does not reduce its output, due to the zero marginal product of labour in that sector, and hence prevents the terms of trade from moving in its favour if the subsistence and modern sectors produce different goods.[3] As dis-guised unemployment disappears, however, income in the subsistence sector increa-ses, which raises the product wage in the modern sector. Furthermore, if the terms of trade move against the modern sector when subsistence output falls (if, as was usually assumed, the modern sector produced manufactured goods and the subsistence sector produced agricultural goods), capitalists in the modern sector have to pay a higher wage in terms of their product. Thus, the product wage in the modern sector increases, profits are squeezed and accumulation slows down. In Lewis's approach, the existence of surplus labour therefore made the process of capital accumulation easier, exactly as in the densely populated regions of Nurkse's analysis.

The foregoing summarizes the first and longer part of Lewis's paper, where the economy is assumed to be a closed one, so that there is no discussion of international issues. It is this closed economy model that has had a major impact on development economics. However, Lewis's paper also has a lengthy section on the open economy, in which he develops a series of open economy models.

One model abstracts from trade altogether (by assuming that there is only one good in the world) but allows for the possibility of capital flows between two countries (in the absence of labour immigration, controlled by immigration restrictions in rich countries). If, in one country, wages increase due to capital accumulation, while in the other country wages are kept low, due to the existence of surplus labour, and if profitability is higher in the latter than in the former, capital will move to the backward country. Lewis (1954: 178–80) notes, however, that backward countries need not have higher profitability, since profitability depends not on wages alone but on natural resources, the quality of the labour force and on the capital already invested there (which affects the quality of other services that the investment projects need to use).

Another model allows each of the two countries to be completely specialized in the production of one good, which they trade with each other. The relative prices of these goods are determined by supply and demand, and capital flows depend on relative profitability in the two regions. Capital flows, however, have the additional effect of increasing the relative supply of the good produced by the capital-importing country, turning the terms of trade against it, which has additional effects on wages and profits in the two countries.

A third model assumes that the two countries produce two goods each: one, a non-traded good (food) in common, and the other, a traded good, steel in the rich country and rubber in the poor one. Lewis assumes that labour is the only factor of production and that labour–output ratios are constant. Then, if there is technological change in rubber production in the poor country, real wages in the country (determined by food productivity) will not change, and the benefits of technological change (perhaps due to capital flows) will be passed on to the rich country through a decline in the relative price of rubber. What is needed to increase real wages in the poor country is an increase in productivity in the food sector.

A final model examines two countries trading with each other in two goods, both of which can be produced in the two countries. In this case, Lewis argues that although comparative advantage will determine the direction of trade, the country that exports the agricultural good and imports the manufactured good will be producing more of the agricultural good than is socially optimal, despite its low productivity, with its manufactured goods producers displaced by imported manufactures. This model is closest to the two-country version of his closed economy model.

Hirschman's (1958) espousal of unbalanced growth, making use of linkage effects, was another important and influential contribution to development economics in the 1950s. Hirschman criticized the advocates of balanced growth with a big push, like Rosenstein–Rodan and Nurkse, by arguing that such a strategy required large amounts of precisely those resources – such as entrepreneurial and managerial ability – that were in scarce supply in poor countries. He also argued that, fortunately, balanced growth was not necessary for these countries either. Unbalanced growth – involving growth in some sectors of the economy – creates surpluses and shortages that could bring into play appropriate responses by private individuals (driven by the profit motive) and state officials (in response to public pressures) which speed up growth. In his support of unbalanced growth, Hirschman emphasized externalities and backward and forward linkages, referring to the pressures created on input-supplying and output-using industries, respectively, of the unbalanced expansion of one particular industry. The proper strategy of economic development is therefore one of identifying and promoting key industries that would be developed in an unbalanced manner in order to maximize these linkage effects and externalities.

Hirschman discussed several international issues related to this analysis. First, he pointed out that imports have a positive impact on the growth of new industries in poor countries. In his opinion, one of the greatest obstacles to the creation of new industries in poor countries is the lack of, or uncertainty about, markets for them. In this situation, the growth of imports plays an important role by developing preferences for products and showing potential domestic entrepreneurs that markets exist for these products, thus inducing domestic producers to enter the market. He argued that when poor countries 'restricted imports too severely, they have been shutting out the awakening and inducing effects which imports have on industrialization' (Hirschman 1958: 124). He recognized the need for protection to allow domestic producers to compete against advanced country producers but argued that protection should be given only after the infant has been established, not before.

Second, Hirschman discussed the possible foreign exchange shortages that can result from unbalanced growth. He noted that foreign exchange shortages do not lead to appropriate responses that would overcome the problem, because importers suffer from a 'foreign exchange illusion' in the sense that they do not receive any clear signals of foreign exchange shortages like they do when there are shortages of domestic supplies of goods (due to price increases or lack of availability), unless there are controls on foreign exchange. To deal with the problem, he recommended the domestic establishment of basic industries, which would clear shortages (Hirschman 1958: 168), and the expansion of imports for industries that produce exportable products (ibid.: 171–72).

Third, he discussed international linkages, arguing that, in general, they are weaker than linkages within different regions in the same country, partly because of political and social considerations that create solidarity within countries, and partly because of frictions due to distance.

### Uneven International Development

The contributions discussed in the previous section attempted to examine the general problem of underdevelopment in LDCs but did not focus specifically on international issues, although, as we saw, they did discuss a variety of them. We now turn to early contributions in development economics that focused primarily on international issues. We concentrate on the contribution of Myrdal (1956, 1957), because he has often been singled out as the major critic of orthodox trade theory and its view of international interactions as being mutually beneficial (see Meier 1958 and Haberler 1959, for instance), and because his work incorporates the contributions of other influential development economists, including Prebisch and Singer.

Myrdal (1957) started with the observation that despite variations within, the capitalist world in the mid-1950s was divided into two parts: a rich part, consisting of former British settler colonies in the temperate zone (including the United States), which was populated mainly by people of European stock and the countries of north-western and west-central Europe; and a poor part, consisting of most of Asia, Africa and Latin America. He then pointed out that countries in the rich part were experiencing continued economic development, while those in the poor part were growing more slowly, or stagnating, or even losing ground. Thus, 'on the whole, in recent decades the economic inequalities between developed and underdeveloped countries has [sic] been increasing' (ibid.: 6).

Next, Myrdal argued that this pattern of increasing global inequality cannot be understood using standard economic theory generally and international trade theory in particular. This was because these theories use the unrealistic assumption of a stable equilibrium and because they confine their attention to a sub-set of the elements of reality that are considered economic factors, leaving out non-economic factors. He argued that this distinction between economic and non-economic factors is 'useless and nonsensical . . . from the view of logic' (ibid.: 10), and is closely linked to the stable equilibrium assumption, since the neglect of non-economic factors removes many mechanisms that lead to disequilibria. He argued that a conceptual tool for the study of international inequality preferable to standard equilibrium theory is the idea of the vicious circle, or the principle of circular and cumulative causation or an unstable process.

The unstable process works within an economy or a region, ignoring interaction between rich and poor regions. This works from the demand side – a rise in income increases demand and leads to further increases in income (and the process will work in reverse as well) – and the supply side, through both market and government mechanisms. A rise in income and production in a region results in increasing returns to scale and external economies favourable for sustaining the rise in income. The rise in income also gives the government a higher tax base, allowing it to spend more on public services, such as roads and railways, and health, which make the region more attractive to firms and workers.

Demographic changes add to these tendencies: poor regions, having higher fertility rates, experience higher population growth, resulting in a more adverse relation between population and natural resources, thereby exacerbating the problem of poverty. Myrdal also mentioned non-economic factors: poorer regions will foster traditional mores and values inimical to growth, while the opposite is true for advanced regions. For all these reasons, rich regions will forge ahead while poor regions will be held back. Some countervailing forces may be at work in the form of external diseconomies, rising wages that increase the costs of firms and the technological obsolescence of machinery in rich regions, but Myrdal asserted that the inequalizing effects are stronger.

Myrdal argued that these inequalizing forces are strengthened by interactions between regions. He analysed the implications of three types of interactions in turn: migration, capital movements and trade. The expanding region attracts immigrants from other regions in search of higher wages, especially those of working age, thereby allowing more expansion as income and demand grow, while the other region falls further behind, with a less productive age distribution. Capital flows to the advancing region in search of higher returns, further increasing income and demand, as well as savings and investment, there; capital flows become an 'instrument for siphoning off the savings from the poorer regions to richer and more progressive ones where returns to capital are high and secure' (Myrdal 1957: 28). Cheap and docile labour in backward regions is generally unable to attract industry to backward areas; it goes instead to centres of economic expansion to enjoy rising demand and external economies.

Regarding trade, the widening of markets will confer a competitive advantage on industries in the advanced region, while hampering handicrafts and industries in backward regions; poor regions remain primarily agricultural and do not experience industrial diversification. Myrdal termed these inequalizing effects across regions 'backwash effects', in contrast to the 'spread effects' of 'expansionary momentum from the centres of economic expansion to other regions' (Myrdal 1957: 31). Growth of industry in rich areas can create a demand for raw materials and other products of backward areas. Rising wages in the rich region can make the poor region's products more competitive. However, Myrdal claimed that these spread effects are likely to be stronger and overcome the backwash effects only within rich countries; thus, in rich countries, inter-regional disparities are smaller and diminish over time, while in poor countries, they are greater and tend to increase over time. This is because the market-mediated spread effects are stronger in richer countries due to improved transport and communications, which lead to stronger demand effects being felt over distances, and because in richer nations, people wish to share their riches with people in poorer areas and engage in greater inter-regional transfers, so that they adopt egalitarian policies.

These inequalizing forces between rich and poor *regions* (within a country) tend to get exacerbated between rich and poor *countries* because the spread effects are weaker and backwash effects stronger. The spread effects are weaker because the barriers due to language, beliefs and government regulations make national barriers a more effective barrier to expansionary spill-overs; moreover, weak spread effects within poor countries dampen the spread effects to poor countries as a whole even after they are felt in outward-oriented sectors. Regarding trade, rich countries specialize in manufacturing industries with strong external economies, while poor countries have small-scale and handicraft industries priced out by cheap imports, and the bulk of their resources are devoted to primary sector production that often meets income-inelastic demand and fluctuating prices. The benefits of technological improvements in these sectors are passed on in the form of lower prices to rich countries, given their low price and income elasticities of demand (Myrdal 1957: 52). Export goods are often produced in enclave sectors with minimal links to the rest of the poor country. Capital movement from rich to poor countries is hampered by insecurity after the breakdown of the colonial system (and the fear of expropriation by nationalist governments), and even when it does move, it goes to economic enclaves that supply inputs to rich country industry and with few links to the rest of the host country (ibid.: 53). If there were no capital controls in many poor countries, capital would move from poor to rich countries in search of more secure returns; the illegal capital flight that occurs should actually be counted as reverse capital flows. Labour migration is severely restricted internationally, especially from countries with non-white populations, preventing the migration of unskilled labour from poor to rich countries.

Turning to policy options open to poor countries, Myrdal (1956, 1957) advocated government intervention and planning in poor countries, and the promotion of trade between poor countries. He was also in favour of government intervention in foreign trade in poor countries, for a number of reasons (see Myrdal 1956: 276–78). First, and most importantly, the need for poor countries to develop requires them to import capital goods, which requires foreign exchange; for this, they need to restrict imports of other goods, mainly consumption goods.

Myrdal's main emphasis, however, was not on restricting imports but on increasing the amount of foreign exchange that could be devoted to development purposes. He focused more on promoting exports than on reducing imports. But, for him, the need to promote exports would not be well served by exclusively emphasizing traditional primary exports, which face inelastic world demand and terms of trade deterioration, as well as price instability. Here, he drew on the work of Prebisch (1950) and Singer (1950). There was therefore a need for promoting a wider range of exports and for entering into manufactured exports. But the promotion of manufactured exports required an increase in production for domestic demand, which required import protection. Myrdal (1956: 257) noted:

> Recognizing these facts . . . does not imply that the industries [the underdeveloped countries] . . . can build up should be relegated altogether to the protected home market. From the point of view of international division of labour this would be entirely unsound, and many opportunities of coming into such export lines where price and income elasticities are great and demand trends rising would be lost. The development of industrial exports is generally apt to instil more of a dynamic spirit of enterprise and competition into a stagnant economy.

Second, it was necessary to create a demand for domestically produced manufactured goods without waiting for the 'natural' growth of demand for such products that accompanies economic development. Third, it was to take advantage of external economies, not only in the narrow sense discussed in mainstream economics in the form of technological spill-overs between producers, but also in the sense of increasing labour productivity through training and increasing consumption levels, and improving the climate of entrepreneurship. Fourth, the existence of surplus labour in agriculture implied that the loss of production in agriculture was smaller than the gain in manufacturing production due to tariff protection. Finally, the structure of prices and costs in poor countries hampered industrialization. Factors such as inertia, which prevents labour from moving from agricultural to industrial areas, and labour legislation made wages higher in manufacturing than in agriculture, with the result that manufacturing production was lower than it would be without such wage differences. Manufacturing protection could compensate for such problems.

Myrdal (1957) was also in favour of international efforts to reduce international inequality. He argued that convergence among regions in advanced countries had been achieved primarily by government policies, which were motivated by feelings of national solidarity and made possible through transfer mechanisms within the framework of the welfare state. Although there was nothing remotely like a world government, he made an impassioned plea for increases in foreign aid by rich countries to poor ones. Years later, Myrdal (1984) was less sanguine about what foreign aid could achieve, especially when misused by corrupt governments in poor countries, but he continued to argue for foreign aid for poverty alleviation in the poorest countries while pushing for internal institutional reform – such as land reform – in them.

### Development Issues in Mainstream Trade Theory

The ideas of the early development economists discussed in the two previous sections seem to be very different from those of the so-called classical theory of trade, as summarized in the theory of comparative advantage, which implies that countries gain from trade and that free trade is the best policy for a country. As is well known, the theory makes a number of assumptions, including either constant or increasing costs of production, perfect competition and the absence of rigidities or imperfections in any market, and the absence of externalities in production or consumption. Moreover, the theory abstracts from dynamic considerations, such as factor accumulation and technological progress (other than as exogenous changes), and the international mobility of factors of production.

The basic idea of the theory is illustrated most simply in the two-goods case, with one good being agricultural (denoted by $A$) and the other being a manufactured good (denoted by $M$). Assume that consumer preferences in the economy can be shown, using the concept of the representative consumer, with indifference curves. Assume that the two goods are produced under conditions of increasing opportunity cost (in terms of each other), with the production possibility frontier shown in Figure 1.

FIGURE 1   *Gains from Trade*

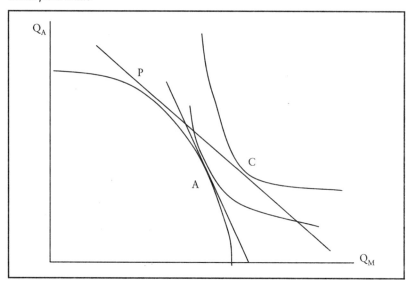

Under autarky, or no trade, the economy must produce and consume at the same point, *A*, at the relative prices shown by the slope of the line tangential to both the production possibilities frontier and the indifference curve through *A*. If the country is able to trade with another country, or the rest of the world, at given terms of trade that imply a lower relative price for the manufactured good, given by the slope of the line through points *P* and *C*, it will produce at point *P* and consume at *C*, and will therefore be able to consume on a higher indifference curve. The country therefore gains from trade – ignoring distributional considerations – since changes in relative prices could hurt some and help others. Several economists, most notably Viner (1952) and Haberler (1959), used this comparative cost argument to argue that foreign trade is beneficial for poor countries.

In his extension and formalization of the Heckscher–Ohlin theory, Samuelson (1948) showed that even without international factor movements, with some additional assumptions, free trade leads to equalization of factor prices between countries. The additional assumptions were constant returns to scale, identical technology between countries, and that the factor endowment difference between countries is not large enough for them to be completely specialized in the production of different goods.[4] Although factors like capital and labour do not move internationally, they move, in effect, through the freely traded goods in which they are embodied. Myrdal (1957) interpreted factor price equalization to imply the convergence of incomes between countries. This happens, provided technology becomes more similar between countries due to technology transfer. Without this tendency, no convergence can be expected. However, the notion of gains from trade – and hence, mutually beneficial exchange – remains valid.

But several economists, especially those concerned with development issues, recognized that if some of the conditions assumed in classical theory failed to hold, the gains from trade theorems would not hold. Haberler (1950) himself provided an early discussion of some of the major types of 'distortions' due to which countries *could* lose from trade. Haberler's list includes: rigidities in factor prices such as wages (due to the existence of labour unions, for instance), which can cause unemployment in a sector – a problem that can be exacerbated by imports of the good produced by the sector; positive production externalities in some sectors, the output of which is reduced by trade; and the infant industry argument, according to which tariff protection for a sector can induce learning and move out the production possibility frontier more rapidly. Some examples of such distortions, which have played an important role in the development literature, can be illustrated by modifying Figure 1.

First, consider the case of differences in wages between sectors. Hagen (1958) examined the case in which there is a fixed wedge between the two, rather than the wage in the two sectors being equalized. The implication of this is shown in Figure 2. In the first place, the economy is not on its production possibility *frontier* (shown by the solid line) but, rather, on a production possibility *curve* (shown by the dashed line) that lies inside it. In the second place, in equilibrium, the marginal rate of product transformation between agricultural and manufactured good is not equal to the relative price between the two goods: too little of the manufactured good is produced compared to the case with equalized wages, because of the relatively higher wage in manufacturing, as in the figure. The autarkic equilibrium for the economy is shown at point *A*, where production and consumption occur at the same point on the distorted production possibility curve (which is drawn for a given wage distortion). Utility-maximizing consumers, assumed to be represented by a representative consumer, will consume in

FIGURE 2 *Losses from Trade with Wage Rigidity*

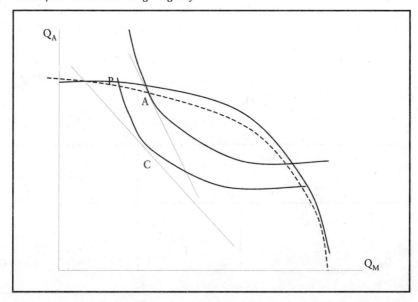

such a manner that the relative price is tangential to the indifference curve.

Suppose, now, that with free trade, the country can import food at a lower price for the manufactured good. The relative price of the manufactured good will therefore be lower, and the production of the manufactured good will be lower than under autarky while output of the agricultural good will be higher, with production moving to a point like $P$. With consumption at point $C$, we find that with free trade, the economy is pushed down to a lower indifference curve than under autarky, so that it loses from trade. Conversely, it can gain from protection. An import tariff raises the domestic relative price of the manufactured good, moves the production point to the right, and possibly leads to a gain. A high enough tariff would, of course, lead to autarky, taking the economy to $A$.

Second, consider the case of different types of production organization in different sectors. Following Lewis's (1954) analysis, assume that the agricultural sector has peasants who share their output equally, while the manufacturing sector is capitalistically organized. Therefore, in the backward sector, peasants earn their average product, not their marginal product of labour, while in the advanced capitalist sector, the wage is equal to the marginal product of labour (with perfectly competitive profit-maximizing employers). If the wage in the manufacturing sector is perfectly flexible, the free inter-sectoral mobility of labour implies that the wage in the manufacturing sector is equal to the value of the *average* product of labour in the agricultural sector.

The resultant allocation of labour between the two sectors is shown in Figure 3 by point $A$, where the average product of labour curve in agriculture (the $APL_A$ curve) intersects the value of marginal product of labour curve in manufacturing (shown by the $VMPL_M$ curve, which shows the value of the mar-

FIGURE 3   *Labour Allocation in the Lewis Model*

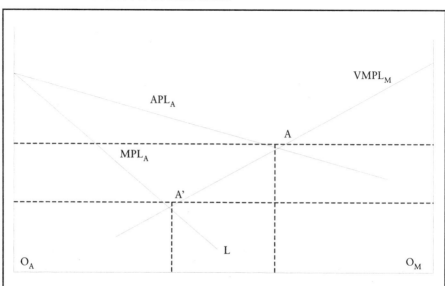

ginal product of labour in manufacturing in terms of the agricultural good, by multiplying the marginal product of labour in that sector by the relative price of the manufactured good). With labour assumed to be the only inter-sectorally mobile factor (under the assumption that agriculture and manufacturing use the specific factors, land and capital), the value of total production is less than what it would be if the allocation of labour is at *A'*, where the value of the *marginal* products of labour in the two sectors is equalized.

This situation is shown using the production possibilities frontier in Figure 4, where points *A* and *A'* correspond to points *A* and *A'* in Figure 3, with the autarkic relative prices used in drawing the $VMPL_M$ curve. The country is now assumed to be able to enter into trade at a relative price of the manufactured good that is lower than the autarkic one. This will imply that the $VMPL_M$ curve in Figure 3 is pushed downwards with free trade, so that the two lines will intersect at a lower level of employment in the manufacturing sector and a higher level in the agricultural sector. Thus, agricultural output is greater and manufacturing output smaller, as shown by production point *P* in Figure 4. With consumption taking place at point *C*, it is possible for the country to lose from trade, as shown in the figure.

Third, consider the implications of external economies existing in manufacturing but not in agriculture, with Haberler's own diagrammatic technique, using Figure 4 again. Under autarky, the economy is at point *A*, with the autarkic price shown by the straight line through point *A*. The slope of the production possibility frontier (which is equal to the ratio of the social marginal costs in the two sectors) is less than the price ratio, and the economy produces too little of the

FIGURE 4 *Losses from Trade in the Lewis Model and with Production Externalities*

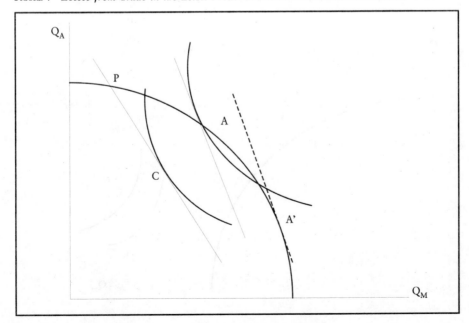

manufactured good compared to what is socially optimal, that is, at *A'*. This is because producers take private costs into account in their production decisions and equate prices to private marginal costs. But the social marginal cost in manufacturing is less than the private marginal cost due to the existence of production externalities. Assuming that the country can obtain the manufactured good abroad relatively more cheaply with free trade, at the international price ratio given by *PC*, the economy produces at *P* (since the manufactured good is less profitable to produce than under autarky, resources will be shifted from manufacturing to agriculture) and consumption occurs at *C*. As shown in the figure, the country can end up losing from trade.

A final example that shows how more trade (due to the lowering of trade restrictions) can lead to losses assumes that the country's terms of trade worsen when it increases its trade. Initially, suppose the LDC imposes a trade tax on the imported good or the exported good (denoted, respectively, by subscripts *M* and *X*), so that there is a divergence between the domestic price (shown by the slope of the line *AB* in Figure 5) and the international price (shown by the slope of the line *PC*). Production takes place at point *P*, the country trades along the line *PC* and consumes at point *C* (with tax revenues being paid back lump sum to consumers), with consumers facing the domestic price ratio. The removal of the tax tends to increase trade and therefore worsens its international terms of trade (because it is what is called a large country), so that the international price ratio is now given by *P'C'*, and production and consumption shift to *P'* and *C'*. As shown in the figure, the country can be made worse off. This problem is dis-

FIGURE 5  *Losses from Trade Expansion due to Terms of Trade Deterioration*

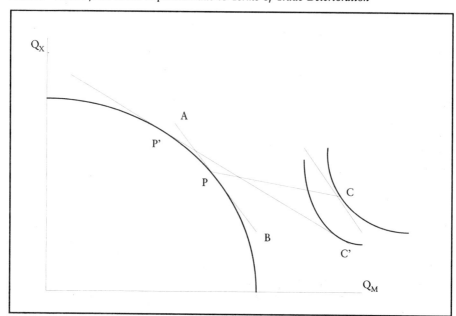

cussed by Viner (1952: 55) as 'a logical flaw of considerable importance in the free trade case'.

The discussion so far provides examples in which a country can lose from trade (in comparison to autarky) or from the expansion of trade. There are other examples which show that with free trade, growth (caused by exogenous factors) can make a country worse off and that the situation can be improved with trade interventions. Bhagwati (1958) analysed the case of immiserizing growth due to deterioration in a country's terms of trade caused by an expansion in the supply of the country's exports. This is shown in Figure 6, where growth (due to factor accumulation or technological change biased towards the export good) implies a deterioration of the terms of trade of the country, from the slope of the line *PC* to the slope of the line *P'C'* (because the country is a large one and pushes the terms of trade against itself when it attempts to export more at the initial terms of trade). Production moves from *P* to *P'*, consumption from *C* to *C'*, and the country is worse off. This loss is not inevitable but can occur if there is a sufficiently large terms of trade loss (which is more likely if foreign demand is more price-inelastic).

Although standard neoclassical trade theory is replete with examples that show how trade can hurt a country and how some form of trade intervention can possibly make it better off, proponents of the theory who discussed the problems of LDCs were not convinced. These critics provided a number of arguments.

First, although they were willing to accept these cases as theoretical

FIGURE 6 *Immiserizing Growth due to Terms of Trade Deterioration*

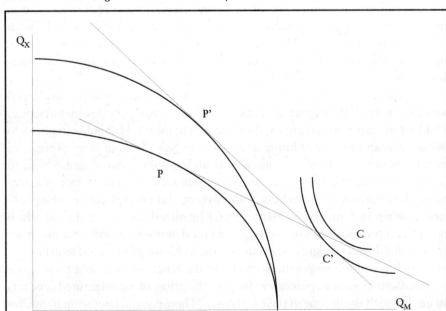

possibilities (or curiosa, as Haberler 1950 put it), they were unwilling to accept them as being important in practice. After his discussion of some distortions that can lead to losses from trade, Haberler (ibid.: 226) wrote that the

> mere enumeration of possible imperfections and deviations from the ideal case does not prove more than the possibility that certain controls might be benefi-cial. . . . On this practically all economists agree. In order to prove that the restriction of international trade . . . is justified, it is necessary to show that there imperfections are persistent (in other words, that there is not even a tendency for the ideal situation to work itself out) and that they persistently operate in such a direction as to weaken (rather than strengthen) the case for free trade.

The arguments put forward by the early development economists can, in fact, be interpreted as attempting to demonstrate that the distortions are empiri-cally important, that in many cases they persist over long periods of time and that they, in fact, make losses from trade very likely. As noted earlier, Myrdal (1956) and, of course, Hagen (1958) argued that wage differentials discriminated against the manufacturing sector. Hagen pointed out that labour was not per-fectly mobile between agricultural and manufacturing sectors in LDCs because a move to the latter required new skills and behaviour patterns to be learnt, and the abandonment of a mode of life one is comfortable with, and that the wage gap was persistent.

Lewis (1954) and Myrdal (1956) discussed the implications of surplus labour in agriculture. Rosenstein–Rodan (1943), Nurkse (1953) and Myrdal (1956), among many other development economists, followed Hamilton and List in stressing the special role of the manufacturing sector in terms of positive exter-nalities, such as creation of labour skills and technological spill-overs, and in invoking the infant industry argument. Singer (1950), Nurkse (1952, 1953), Prebisch (1950), Lewis (1954) and Myrdal (1956, 1957), among others, examined the implications of terms of trade deterioration for poor countries, and the implica-tions of primary export-oriented growth.

The critics remained unconvinced. Viner (1952: 60–61, also 62–63) wondered why, 'if the export of primary products in exchange for manufactures is bad for the exporting countries, the sympathy of the world should not go out to Denmark as an exporter of butter and bacon; to New Zealand as an exporter of mutton, butter and wool; to Australia as an exporter of wool and wheat; to California, Iowa, and Nebraska, and so on.' He accused these writers of a dog-matic identification of agriculture with poverty, and an explanation of agricul-tural poverty in terms of inherent natural historical laws by virtue of which agricultural products tend to exchange on ever-deteriorating terms for manufac-tures, technological progress tends to confine its blessings to manufacturing ind-ustry, and agricultural populations do not get the benefit of technological progress in manufactures even as purchasers because the prices of manufactured products do not fall with the decline in their real costs. 'These natural laws seem to me, for the most part mischievous fantasies, or conjectural or distorted history, or, at the best, mere hypotheses relating to specific periods and calling for sober and objective testing' (ibid.: 62).

Viner (1952: 63–65), in attempting to oppose Manilesco and Prebisch (1950), argued that the fact that rich countries are primarily engaged in manufactures and services, and poor countries are primarily agricultural, does not imply that agriculture causes poverty; poverty, rather, leads to the greater weight of agriculture. He (ibid.: 102) argued that, to the extent that free trade creates problems for poor countries and protectionism appears to be beneficial, it is because of other distortions that their governments introduce in them through their planning and control approach. That approach, and not trade, is the source of the problem.

Critics like Meier (1958) recognized that there were many types of distortions in LDCs, not all of which were the results of government intervention. Many of these problems were, indeed, located in the agricultural sector and the neglect of that sector by development economists, who were enamoured with and wanted to protect the manufacturing sector, and were therefore focusing on the wrong issues. Meier also took development economists to task for stressing the terms of trade problem for poor countries. He produced various arguments to question the statistical validity of the terms of trade deterioration phenomenon, and said that even if there was such deterioration, it had no necessary implications for the growth of LDCs, since it could be the result of improvements in productivity.

Second, the critics argued that protectionism is not the optimal intervention, even if the distortions exist. Viner (1952: 59), for instance, held that infant industry protection was problematic because

> it entails costs for the nation as a whole, including other industries which have to operate without the benefit of special aid. . . . [It will be] . . . advisable to aid it during its immaturity by subsidy rather than protection . . . The burden of support can then be placed where it rationally belongs, or where it is desired where it shall fall, instead of falling fortuitously on those who happen to be users of the industry's product.

This issue was recognized by many protagonists of trade intervention. Hagen (1958), for instance, pointed out that the best policy to deal with the wage distortion in his model is to introduce a wage subsidy to the high-wage sector that would neutralize the effect of the distortion. Such a policy, with free trade, would produce the optimum equilibrium for the economy. The idea that the first-best intervention is the one that addresses the distortion at its source, and that other interventions are not 'first best' because they introduce new distortions in the economy, was subsequently systematized by Bhagwati (1971). Thus, for instance, the first-best kind of policy intervention to deal with a production externality is a production subsidy or tax, rather than an import tax.

These results are valid within the confines of the simple Heckscher–Ohlin framework. However, it is one thing to show theoretically with a simple model that one kind of policy works best in a given situation, but it is quite another thing to argue that this is the best policy in real economies encumbered with administrative and budgetary constraints. It is, arguably, far more feasible to impose a tax on imports than to subsidize a large number of domestic producers scattered around a poor country.

Third, the critics asked if governments could actually improve the situation through trade intervention. Do they have the means to do so? Can they decide on what sectors to protect? Can they stay clear of the influence of interest groups and rent-seeking behaviour, and other behaviour that leads to losses? Viner (1952) argued against the infant industry argument on some of these grounds after noting its theoretical validity. He stated that:

> (1) the selection of industries to be protected has often been arbitrary or irrational; (2) once protection is granted on any grounds, it opens the door to promiscuous protection: (3) protection to a particular industry is as likely to stifle or delay its genuine progress toward economic independence as to stimulate it, since it provides to those engaged in the industry a shelter against the normal consequences of inertia, inefficiency, or restrictive monopoly; (4) in past experience, the protection has generally tended to become permanent, instead of being removed either as the industry no longer needs it or as the industry has revealed permanent incapacity to operate without artificial support. (ibid. 1952: 59)

It is possible to argue that early development economists did not give much attention to these problems. They could certainly not foresee all the excesses and irrationalities of highly interventionist and autarkic regimes in LDCs. But not many of them recognized the importance of such issues, not even their critics. However, the problems related to corruption and inefficiency did not completely escape the attention of the early development economists either.

Myrdal (1956: 283) was in favour of tariffs, rather than quantitative restrictions, on the ground that, in addition to the revenues the government can obtain from tariffs, the latter tend easily to create cancerous tumours of partiality and corruption in the very centre of the administration, where the sickness is continually nurtured by the favours distributed and grafts realized, and from which it tends to spread to every limb of society. Industrialists and businessmen are tempted to go in for shady deals. Individuals who might have performed useful tasks in the economic development of their country become idle hangers-on, watching for loopholes in the decrees and dishonesty in their implementation. Myrdal did not discuss the fact that similar problems can also beset tariffs, but that is probably because he recommended either a flat-rate tariff on manufactured imports or regular tariffs set at different levels by semi-permanent legislation, and not changed frequently in a manner that would lend themselves to the type of problems created by quantitative restrictions.

Fourth, the critics argued that the benefits of trade are not fully captured within the confines of the Heckscher–Ohlin framework. For instance, Haberler (1959) argued that dynamic considerations, left out of the static framework of the classical approach, strengthen the case for free trade. The next section turns to issues beyond the confines of this approach, to discuss Haberler's arguments, and also to review and discuss the contributions of the early development economists who, after all, were not using the classical approach, even though – as seen in this section – some of their arguments can be couched within it.

### International Trade Theory and Development Economics

Haberler (1959) argued that dynamic factors strengthen the case for free trade for a number of reasons. First, trade enables poor countries to have access to goods – like machinery and raw materials – essential for economic development because they are necessary for increasing production. Second, by importing goods, especially capital goods, poor countries are able to import technical know-how, skills, managerial talents and entrepreneurship; although it is not the only vehicle for technology transfers, for Haberler, it is the most important one. Third, trade 'serves as a transmission belt for capital' because it is easier to get foreign capital for export industries, and because a large volume of trade makes it easier to make payments for foreign capital (ibid. 1959: 110). Finally, foreign trade fosters competition and keeps inefficient monopolies in check, an issue of importance in poor countries with small markets in which infant industry protection can create domestic monopolies. These arguments go well beyond the framework of the classical approach in a number of ways: by introducing produced inputs like machinery, by allowing for technological change, by incorporating international capital flows and, finally, by taking monopolies into account.

Other departures from the classical theory of trade can lead us to recognize additional benefits from trade. Smith's productivity theory of trade, according to which international trade can lead to dynamic and irreversible increasing returns due to specialization, was used by Myint (1958) to argue in favour of dynamic benefits from trade. However, he did not attach much importance to such benefits for LDCs because productivity increases were once for all, and labour shortages led to labour migration rather than productivity growth. He could have added that if the pattern of specialization due to trade was such that rich countries produced manufactured goods and poor countries mainly produced primary products, both static and dynamic gains would accrue to rich countries, and only static gains would accrue to poor ones.

Myint (1958) also drew on Smith's vent-for-surplus approach to argue that many poor countries do not use their resources fully because there is no domestic demand for these. Once the poor countries are opened up to international trade, they are able to expand their exports rapidly because of foreign demand for these resources, without (significantly) taking resources away from other sectors. An example of such trade can involve minerals or plantation crops, for which there is little or no domestic demand in poor subsistence economies, but for which there is foreign demand as intermediate goods. If the labour requirements for these sectors are small, then, an expansion in imports of these products can take place rapidly, as in many poor countries in the colonial period.

If the labour requirements were large, they were supplied in the past with immigration from other poor countries (like China and India), which allowed wages to be kept low.

In a colonial setting, the rapid expansion of such exports did not benefit poor countries significantly, partly because of high profits being remitted abroad by corporations that often had monopsonistic relations with sellers of products in poor countries. Myint (1954–55) argued that these problems were more important than factors that other development economists thought had led to an inherent tendency for the relative prices of primary products to fall. However, Myint was in favour of the expansion of such exports, since poor countries would have greater control over prices and profits with independence. He argued that further expansion of such exports could provide the foreign exchange necessary for their development plans. This vent-for-surplus approach is very different from the classical theory because it allows for the existence of unemployed resources. But it is unclear to what extent, and to how many LDCs, it is of relevance in the post-colonial period.

A departure from the classical approach does not necessarily imply that free trade makes poor countries better off, or that interaction between rich and poor countries can lead to a narrowing of international inequality. In an earlier section, we discussed the implications of Ricardo's dynamic model, which had asymmetric effects for rich and poor countries because of the kinds of goods they exported. In this section, we have already remarked on the implications of the Smithian productivity theory, due to the greater importance of the division of labour and increasing returns in some sectors than in others.

As noted earlier, the positive externalities that accrued from manufacturing production were an important theme in the writings of the early development economists. Although some aspects can be understood in terms of the static classic theory of international trade (as the difference between private and social marginal cost) or in terms of the infant industry argument, in which costs fall over time due to learning, it is more properly characterized as a dynamic phenomenon – along the lines of Smithian productivity growth – which is irreversible and takes place as capital accumulates, taking into account externalities between firms in the same industry and externalities across industries as well.

This is clear from the writings of Singer, who argued that international trade according to comparative advantage (and international investment), in which poor countries were primarily specialized in primary production, may

> spread present static benefits fairly over both. They may have had very different effects if we think from the point of view, not of static comparative advantages, but of the flow of history of a country. Of this latter school of thought the 'infant' argument for protection is but a sickly and often illegitimate offspring. (Singer 1950: 477)

He argued that international trade according to comparative advantage, and international investment in primary producing and extractive sectors had resulted in the growth of manufactured imports into LDCs, and the diversion of whatever little domestic entrepreneurship and investment they had to the export sectors. The result is that they have not been able to develop manufacturing, which, he argued, is of crucial importance:

> In the economic life of a country and in its economic history, a most important element is the mechanism by which 'one thing leads to another', and the most important contribution of an industry is not its immediate product . . . and not even its effect on other industries and immediate social benefits (thus far economists have been led to go by Marshall and Pigou) but perhaps beyond this its effect on the general level of education, skill, way of life, inventiveness, habits, store of technology, creation of new demand, etc. And this is perhaps precisely the reason why manufacturing industries are so universally desired by underdeveloped countries: they provide the growing points for increased technical knowledge, urban education and the dynamism and resilience that goes with urban civilization, as well as the direct Marshallian external economies. No doubt under different circumstances commerce, farming, and plantation agriculture have proved capable of being such growth points, but manufacturing industry is unmatched in our present age. (ibid.: 476–77)

The view of the early development economists regarding international issues appears to make much more sense when examined in dynamic terms, free of the static framework of classical trade theory. This can be appreciated with the following three remarks. First, these economists were not arguing that manufacturing should be promoted at the expense of agriculture. Many of them held that the development of agriculture is essential for economic development. Myrdal (1956: 206–09), for instance, discussed the need for reorganizing of agriculture and for increasing agricultural productivity. Lewis (1954), as we have seen, stressed the need for increasing productivity in agriculture to raise real wages in LDCs. This perspective, however, is essentially a dynamic one that involves capital accumulation and productivity growth, and which is alien to the world of static trade theory. In it, as Meier (1958) believed, any move protecting manufacturing is a move along the production possibility frontier, which reduces agricultural production.

Second, these economists were not arguing that both imports and exports should be reduced. They were certainly not for autarky, but for increasing exports and reducing imports. Protection of the importable sector in static trade theory implies shifting resources away from exportable production to importable production. But in a setting in which economies are constrained by foreign exchange bottlenecks, so that they are not using all their domestic resources, it is possible to reorganize production so as to increase the production of both importables and exportables. Moreover, in a dynamic framework, protection of selected manufactured goods can lead to increases in productivity – due to 'learning by doing' and external effects – which can then make these manufacturing sectors more competitive in world markets, allowing exports to be increased.

Third, these economists took the causes and consequences of technological change seriously. Instead of assuming that technological change could costlessly and easily result from the transfer of technology from advanced countries, or be left to foreign investors willing to invest and bring in new technology, or just be brought in by importing equipment, they examined the mechanisms by which technological capabilities could be built up. Other mechanisms of technological change could have worked in the past, when the migration of skilled and semi-skilled workers could bring in skills, or when education levels between technology-exporting and technology-importing regions were comparable. Thus, there may be good reasons as to why Australia, New Zealand and Denmark, not to speak of California and Iowa, may have developed despite being heavily agricultural. But to simply assert that LDCs could expect to develop in their footsteps without analysing the causes and consequences of technological change in the modern global economy, is unacceptable.

### Conclusion
The main contributions of early development theory to the study of international issues may be summarized as follows:

1. Trade can create problems for less developed countries and trade restrictions can help under some circumstances. Losses due to trade can be represented, to some extent, using the tools of orthodox trade theory, but are better discussed in more dynamic terms, involving increasing returns, externalities and technological change, rather than by using the orthodox static trade theory models.

2. There are many ways in which trade can help development, so that care should be taken to see that interference with trade does not become counterproductive. In particular, LDCs should try to promote exports, mainly those of manufactured goods.

3. International capital flows often do not come to poor countries, and when they do come, they may not contribute very much to development there because they tend to be primarily concentrated in enclave sectors, and in primary and extractive industries that exacerbate the pattern of comparative advantage.

4. Inequality between rich and poor countries has been growing over time.

5. International interactions between rich and poor countries have been contributing to widening the gap between these countries, due to the nature of trade and factor movements, and due to non-economic mechanisms.

6. International efforts, through foreign aid and other international agreements, should supplement efforts by the LDCs themselves to reduce international inequality.

Early development economics has been criticized by orthodox economists, especially after the neoclassical revival in development economics in the 1970s and 1980s, for neglecting the role of foreign trade in development and for recommending excessive state direction in the economy, including its foreign trade. It is argued that such neglect and intervention has led to various inefficiencies in the economy, and to poor economic performance in many LDCs. It is claimed that countries in East Asia that pursued outward-oriented policies performed much better than more inward-oriented economies. It is also argued that poor countries, on the whole, were growing faster than rich countries (see Lal 1985: 24) when world trade was also growing.

A longer look at developments in the real world and at theoretical developments provides a different picture.

1. Trade controls and other government policies can help establish industries in LDCs, which can then lead to growth with export growth after import substitution policies have developed industries. The experience of East Asian countries is best interpreted in this way (see, for instance, Amsden 2001). The promotion of primary and extractive industries has not been an engine of growth in LDCs. Theoretical models involving increasing returns and externalities have been developed to show how countries can lose due to freer trade.

2. Excessive intervention in trade has stifled competition and led to various kinds of inefficiencies in some countries. Orthodox critics of early development economists have belaboured this point (see Lal 1985, for instance).

3. Capital, in the form of foreign direct investment, has flowed to relatively few LDCs, and when it has flowed, has played a positive development role when it has gone into manufacturing and infrastructural sectors, and not into agricultural and extractive sectors. Theoretical developments, even in orthodox economics, have suggested why capital does not flow from rich to poor countries (Lucas 1990).

4. The inequality between rich and poor countries has been growing by a number of definitions. This is true if one considers long periods of history and makes conjectures about growth rates in poor and advanced countries (see Pritchett 1997), or if one uses currently popular measures of convergence, namely, beta convergence and sigma convergence (see Sala-i-Martin 1996). There is room for debate here, because some argue that the respectable recent growth of China and India has reduced inequality between nations.

5. Theoretical models have been developed to show that interaction between rich and poor countries can lead to a widening of the gap between these countries. This is true of orthodox models with full employment of resources (see Stokey 1991, for instance), and also using structuralist North–South models that incorporate various kinds of structural 'rigidities' in them (see Dutt 1990). Uneven development in these models can occur due to the pattern of trade specialization, with the rich North exporting goods involving learning by doing, and the poor South exporting goods that involve little or no learning (for example, primary goods

or low-skill manufactures). But uneven development can also occur with capital flows and technology transfers.

6. International institutions have not evolved in ways that provide LDCs with more chances to catch up. By pushing severe austerity measures, the International Monetary Fund has forced LDCs to contract even more than warranted by the adverse shocks they have faced. The World Bank has pushed structural adjustment, involving trade liberalization and other changes that have severely limited the ability of poor countries to determine their own trade policies. Trade liberalization has also been promoted through the World Trade Organization, which has extended its jurisdiction over restrictions on foreign direct investment and intellectual property rights. With aid flows falling as well, this is a far cry from Myrdal's call for international efforts to reduce global inequality.

Early development economists did not tell us everything we now know or need to know about the role of international factors in development. But they provided a fine start, and certainly a better one than what is sometimes attributed to them. The least we can do is to not forget or misrepresent them.

**Notes**

1 See Little (1982) and Lal (1985) for early criticisms of these allegedly autarkic views. Some critics, like Lal, distinguish between free trade and free market views, and claim that they are against autarky but not in favour of unfettered free markets. Such negative views of the early development economists prevail today, arguably with even greater force, among mainstream neoliberal proponents of globalization and openness.

2 Space limitations require this review to be brief and selective, focusing on the mercantilists – Smith, Ricardo, Hamilton, List – and neoclassical trade theory. We will not discuss the contribution of Marx, who argued that poor countries received both creative and destructive influences from rich countries as a result of colonial domination – creative due to the entry of capitalist forces in otherwise stagnant societies, and destructive due to the destruction of their industries, as in India. Marx's work provides an important background for the work of later Marxist and dependency theorists, who are not dealt with in this chapter.

3 There are some technical problems with this argument. If the marginal product of labour is zero in the subsistence sector, the withdrawal of peasants in that sector can imply a rise in average earnings in the subsistence sector. The problem is not insurmountable, however, if it is assumed that subsistence workers who migrate retain their share of the product, or that landlords keep average earnings of peasants in the subsistence sector constant.

4 There is also the assumption that goods can be unambiguously defined as having high or low capital intensity, that is, there are no factor intensity reversals.

**References**

Amsden, Alice (2001), *The Rise of 'The Rest': Challenges to the West from Late-Industrializing Economies* (New York: Oxford University Press).

Baran, Paul (1957), *The Political Economy of Growth* (New York: Monthly Review Press).

Bhagwati, Jagdish N. (1958), 'Immiserizing Growth: A Geometric Note', *Review of Economic Studies*, 25, 201–05.

—— (1971), 'The Generalized Theory of Distortions and Welfare', in Jagdish N. Bhagwati, Ronald W. Jones, Robert A. Mundell and Jaroslav Vanek, eds, *Trade, Balance of*

*Payments, and Growth: Essays in Honor of Charles P. Kindleberger* (Amsterdam: North-Holland).

Chang, Ha-Joon (2002), *Kicking Away the Ladder: Development Strategy in Historical Perspective* (London: Anthem Press).

Dutt, Amitava K. (1990), *Growth, Distribution and Uneven Development* (Cambridge: Cambridge University Press).

Haberler, Gottfried (1950), 'Some Problems in the Pure Theory of International Trade', *Economic Journal*, 60, June: 223–40.

—— (1959), 'International Trade and Economic Development', Fiftieth Anniversary Commemoration Lectures, National Bank of Egypt, Cairo; reprinted in James D. Theberge, ed., *Economics of Trade and Development* (New York: John Wiley), 1968.

Hagen, Everett E. (1958), 'An Economic Justification of Protectionism', *Quarterly Journal of Economics*, 72 (4), November: 496–514.

Hirschman, Albert O. (1958), *The Strategy of Economic Development* (New York: Norton).

Lal, Deepak (1985), *The Poverty of 'Development Economics'* (Cambridge, Massachusetts: Harvard University Press).

Lewis, W. Arthur (1954), 'Economic Development with Unlimited Supplies of Labour', *Manchester School*, 22 (2): 131–91.

Little, Ian M.D. (1982), *Economic Development* (New York: Basic Books).

Lucas, Robert E. (1990), 'Why Doesn't Capital Flow from Rich to Poor Countries?', *American Economic Review*, 80: 92–96.

Meier, Gerald M. (1958), 'International Trade and International Inequality', *Oxford Economic Papers*, October.

Myint, Hla (1954–55), 'The Gains from International Trade and Backward Countries', *Review of Economic Studies*, 22 (2), No. 58.

—— (1958), 'The "Classical Theory" of International Trade and Underdeveloped Countries', *Economic Journal*, June: 317–37.

Myrdal, Gunnar (1956), *An International Economy* (New York: Harper Brothers).

—— (1957), *Rich Lands and Poor Lands* (New York: Harper Brothers).

—— (1984), 'International Inequality and Foreign Aid in Retrospect', in Gerald M. Meier and Dudley Seers, eds, *Pioneers in Development* (New York: Oxford University Press for World Bank).

Nurkse, Ragnar (1952), 'Some International Aspects of the Problem of Economic Development', *American Economic Review*, May.

—— (1953), *Problems of Capital Formation in Underdeveloped Countries* (Oxford: Oxford University Press).

Prebisch, Raul (1950), *The Economic Development of Latin America and its Principal Problems*, Lake Success (New York: United Nations).

Pritchett, Lant (1997), 'Divergence, Big Time', *Journal of Economic Perspectives*, 11 (3): 3–17.

Rosenstein-Rodan, P.N. (1943), 'Problems of Industrialization in Eastern and South-Eastern Europe', *Economic Journal*, June–September: 202–11.

Sala-i-Martin, Xavier (1996), 'The Classical Approach to Convergence Analysis', *Economic Journal*, 106: 1019–36.

Samuelson, Paul A. (1948), 'International Trade and the Equalization of Factor Prices', *Economic Journal*, 58 (2): 165–84.

Singer, Hans (1950), 'The Distribution of Gains between Investing and Borrowing Countries', *American Economic Review*, 4 (2), Papers and Proceedings, May: 473–85.

Stokey, Nancy J. (1991), 'Human Capital, Product Quality and Growth', *Quarterly Journal of Economics*, 106 (2), May: 587–616.

Viner, Jacob (1952), *International Trade and Economic Development* (Glencoe, Illinois: Free Press).

# The Rise and Decline of Latin American Structuralism and Dependency Theory

*Alfredo Saad–Filho*

Structuralism and dependency theory were the first significant contributions to political economy to arise from the Latin American periphery. Their enduring influence can be gauged by the casual manner in which the previous sentence uses the term 'periphery' – no explanation is required, because it seems to express an obvious feature of the contemporary world. Yet, on reflection, there is nothing simple about it: dividing the world into 'centre' and 'periphery' implies the existence of systemic and possibly insurmountable differences between rich and poor countries, which must themselves be explained, both historically and analytically. This is what these theories set out to do, initially in the context of the Latin American transition from primary export-led growth to import-substituting industrialization (ISI). In spite of this geographically and historically specific frame of reference, the insights of structuralists and dependency theorists have been incorporated into a rich literature on development policy and the condition of underdevelopment, spanning most of the world.

There is a close theoretical and historical relationship between these two schools of thought. This is partly because they share key principles and perspectives on development and underdevelopment, and partly because prominent structuralists played an important role in the development of dependency theory in the 1960s. In spite of their similarities, explained below, there is a fundamental difference between structuralism and dependency theory: while the former claims that capitalist development is possible in the periphery through industrialization and comprehensive social reforms, the latter is more pessimistic, arguing that capitalism systematically *underdevelops* poor countries. For most *dependentistas*, socialism is the only alternative.

There is much to commend structuralism and dependency theory. They challenge mainstream economics perceptively and insightfully; usefully highlight the importance of interdisciplinary studies in the social sciences; rightly argue that activist state policies are essential for equitable and sustainable economic growth; forcefully bring out the connections between social relations and economic structure, policy and performance; and provocatively claim that democratic social; and economic reforms are preconditions for development. Many paid dearly for holding these iconoclastic views, especially during the 1960s and

1970s, when military regimes held sway throughout Latin America. In spite of their important insights into the problems of underdevelopment and their lasting influence among development theorists, practitioners and the wider community, the theoretical shortcomings of structuralism and dependency theory have contributed to their declining popularity. The first section of this chapter explains the context in which structuralism and dependency theory developed. The following section critically reviews the rise of structuralism in the wake of ISI and its transformation over time. The third section outlines dependency theory and its main shortcomings. The last section concludes this chapter.

### Import-Substituting Industrialization (ISI)

Most Latin American countries went through a process of ISI between the early 1930s and the mid-1980s. ISI is an industrialization strategy based on the systematic deepening and horizontal integration of manufacturing industry, with the primary objective of replacing imports. Different countries experienced ISI in distinct ways, depending on the modalities and extent of state intervention, the form and severity of balance of payments and financial constraints (especially the structure of exports, the efficiency of the domestic financial system and the role of foreign capital), the level and distribution of national income, the size of the domestic market, the composition of the labour force and other variables.

Under ISI, manufacturing expansion typically departs from the internalization of production of non-durable consumer goods, such as processed foods, beverages, tobacco products and cotton textiles. It later deepens to include production of more complex durable consumer goods, especially household appliances and automobile assembly, oil refining, simple chemical products and cement. In a few countries, ISI can reach a third stage, when the manufacturing structure becomes 'complete' (in the jargon of structuralism and dependency theory), with the production of basic and capital goods, and technologically advanced products, including industrial machinery, electronic instruments, and even modern ships and aircraft designed with domestic technology. Although no Latin American country 'completed' ISI in this sense, especially because of the insufficient development of their technological capability, most countries industrialized to some extent, and, by the mid-1980s, Argentina, Brazil and Mexico had made significant inroads into the last stage of import substitution. At that point, ISI was interrupted, and most Latin American countries shifted towards a neoliberal policy model. Although this policy change has helped to address some of the shortcomings of ISI, especially the propensity to high inflation, it has left unresolved other deficiencies of the previous model, particularly the extreme concentration of income and wealth, and the chronic weakness of the local financial system. Neoliberalism has also blocked employment creation in most countries, and led to the hollowing out of the manufacturing base of every country where it was implemented. Policy-induced deindustrialization was especially severe in Argentina, Chile and Peru, where local industry has been profoundly disarticulated or nearly wiped out.

In Latin America, ISI was not usually due to deliberate policy choices, although state support was essential for its continuity and relative success. In most countries, ISI was the outcome of the *success* of primary product exports, including sugar, coffee, cereals, meat, guano, bananas, rubber, copper and tin. Success in traditional activities fostered the expansion of complementary economic sectors, especially transport, storage, trading, finance and other service industries. It also led to the emergence of a professional urban middle class and rapid expansion of the waged working class, whether through state-managed transformation of the pre-existing (largely peasant) work force or through state-sponsored mass immigration. Urbanization, capital accumulation and income growth created markets for low-technology, non-durable consumer goods that were too bulky or uneconomical to be profitably imported. For these reasons, manufacturing development was normally located near the centres of primary production, such as Buenos Aires and São Paulo, where the essential requisites for capitalist production were already present: wage workers, money capital, some degree of mechanization of production, markets, transport and trade links, and finance (see Bulmer–Thomas 2003; Hirschman 1968; Thorp 1992). In sum, early manufacturing development was almost invariably pro-cyclical and non-dualistic: it depended heavily on the prosperity of the primary export sector, rather than being autonomous from or antagonistic to it. At a later stage, manufacturing would expand during downturns of the export sector, supplying the domestic market when imports were not available. At an even later stage, it would become largely independent of the fortunes of the primary export sector, finally becoming large enough to lead the economy.

The two world wars and the Great Depression powerfully accelerated ISI. These events were experienced in Latin America as strongly adverse exogenous shocks. The Depression caused a sharp contraction of the region's external markets and reduction of its commodity export prices, leading to a substantial decline in Latin America's capacity to import. In most countries, the purchasing power of exports declined by at least one-third; in some cases (especially Chile and El Salvador), by more than two-thirds. The world wars also significantly reduced the availability of imports because of disruptions in the main sources of manufactured exports and in the Atlantic trading system. Less obviously, these adverse shocks also triggered large fiscal deficits in most Latin American countries, because import tariffs were normally the most important source of tax revenue (in many countries, tariffs generated 50 per cent of government revenue in the late 1920s; see Bulmer–Thomas 2003: 178, 192.

In normal circumstances, trade and fiscal deficits would have been financed externally, but this was not possible during the wars or the Depression. Governments were forced to choose between accepting vigorously expansionary monetary policies and sharp devaluations of the exchange rate, and seeking to impose fiscal balance through harshly contractionary fiscal policies that would inevitably worsen the economic crisis. In the large countries, where markets were relatively developed and there was unused capacity in the non-export sector, proto-Keynesian expansionary policies generally led to a rapid economic recovery based on domestic manufacturing growth. In contrast, in the smaller countries, where markets were relatively undeveloped and there was little unused capacity, expansionary fiscal and monetary policies frequently triggered inflation and a collapse of the exchange rate.

Latin American ISI was unquestionably successful on several grounds; for example, it fostered extraordinarily rapid rates of economic growth for over half a century, and led to profound economic, social and political transformations across the region. In several countries, primary exports ceased being the main dynamic force of the economy as early as the 1940s, allowing national income to grow regardless of the fluctuations of export revenues. However, the extent of this shift varied greatly, and manufacturing expansion was rarely smooth. It was frequently hampered by political instability, administrative incompetence, institutional inadequacies, poor infrastructure, lack of finance and skilled workers, insufficient market size, and lack of consensus around the industrialization strategy, for either economic or ideological reasons. Different combinations of these factors explain why Brazil and Mexico advanced farther than Argentina and Peru on the road to industrialization, while Paraguay and Honduras hardly moved at all.

Latin American economies showed increasing signs of stress from the 1950s. Growth rates declined, political crises followed in rapid succession and there was mass discontent in several countries. Political democracy, often closely associated with populism, exhausted itself and was replaced by military dictatorships almost everywhere between the mid-1960s and mid-1970s. It was clear that ISI was plagued by severe shortcomings. Its decline was closely followed by the crisis of structuralism and the swift rise of dependency theory. However, dependency did not thrive for long. When Latin American ISI entered into terminal decline in the 1970s and 1980s, through bouts of financial instability, foreign debt crises, economic stagnation and hyperinflation, dependency theory also yielded to the combined weight of its internal inconsistencies, persecution at home and ideological defeat abroad, as monetarism and neoliberalism became hegemonic around the world.

### Structuralism

World War II turned several Latin American countries into net creditors for the first time, and, by the end of the war, the region held large foreign currency reserves. Latin America seemed to be poised for a long period of sustained growth; in fact, average GDP growth rates reached 5.8 per cent between 1945 and 1954, pushed by the expansion of the manufacturing sector. In spite of this, there were severe doubts in Latin America and abroad about the viability and economic efficiency of continuing industrialization.

In 1950, Raúl Prebisch, the Argentine central banker who was appointed executive secretary of the newly created United Nations Economic Commission for Latin America (ECLA or, in Spanish and Portuguese, Cepal), outlined an innovative interpretation of the ongoing Latin American transition from primary export-led growth (*desarrollo hacia afuera*) to internally-oriented urban-industrial development (*desarrollo hacia adentro*) (Prebisch 1950). This report became the founding document of Latin American structuralism. In it, Prebisch reviewed the limitations of the previous growth model, explained the origins of ISI, rationalized the developmentalist (*desarrollista*) role of Latin American states, and submitted a compelling case for industrialization in order to overcome poverty and underdevelopment. Prebisch's report captured the spirit of the times and caused an immediate sensation. During the next few years, an extraordinarily talented group of Latin American economists would gravitate around the Cepal office in Santiago (Chile), among them Celso Furtado, Octavio Paz, Aníbal Pinto, Osvaldo Sunkel and Maria da Conceição Tavares. There, or in economic planning and finance ministries or development agencies throughout the region, structuralists produced influential papers, reports and economic plans that interpreted, legitimized and directed the region's process of industrialization. The next subsection reviews the principles of structuralism and its policy prescriptions, and the most important critiques of structuralism.

### Principles and Policies

The structuralists were heavily influenced by Keynesianism and, at a further remove, by the Veblen school of institutional political economy. They claimed that markets do not always work well in poor countries (the food and labour markets are especially prone to failure), argued that the state should promote manufacturing growth at the expense of such primary activities as agriculture and mining, did not shy away from recommending the nationalization of strategic industries, and vigorously advocated the democratization of social and economic life, including the promotion of social welfare, rising wages and redistribution of income and land. However, in contrast to their Keynesian colleagues in the developed countries, the Latin American structuralists did not suggest that states should fine-tune the level of demand in order to achieve short-term economic stability. For them, rapid long-term growth was more important than stability; the state should focus primarily on the former, rather than the latter (see Bielschowsky 2000; Rodríguez 1981; Sunkel and Paz 1970; for didactic introductions to structuralism, see FitzGerald 2000; Kay 1989; Larraín 1989).

Latin American structuralism is dualist. Structuralists traditionally argue that the production structures in the centre and the periphery are very distinct, and that these regions fulfil different functions in the international division of labour. Dualism in the world economy is replicated within the peripheral countries. While productivity is high in all sectors of the economy in the industrialized countries, the peripheral economies are heterogeneous. In these countries, productivity is generally high in the primary export sector, but this sector tends to be a relatively small enclave, often owned by foreign capital, and only loosely connected to the rest of the economy. Although profits in this sector are high, they are also highly concentrated, and tend to be either repatriated abroad by exporting firms or wasted through luxury goods imports by the solvent classes. In addition to the highly profitable export sector, there is also a relatively ineffi-cient sector in the periphery producing agricultural and manufactured goods for domestic consumption, as well as a vast subsistence sector where masses of iso-lated peasants scrape a living outside the market economy. Dualism in the peri-phery and in the world economy is due to the exploitative social and economic relations imposed by the process of colonization. These unequal relations are continually reinforced by commercial, financial and cultural exchanges between rich and poor regions; therefore, they do not tend to be overcome 'spontaneously' by market processes.

Structuralism is heavily critical of neoclassical economic theory, espe-cially its presumptions that markets work, that countries should specialize in international trade according to their comparative advantage, and that economic efficiency can be ascertained by microeconomic cost–benefit analysis. Structur-alists claim, instead, that markets do not work well in the periphery because of structural (non-market) factors. These include strong trade unions in urban are-as, monopoly power in the manufacturing sector, concentration of power and income in society, and the prevalence of large unproductive landholdings in the countryside. These *latifúndios* are held for reasons of prestige rather than econo-mic profit, and do not respond to price signals. For example, they systematically fail to raise output when food prices increase due to the growth of urban demand, contributing to food scarcity and inflation (the subsistence sector also fails to respond to market incentives, squeezing food supplies simultaneously from two sides). Structuralists also argue that free trade and the existing international division of labour systematically benefit the centre at the expense of the periph-ery, because of the secular decline of the periphery's terms of trade (see below). Finally, they suggest that investment projects should be assessed macroeconomically (presumably, by state agencies) because economic development generates strong externalities that must be factored into cost–benefit analyses. Loss-making ven-tures may therefore deserve subsidies, or may be undertaken by state-owned enterprises, because of their growth or employment-creating potential or positive implications for other sectors of the economy.

Deterioration of the periphery's terms of trade (the 'Prebisch–Singer hypo-thesis': see Prebisch 1950; Singer 1950) is one of the distinguishing features of Latin American structuralism, and has generated a vast and continuing debate. Terms of trade are the ratio between the unit prices of exports and imports of a given country. Starting from trade equilibrium and ignoring financial flows, a country's terms of trade improve if its exports become relatively more valuable, allowing it to accumulate trade surpluses (or import more) with the same quan-tum of exports. Conversely, if the relative price of the country's imports increases, its terms of trade decline. In this case, the country will run a trade deficit or, alternatively, it will have to export more in order to restore its trade balance. In a world with financial flows, deterioration of terms of trade may also be tempo-rarily compensated by foreign debt, foreign investment, or aid flows.

Deterioration of terms of trade can be analysed from the supply or demand side. Let us start from the supply side. In the periphery, there is a large pool of unemployed and underemployed workers, mostly based in the rural subsistence sector, but also, increasingly, in urban areas, preventing modern (manufacturing and export) sector wages from rising – the employers can hire all the workers they need at the going wage. In this case, if there is productivity growth in the modern sector, unit costs decline and output prices tend to fall because of competition, transferring to the buyers (based in the centre) a large part of the benefits of productivity growth in the periphery. In contrast, in the centre, unemployment is low, the workers are unionized and they resist nominal wage cuts. In this case, productivity growth reduces unit costs but prices do not fall: the gains are appropriated by the workers and their employers through higher wages and profits. Since primary product prices tend to fall while the prices of manufactures remain constant, the periphery's terms of trade tend to decline over time.

Let us now shift to the demand side. Goods can be divided into necessities (food and other primary products) and luxuries (manufactures). The economic difference between them is that the demand for necessities grows more slowly than income (that is, their income elasticity of demand is less than one), while the demand for luxuries grows more rapidly than income (their income elasticity of demand is greater than one). If the periphery exports necessities and imports luxury goods, as income rises in the periphery of the world economy, its ratio of imports to consumption tends to increase, leading to excess demand for imports, higher prices for manufactures and balance of trade deficits. In contrast, as income rises in the centre, its ratio of imports to consumption tends to decline, primary product prices tend to fall and the centre's balance of payments tends to improve.

Structuralists claim that the periphery can escape from this vicious circle only through industrialization. Manufacturing expansion would allow peripheral countries to avoid the tendency towards deterioration of their terms of trade and, instead, benefit from rising terms of trade. It would also alleviate their balance of payments constraint, permit export diversification, provide an alternative engine of growth, offer an important source of employment and contribute to rapid productivity growth, raising living standards and helping to eliminate poverty. Industrialization would also modernize society through introduction of new technologies and new (urban, sophisticated, *developed*) values. For the structuralists, writing in mid-twentieth-century Latin America, import substitution was the only realistic industrialization strategy. Manufacturing exports to the centre seemed to be unfeasible because of protectionism, the poor quality of Latin American goods and their high prices, due partly to low productivity and partly to the overvalued exchange rates in most countries (which cheapens the capital goods imports required by manufacturing development but makes exports more expensive in dollar terms). Finally, industrialization in the periphery could be successful only with state support. 'Spontaneous' ISI is limited because of competition from established foreign producers, lack of infrastructure (which could not be supplied by a weak private sector lacking technology and finance), insufficient coordination of production and investment decisions, and resistance by powerful interests, preventing the indispensable transfer of resources from the primary sector. Industrial success necessitates state subsidies, affordable credit, trade protection for infant industries, foreign exchange controls, and the attraction of foreign capital and technology to the growing manufacturing sector.

Finally, the structuralists claim that Latin American industrialization is severely limited by the lack of savings to finance investment in the 'modern' sector. On the one hand, public savings are low because the tax system is both regressive and inefficient. On the other hand, private savings are insufficient because the periphery's large labour surplus and low average productivity limits incomes and savings; moreover, the wealthy groups tend to mimic the luxury consumption patterns originating from the centre, which drains away the country's savings and foreign exchange. Here, too, state intervention is essential in order to stimulate the growth of savings and productivity, and direct resources away from wasteful luxury goods imports.

### Critiques of Structuralism

Structuralism was criticized from different angles, especially by mainstream economists, and the dependency and Marxist schools. Their arguments are briefly reviewed below.

### The Neoclassical Critique

Mainstream economists often conflate structuralism with ISI (see, for example, Bruton 1981, 1998; Little, Scitovsky and Scott 1970). Although this oversimplifies the process of industrialization in Latin America and grossly exaggerates the role of structuralism in bringing about ISI, it facilitates a critique of structuralism because it can be blamed even for those shortcomings of ISI that were first highlighted by Cepal.

Neoclassical economists claim that structuralism and ISI were misguided theoretically and costly in practice. They argue that there is no harm specializing in primary exports because: first, attempts to demonstrate the Prebisch–Singer hypothesis have been either inconclusive or methodologically flawed; and, second, the shift of incentives towards the manufacturing sector, in which Latin America does not have comparative advantage, misallocates resources in the present and reduces growth rates in the future. Manufacturing inefficiency is due to inadequate (excessively capital-intensive) technologies imported from the developed countries. These technologies are not conducive to cost efficiency because Latin America lacks the adequate combination of factors of production as well as market size needed for efficient use of these technologies. They also lead to urban unemployment, since rural dwellers tend to flock into the cities looking for non-existent 'good' urban jobs. Since these causes of inefficiency could not be eliminated rapidly, Latin American industries would need to be protected indefinitely, which would be enormously expensive and hugely wasteful (it would be much more efficient to direct resources towards the further expansion of the primary sector, in which Latin America had comparative advantage). Moreover, blanket infant industry protection, as was often the case in Latin America, would foster the over-diversification of manufacturing, replicating the problems of techno-logical inadequacy and economic inefficiency across several sectors, and leading to rent-seeking behaviour as entrepreneurs looked for profit opportunities gene-rated by protection, other incentives, legal loopholes or corruption. Finally, neo-classical economists claim that state economic activism is inflationary because subsidies to private and state-owned enterprises, and 'populist' funding of public services, generate large fiscal deficits that tend to be financed by printing money.

In sum, although ISI may lead to a limited period of rapid growth, it is unsustainable in the long term because of its cumulative inefficiencies, and bec-ause it causes rising inflation and unemployment. Economic recovery requires a shift of investment towards the primary sector, export diversification, industrial rationalization (eliminating the inefficient producers), and public expenditure cuts to control inflation and reduce the economic role of the state.

### The Left Critique

Left-wing critics of structuralism, especially the dependency theorists and Marxists, have an altogether different view of structuralism and ISI.[1] Many of them had worked with Cepal or reformist governments, and their critique is often based on first-hand experience of the limitations of manufacturing develop-ment in Latin America and profound familiarity with structuralist theory.

Dependency theorists and Marxists rightly acknowledge that structural-ism cannot be blamed for many of the shortcomings of ISI. Their critique is, therefore, largely conceptual. First, dependency theorists and Marxists claim that the theory of structural duality does not provide a satisfactory account of the different forms of labour in Latin America, including the persistence of (low productivity) remnants of feudalism and slavery, the diffusion of subsistence pro-duction and their intricate relationship to the (high productivity) modern sector.

Second, Cepal expected the urban bourgeoisie to lead the process of industrialization, and the majority of the population was normally included in the analysis only as consumers or wage workers, rather than as independent social and political agents. This is insufficient, because the structuralists them-selves gradually realized that the local bourgeoisie is profoundly dependent on their foreign counterparts, and will never engage in a consistent (and necessarily radical) project of autonomous national development. Moreover, it gradually became clear that the fruits of manufacturing development would not spontane-ously trickle down to the poor, as the structuralists initially expected. For the left-wing critics of structuralism, sustained manufacturing development and distribu-tion of income, wealth and power can be achieved only through popular or socialist governments (see below).

Third, the Prebisch–Singer hypothesis is untenable and should be rej-ected. Its use of the undifferentiated concepts of 'primary products' and 'manufactures' is not helpful, since they cannot be distinguished unambiguously (at what stage of processing does a primary product become a manufactured good?), and because no country exports 'primary products' as such – the international markets for coffee, copper, meat and other primary products are profoundly different from one another, and these differences should be taken into account in any study of price trends and their implications for specialization. Finally, the use of international commodity prices is misleading. They are only loosely related to the farm-gate prices received by producers in the periphery and, therefore, cannot explain their economic behaviour.

Fourth, it became clear in the late 1950s that ISI suffered from fundamental problems that structuralism was ill equipped to address. ISI had worsened the balance of payments constraint, both because the transfers from the primary sector (required to support industrial development) had sapped export performance, and because imports had become increasingly incompressible. While consumer goods imports can be cut relatively painlessly in the event of adverse fluctuations of primary product prices, industrial inputs are rigid. With ISI, crises affecting the export sector often triggered the contraction of manufacturing output and urban unemployment. ISI had also increased the concentration of income and the degree of foreign dependence, now including technology, finance, ownership of industry, culture, patterns of consumption and so on. Finally, being based on imported technology, the Latin American industrial plants normally had excess capacity, which contributed to industrial concentration and reduced competition. In sum, contrary to all expectations, ISI had *increased* the power of large players and the economy's vulnerability to adverse external shocks.

### Dependency Theory
Dependency theory was developed in the 1960s and 1970s by Fernando Henrique Cardoso, André Gunder Frank, Ruy Mauro Marini, Theotonio dos Santos, Immanuel Wallerstein and others.[2] They offered a radical critique of capitalism in the periphery, in the context of the exhaustion of the post-war boom in the centre, and the crisis of ISI, the collapse of populism and the theoretical decline of structuralism in Latin America. Dependency theory is concerned primarily with the exploitation of the periphery by the centre, including the different forms of extraction of economic surplus and the mechanisms of surplus transfer to the centre. This approach rapidly became a leading paradigm in many countries and, even today, continues to be influential among left-wing organizations and movements, for example, in the global justice, anti-globalization and anti-capitalist movements.

#### Intellectual Sources and Features
Dependency theory was inspired primarily by Latin American structuralism and the US 'monopoly capital' school. The influence of structuralism hardly needs mentioning. It includes the division of the world economy into centre and periphery, the claim that polarization is furthered by unequal exchange between

these areas (drawing inspiration, in part, from the Prebisch–Singer hypothesis), the view that the existing distribution of assets (especially land) prevents the expansion of the domestic market in the periphery, the argument that economic development requires political autonomy, completion of the manufacturing base, independent technological capacity, and so on.

Monopoly capital theory was developed by the American economists Paul Sweezy and Paul Baran (see Baran 1957; Baran and Sweezy 1966) and their associates in the journal *Monthly Review*. This interpretation of contemporary capitalism is based on the theories of Marx, Keynes, Kalecki and Steindl. It claims, first, that modern capitalism is dominated by large corporations (monopolies). Concentration and centralization of capital facilitates the increase of prices relative to wages, concentrating income and reducing the intensity of competition. The latter, in turn, slows down technical change and contributes to the stagnating tendency of modern capitalism (see, especially, Steindl 1952). Second, in developed capitalist economies, there is a problem of absorption of the (growing) surplus produced by firms. The actual surplus is defined at the macroeconomic level as the difference between actual output and essential consumption (with wages fixed at the subsistence level), while, at the level of the firm, surplus is the excess of revenue over costs, which includes profits and such 'unnecessary' costs as advertising and sales promotion expenditure. The surplus tends to rise because of the relative decline of costs, including wages, which creates a potential (macroeconomic) problem of lack of demand in developed economies. Insufficient demand can be addressed in different ways, including wasteful sales effort, state expenditure, militarism and imperialism (see Sawyer 1999).

Baran (1957) applied these insights to the relationship between centre and periphery. For him, development and underdevelopment are inseparable because the centre developed historically on the basis of colonialism, imperialism and plunder, which, in turn, created underdevelopment in the periphery. Today, the centre profits from the capture of surplus from the periphery through unequal trading and financial relations, perpetuating the subordination of this area of the world economy. These elements were combined into several dependency approaches, whose core is summarized below.

First, dependency theory is historical and rejects dualism. It focuses, instead, on an integrated world system based on a network of exchange relations in which centre and periphery fulfil different but inseparable roles. The periphery was incorporated into the world system by the expansion of commercial capitalism in the late fifteenth century and, since then, it has been subjected to different types of dependence: mercantile during the colonial era, industrial–financial from the late nineteenth century, and technological–industrial since the mid-twentieth century. During these phases, colonialism, imperialism, and unequal trade and financial relations led to surplus transfers to the centre. There are no sharp differences between 'modern' and 'backward' areas in the underdeveloped economies – peripheral countries are capitalist by virtue of their articulation with the world market, even if (for functional or historical reasons) distinct modes of labour exploitation can be found there. In sum, the backwardness of the periphery is not due to the 'lack' of capitalist development, as argued by Cepal (and neoclassical economists), but to prevailing international relations of capitalist exploitation and subordination.

Second, dependence has created peculiar social structures in the periphery, especially a parasitic *comprador* ruling class, or *lumpenbourgeoisie*. Typically, this class manages the exploitation of the locals on behalf of the centre, exports the products of their labour (and the corresponding surplus), and purchases from abroad goods allowing it to live in luxury amidst the squalor of a despoiled land. Its high living standards, and the transfers to the centre, are possible only because of the extremely high rates of exploitation in the periphery; however, as a result, this region lacks both resources and markets for autonomous development. In sum, dependence is based on a coincidence of interests between the elites based in the centre and the peripheral *comprador* class, and marginalizes and impoverishes the masses.

Third, surplus is transferred to the centre by unequal exchange, profit remittances by transnational companies and financial transactions, especially debt repayment and capital flight. These transfers depress incomes, welfare standards and investment in the periphery, and produce a distorted growth pattern favouring the production of primary products for export and of luxury goods for domestic consumption.

For Frank and other *dependentistas*, the relations binding the centre and the periphery have generated a process of 'development of underdevelopment': underdevelopment is not a transitional stage through which countries must pass but, rather, a condition that plagues regions involved in the international economy in a subordinate position. For them, dependent capitalism is not progressive because it does not lead to the systematic development of labour productivity and the satisfaction of wants in the periphery, while capitalism in the centre is no longer progressive because it is parasitical on the periphery. Therefore, the periphery can develop only after radical political change including, for many *dependentistas*, the elimination of relations of dependence (and the *comprador* class) and the institution of socialism.

### Critiques of Dependency Theory

Dependency theory has been criticized from several angles (see, for example, Brenner 1977; Laclau 1971; Lall 1975). In what follows, two critically important shortcomings of dependency theory are addressed.

### Structuralism

The shortcomings of structuralist theory were reviewed above and do not need to be repeated here; only two implications for dependency will be pointed out. First, dependency theory turns the evolutionist aspects of structuralism on their head. Drawing upon structuralism (and modernization theory, more generally), dependency writers often select certain supposedly progressive tendencies in western capitalist development. These tendencies are transformed into a general model and what is perceived to have taken place in the periphery is a distortion from the model, due to the exploitation of the periphery by the developed centre. Consequently, the usual conclusions are reversed: metropolitan policy and technology exports are malevolent, rather than beneficial; the net balance of payments' impact of foreign direct investment is negative; the local elite is an exploiting clique, rather than a modernizing bourgeoisie; international trade perpetuates underdevelopment; and attempts at capitalist development bring stagnation and deepen the underdevelopment of the periphery.

Second, dependency theory is even more overtly functionalist than structuralism. It subordinates agency to structure, and assumes that the historical development and social structure of the periphery can be explained by their functionality to western capitalism. Development is ultimately impossible under capitalism because there is no scope for independent agency: dependent countries tied to the world market *cannot* develop. The obvious alternative is to *delink* from the capitalist world system through a socialist revolution – however, this conclusion is never rendered compatible with the subordination of agency to structure at every stage in the analysis. More generally, dependency theory frequently fails to analyse how social relations in the periphery change, and how human agency in the centre and the periphery shapes the relationship between these regions.[3]

### Monopoly Capital

The monopoly capital school argues that the concentration and centralization of capital are defining features of modern capitalism; that they lead to monopoly and loss of economic dynamism, and create a tendency towards under-consumption; and that these difficulties can be addressed only through wasteful expenditures and militarism at home, and imperialism abroad.

These elements of dependency theory are vulnerable on four grounds (see Bleaney 1976; Chattopadhyay 2000; Fine and Murfin 1984). First, dependency theory and the monopoly capital school do not define monopoly power clearly or consistently, and do not adequately explain how it arises and influences the reproduction of industrial capital, the circulation of money and the distribution of income. The theory of monopoly pricing is especially weak, being little more than a collation of the ideas of the Austrian Marxist Rudolf Hilferding and the Polish precursor of Keynes, Michal Kalecki. Monopoly capital and dependency tend to underestimate the role of demand in the determination of prices, and to exaggerate the importance of firm size, rather than focus on the (transnational) structure of supply chains, in which case, size would become a secondary and possibly unimportant issue. They also fail to consider the extent to which state regulation and the potential entry of (domestic or foreign) competitors might compel even large firms to follow competitive strategies, and to what extent monopoly power makes stagnation and crises inevitable. Finally, they pay scant regard to the counter-tendencies to the concentration and centralization of capital, claiming that monopolization is not only a basic, but also a largely unavoidable tendency in modern capitalism.

Second, the concept of surplus developed by Baran and Sweezy, and adopted by dependency theory, is analytically unsatisfactory. It rests on an arbitrary definition of 'essential consumption' on the part of workers, whose level is determined normatively by the analyst, and on an external distinction between 'necessary' and 'surplus' elements of the social product (in which case, even adornments in otherwise useful goods, such as automobiles, are part of the surplus). This concept is, therefore, inevitably subjective.

Third, the monopoly capital and dependency approaches claim that all countries involved in international trade are equally capitalist, and that connections to the world trading system (and the ensuing surplus transfers) play a determining role in the underdevelopment of the periphery – leaving unexplained the economic development of such countries as Canada, Ireland, Japan and South Korea, and suggesting that relatively isolated countries in Latin America and Sub-Saharan Africa are more likely to grow 'autonomously' than wealthier countries closely linked to international trade and financial flows.

Finally, dependency theory and the monopoly capital school make an inconsistent case for socialism, because their claim that capitalist development is impossible in the periphery is insufficient to support the case for revolution. At best, the argument – that the periphery is exploited by the centre – implicitly makes a case for *nationalism* for, if underdevelopment is due to international integration, the logical solution is not socialism but a (delinked) national development strategy. Perception of this limitation in the dependency school is supported by the fact that only exceptionally does it directly address domestic relations of exploitation. In practice, this approach leaves the state as the most important agent of national emancipation, which, again, is incompatible with its purported socialist strategic objectives.

### Conclusion

Structuralism and dependency theory have shown the limitations of neoclassical development economics. They have also demolished old (self-serving) prejudices about the periphery's place in the world, which claimed that its specialization in primary product exports was both 'natural' and 'desirable', and that these countries were unsuited for industrial development. Structuralism and dependency have creatively explained the shifts in Latin America's productive structure since the colonial era, showed that comparative advantage is created rather than divinely ordained, and outlined a compelling case for national economic autonomy. These approaches evolved over time and tended to become increasingly radical, in response to the limitations of ISI, the perceived deterioration of the economic, social and political conditions in the periphery since the 1960s, and their increasing awareness of the obstacles to the realization of Latin America's potential. They were, however, essentially *nationalist* and *developmentalist* theories, drawing upon Keynesian, Marxist and other insights, and focusing their hopes of economic and social change on different agents – in one case, the industrial bourgeoisie and, in the other, the state – as vehicles for the realization of the economic aspirations of the urban and rural masses.

Several reasons explain why structuralism and dependency theory lost the battle of ideas. These include, on the one hand, increasing political, ideological and economic pressure emanating from the centre, combined with the onslaught of local dictatorships against dissenting intellectuals, frequently leading to denial of employment, imprisonment, exile and (for those unprotected by fame or powerful connections) even execution. On the other hand, these schools of thought failed because of their own theoretical insufficiencies.

For example, structuralism was unable to outline viable short-term stabilization policies addressing the disequilibria induced by ISI, or consistent development policies after exhaustion of ISI had taken hold in the late 1950s and early 1960s. The latter was especially problematic, given the lack of interest of domestic capitalists in the structuralist strategy of market expansion through land reform, higher wages and regional economic integration. Structuralism also signally failed to evaluate, in a timely manner, the implications of the changes in the international financial system, which eliminated the scarcity of dollars plaguing the early post-war economy, and the evolution of the international division of labour, which created integrated production chains spanning the world. The collapse of the Bretton Woods system in 1971 and the international debt crisis from 1982 posed challenges that structuralism was simply unable to address. Its telling denunciation of the costs of structural adjustment could not mask the fact that the structuralists had nothing new to offer. Many followers became disillusioned and adhered to the mainstream, or simply abandoned attempts to offer alternatives to the Washington Consensus. Cepal still produces insightful reports that must be read by anyone interested in Latin America, and its data-set remains indispensable, but its influence in academic and political circles has declined significantly, and it has been unable to provide a much-needed counterweight to the hegemony of neoliberalism in the region.[4]

In turn, dependency theory collapsed because of the theoretical inconsistencies explained above, and because of its inability to provide a convincing explanation of the changes in the world economy in the 1980s and 1990s, including the accelerated transnationalization of productive capital and finance, the rapid development of many East Asian countries and the continuing stagnation of other regions. Elements of dependency theory can still be found in several critical approaches, and left-wing NGOs and activist movements can readily incorporate dependency views, but they continue to lack consistent foundations.

The claim, made by structuralism and dependency theory, that subordination to the world market seals the fate of nations, is wrong. Inequality, poverty, low productivity and sluggish growth in countries of the periphery, their propensity to import luxury goods and transfer profits to the centre, and their lack of coordination of economic activity are due primarily to the social structures prevailing in them, rather than their international trade relations. One of the most significant implications of this conclusion is that Latin American ISI was limited by an elite pact with two key features, which were perceived clearly only retrospectively. First, property rights were untouchable. Consequently, no significant land reform could be achieved (except through revolutionary processes), which limited the capitalist transformation of the region to the relatively undemocratic 'Prussian' path.[5] For the same reason, reorganization of the financial system for adequate funding of rapid industrialization was also impossible in Latin America. Second, the elite pact sheltered the agro-export interests and maximized their influence upon the state, to the detriment of the rising industrial capitalists, and the urban middle and working classes (who were not party to the pact). While the industrial capitalists defended their interests through negotiations, brokered by the state, with other elite segments, the other urban actors found it difficult to be heard. Their attempt to bypass strongly conservative state institutions (especially the legislature and the judiciary) through populism was, however, limited and essentially conservative. The promotion of economic change and the management of social conflicts by a powerful populist executive hindered the consolidation of democratic representative institutions in most of Latin America, at least until the 1980s.

In Latin America and other parts of the world, income, wealth and power remain concentrated in the hands of powerful elites. Limited democracy, weak states and stunted growth have also contributed to perpetuation of the features of underdevelopment that originally motivated structuralism and dependency theory. Their concerns remain valid in the early twenty-first century and there is scope for the development of alternatives to the mainstream, responding to old as well as other concerns, such as environmental sustainability, gender equality, the coexistence of underemployment, personal debt and overwork, and other urgent problems of rich and poor nations.

### Notes

[1] The most comprehensive left-wing critiques of ISI and structuralism are provided by Cardoso and Falleto (1979) and Tavares (1978).

[2] See, among others, Cardoso and Falleto (1979), Frank (1966, 1972), Marini (1973), Santos (1970) and Wallerstein (1974, 1980, 1989).

[3] Cardoso and Faletto (1979) sought to analyse concrete situations of dependence in Latin America, but with only limited success; see Weeks and Dore (1979).

[4] For a sample of recent work, see the Cepal website (www.cepal.org) and Ocampo (2002).

[5] For a detailed contrast between the 'Prussian' and 'American' paths of agrarian transformation and capitalist accumulation, see Byres (1996).

### References

Baran, Paul (1957), *The Political Economy of Growth* (New York: Monthly Review Press).

Baran, Paul and Paul M. Sweezy (1966), *Monopoly Capital* (New York: Monthly Review Press).

Bielschowsky, Ricardo, ed. (2000), *Cinqüenta Anos de Pensamento na CEPA*, Record (Rio de Janeiro).

Bleaney, Michael (1976), *Underconsumption Theories: A History and Critical Analysis* (London: Lawrence and Wishart).

Brenner, Robert (1977), 'The Origins of Capitalist Development: A Critique of Neo-Smithian Marxism', *New Left Review*, 104: 25–92.

Brewer, Anthony (1989), *Marxist Theories of Imperialism: A Critical Survey* (London: Routledge): Chapters 7–9, 136–224.

Bruton, Henry J. (1981), 'The Import-Substitution Strategy of Economic Development: A Survey', *Pakistan Development Review*, 10 (2): 123–46.

—— (1998), 'A Reconsideration of Import Substitution', *Journal of Economic Literature*, 36: 903–36.

Bulmer–Thomas, Victor (2003), *The Economic History of Latin America since Independence*, second edition (Cambridge: Cambridge University Press).

Byres, Terry J. (1996), *Capitalism from Above and Capitalism from Below* (London: Macmillan).

Cardoso, Fernando H. and Enzo Faletto (1979), *Dependency and Development in Latin America* (Berkeley: University of California Press).

Chattopadhyay, Paresh (2000), *Surplus School and Marx: On Garegnani's Marx Reading*, Papers and Sessions for International Working Group in Value Theory Mini-Conference at the Eastern Economic Association, 24–26 March (Washington: Crystal City).

Emmanuel, Arghiri (1972), *Unequal Exchange: A Study of the Imperialism of Trade* (New York: Monthly Review Press).

—— (1975), 'Unequal Exchange Revisited', IDS Discussion Paper No. 77, Institute of Development Studies, University of Sussex, Brighton.

Fine, Ben (2001), *Social Capital versus Social Theory: Political Economic and Social Science at the Turn of the Millennium* (London: Routledge).

Fine, Ben and Andy Murfin (1984), *Macroeconomics and Monopoly Capitalism* (Brighton: Wheatsheaf).

FitzGerald, Edmund V.K. (2000), 'ECLA and the Theory of Import-Substituting Industrialization in Latin America', in Enrique Cárdenas, J.A. Ocampo and Rosemary Thorp, eds, *An Economic History of Latin America*, Vol. 3 (London: Palgrave).

Frank, André G. (1966), 'The Underdevelopment of Development', *Monthly Review*, 18 (4): 17–31.

—— (1972), *Lumpen-Bourgeoisie, Lumpen-Development: Dependence, Class, and Politics in Latin America* (New York: Monthly Review Press).

Hirschman, Albert O. (1968), 'The Political Economy of Import-Substituting Industrialization in Latin America', *Quarterly Journal of Economics*, 82 (1): 1–32.

Kay, Cristobál (1989), *Latin American Theories of Development and Underdevelopment* (London: Routledge): Chapter 2.

Laclau, Ernesto (1971), 'Feudalism and Capitalism in Latin America', *New Left Review*, 67: 19–38.

Lall, Sanjaya (1975), 'Is "Dependence" a Useful Concept in Analysing Underdevelopment?', *World Development*, 3 (11–12): 799–810.

Larrain, Jorge (1989), *Theories of Development: Capitalism, Colonialism and Dependency* (Cambridge, Massachusetts: Polity Press): Chapter 3.

Little, Ian, Tibor Scitovsky and Maurice Scott (1970), *Industry and Trade in Some Developing Countries: A Comparative Study* (Oxford: Oxford University Press).

Marini, Ruy M. (1973), *La Dialéctica de lá Dependencia* (Mexico: Ediciones Era).

Ocampo, José A. (2002), *Globalization and Development* (New York: United Nations).

Prebisch, Raúl (1950), *The Economic Development of Latin America and its Principal Problems* (New York: Economic Commission for Latin America).

Rodríguez, Octavio (1981), *La Teoría del Subdesarrollo de la Cepal* (Mexico: Siglo Veintiuno).

Rouquié, Alain (1998), 'The Military in Latin American Politics since 1930', in Leslie Bethell, ed., *Latin America: Politics and Society since 1930* (Cambridge: Cambridge University Press).

Saad–Filho, Alfredo (1993), 'Labour, Money and "Labour-Money": A Review of Marx's Critique of John Gray's Monetary Analysis', *History of Political Economy*, 25 (1): 65–84.

—— (2002), *The Value of Marx: Political Economy for Contemporary Capitalism* (London: Routledge).

Santos, Theotonio dos (1970), 'The Structure of Dependence', *American Economic Review*, 60 (2): 231–36.

Sawyer, Malcolm (1999), 'Monopoly Capitalism', in Philip A. O'Hara, ed., *Encyclopedia of Political Economy*, Vol. 2 (London: Routledge).

Singer, Hans (1950), 'The Distribution of Gains between Investing and Borrowing Countries', *American Economic Review*, 40 (2): 473–85.

Steedman, Ian (1977), *Marx after Sraffa* (London: New Left Books).

Steindl, Josef (1952), *Maturity and Stagnation in American Capitalism* (New York: Monthly Review Press).

Sunkel, Osvaldo and Pedro Paz (1970), *El Subdesarrollo Latinoamericano y la Teoría del Desarrollo* (Mexico: Siglo Veintiuno).

Tavares, Maria C. (1978), *Da Substituição de Importações ao Capitalismo Financeiro* (Rio de Janeiro: Zahar).

Thorp, Rosemary (1992), 'A Reappraisal of the Origins of Import-Substituting Industrialization, 1930–1950', *Journal of Latin American Studies*, 24, Quincentenary Supplement: 181–95.

Wallerstein, Immanuel (1974), *The Modern World-System*, Vol. 1: *Capitalist Agriculture and the Origins of the European World-Economy in the Sixteenth Century* (New York: Academic Press).

—— (1980), *The Modern World-System*, Vol. 2: *Mercantilism and the Consolidation of the European World-Economy, 1600–1750* (New York: Academic Press).

—— (1989), *The Modern World-System*, Vol. 3: *The Second Era of the Great Expansion of the Capitalist World-Economy, 1730–1840s* (New York: Academic Press).

Weeks, J. and E. Dore (1979), 'International Exchange and the Causes of Backwardness', *Latin American Perspectives* 6(2): 62–87.

# Development in the History of Economics

*Tamás Szentes*

Although development economics as a separate field of studies was 'born' after World War II, it does not mean that its concerns had been neglected in the social sciences before that. On the contrary, since the very beginning of modern economic thought, a major concern of all theoretical streams of economics has been – directly or indirectly, explicitly or implicitly – the sources of economic development, the origins of the 'wealth of nations', as well as the ways and means, conditions and factors, promoting development[1] (often in the context of a particular economic system).

Early and somewhat primitive economic theories of, and policies for, the capitalist market economy were born in the great historical transformations of the sixteenth and seventeenth centuries, leading to the rise of industrial capitalism in western Europe, first of all in Britain and France. These raised, and answered, in one way or another, some of the fundamental questions and dilemmas of economic development still in the literature of post-World War II development economics: what does the economic development of a nation imply; what are its forces and sources; where and how can 'surplus' (the excess over subsistence needs) be created and mobilized; the implications of 'outward' and inward-oriented policies; whether international trade or domestic production; whether monetary or real processes; whether merchants or producers are the 'agents of development'; choosing between manufacturing and agriculture; whether equilibrium or disequilibrium, balanced or unbalanced growth; and whether state interventions or market spontaneity promote economic development, contribute more to national progress and increase the 'surplus', thereby increasing the wealth, welfare and strength of the nation.

### Classical Economics

The views associated with classical economics were not only much more diverse than those of their mercantilist and physiocratic predecessors (discussed elsewhere in this volume), but also presented far more complex perceptions of the economy and its development. While answering practically the same questions of development, albeit in somewhat different ways, as their predecessors, the classical economists also added new issues, mainly due to the new historical circumstances.

One feature of classical economics (at least, of its most characteristic representatives, such as Adam Smith and David Ricardo) that is distinct from the theoretical streams following it is that it combines the labour theory of value with the principles of liberalism. In other words, it preserves the concept of 'natural prices' (that is, 'value' as the basis of market price formation) being determined by the quantity of human labour used in production. It logically follows that incomes are determined by the labour performed, and belief in the economically rational and socially favourable operations of an unregulated market economy.

Thus, the classical economists attributed equally important roles in economic development, in the growth of the 'wealth of nations', to human labour (as the source of all value) and to the free, spontaneous operations of the market (that is, to a system of economic liberalism). They believed that if individuals can freely pursue their own selfish interests, the 'invisible hand' (owing to spontaneous operations of the market) will coordinate their actions to ensure social rationality, efficient allocation of resources, better welfare and fair income distribution, and also that their behaviour will be socially responsible. But, unlike their predecessors, they could find the 'surplus' in both production (including industrial production) and foreign trade (even without unequal exchange and disequilibria).

While the classical economists were quite aware of the need for all 'three factors of production' (nature, labour and capital) in several respects, they emphasized human labour (which also could be considered the source of capital, producing tools and equipment, and whose performance is supported by nature) and the increase in its productivity (hopefully countervailing the 'law of diminishing returns') as following not only from improved techniques (tools and equipment) of production, but also from acquired experience, from 'learning by doing', from dexterity. Therefore, they also pointed to the progressive role of specialization, that is, the division of labour, both within and among nations, which contributes to accumulation of skill and knowledge in production. It may also add to the 'surplus', through international trade based on 'absolute advantage' (Smith) or 'comparative advantage' (Ricardo), increasing wealth and mutual benefit for all without unequal exchange and disequilibria.

The representatives of classical economics perceived the historical process of development as leading from early stages (or systems) characterized by primitive activities (such as hunting, gathering and fishing) and then primary activities, to the most developed industrial economy and society, based on a spontaneously operating market, on harmonious cooperation among owners of factors of production as well as trading nations, and on the freedom of individuals who act according to their interests and thus unwittingly contribute to social welfare for all. This perspective not only incorporates a unilinear concept of development, but also confidence in the capitalist market economy. However, the classical economists were quite aware of some imperfections of the prevailing system, in their own country and in other countries. They also expressed their worry about the prospects of a 'stationary state'.

The classical economists pointed, in one way or another, implicitly or explicitly, to almost all of the main conditions, factors and aspects of economic development. These included natural conditions and the growth of population, that is, the number of both consumers and producers; the conditions for equilibrium both within and between national economies; labour productivity, depending on specialization, dexterity, skill, education and technical equipment, as a source of surplus both in agriculture and industry; savings and capital formation, depending not only on the rate of interest, but also, more generally, on incomes and income distribution; investment, competition and technical progress (science and innovations); international trade and division of labour; certain moral, cultural, social and institutional aspects of development; and even the role and responsibilities of government in a market economy. If they overemphasized one or the other of the various issues of development (although far less than often attributed to them), it was mainly because of the historical conditions and/or their own hopes for change.

### Marxian Economics

The economic theory of Karl Marx can also be considered a theory of development for at least three reasons. First, apart from its utopian and political-ideological elements, it contributed a lot to theoretical discussion of contemporary development issues, many of which are still relevant for the economics of development today.[2] Second, by interpreting economic phenomena and processes in a socio-political context, Marxian theory was a precursor of the kind of interdisciplinary approach considered a distinctive feature of development economics after World War II. Third, it presented an overall approach to the historical development of human society.

Marxian political economy emerged from the 'soil' of British classical economics, but was also influenced by German philosophy (particularly Hegel) and the French 'utopian socialists'. Marx, however, rejected and criticized the liberalism of classical economics, and the belief in socially and internationally harmonious operations of the capitalist market economy; he further elaborated the labour theory of value to explain exploitation without the use of (non-economic) force.

Marx not only applied a more holistic, that is, interdisciplinary approach in his analysis of the contemporary capitalist system, but, in addition to the 'stock' and 'flow' approach (already applied and combined in classical economics), he introduced a 'relations approach' by identifying lasting relations between classes of society or nations, underlying their positions, actions and behaviour. Accordingly, the economy consists not only of certain 'stocks', or endowments, and of certain transactions, or 'flows', among economic actors, but also of 'social relations of production and distribution' among classes or nations. Development thus involves, in his view, both progress, or evolution of 'productive forces', and changes in the 'social relations of production', with concomitant changes in the institutional, political and legal systems (the so-called 'superstructure').

The primary 'force of production' is human labour, the only source of social value, the creator of capital and technology.[3] Productive forces also include the 'means of production', that is, 'physical capital' (tools, equipment, machinery, etc.), which are, in the final analysis, products of human labour. Production in all societies must be sustained but development requires 'expanded reproduction', that is, production at ever-higher levels. Since such expanded reproduction implies not only growth of the output, but also a process of distribution and a corresponding pattern of use of products, Marx referred to 'social reproduction', which includes distribution and use of products.

The 'engine' of economic development is the progress of 'productive forces', that is, improvement (with experience, skills, education, culture) of the quality and performance of the labour force, and introduction of better techniques, that is, new technologies. But the development of productive forces, without which a society cannot develop, can proceed rapidly or slowly, or can even be retarded, depending on the prevailing pattern of the 'social relations of production'. The latter involve 'property relations', namely, the pattern of ownership over the main 'means of production' (including land and 'physical capital'), and the 'division of labour' within society or internationally, that is, the pattern of occupations, trades, activities and specialization, and, last but not the least, 'distribution relations'. Marx considered the actual 'social relations of production' with concomitant development of 'productive forces' as the 'economic base' of society, on which a kind of political, institutional, legal, moral, religious and cultural 'superstructure' is built. Social development must involve both the 'economic base' and the 'superstructure', which are in 'dialectical' interaction with each other.

Contrary to the classical view, Marx stressed the contradictory nature of the development process and, like Hegel, considered these contradictions as factors promoting development. He perceived the process of development as involving both evolution and revolution, with gradual changes in quantity leading to sudden qualitative transformations, and as a process not only creating new contradictions, but also being pushed forward by them. Such contradictions regularly appeared, according to Marx, in the historical development of human societies, between their evolving productive forces and the social relations of production at the beginning, promoting but later hindering the growth of the latter. Since this manifests itself socially in 'class struggle', and politically in the struggle between the *ancien régime* and revolutionary forces of the oppressed, it finally leads to revolutionary change, that is, qualitative transformation of the so-called 'social formation'.[4] The 'economic base' in a 'mode of production' involves certain social relations of production besides the forces of production, while its 'superstructure' involves a corresponding power structure with a ruling class.[5]

Marx distinguished capitalism as a system based on 'economic coercion', that is, upon the economic need of otherwise free workers to perform wage labour for capitalists, in contrast to all pre-capitalist class societies, in which the ruling classes used non-economic force to appropriate the surplus. Nevertheless, he and his followers envisaged and recommended non-economic violence, instead of 'countervailing economic power', as the only way of changing the system. In other words, while stressing the ability of capitalism to operate without non-economic force as its distinctive feature versus other socio-economic systems, Marx assumed force to be necessary for transitions. For Marx, force was a precondition not only for the emergence of this system (including 'primitive' or 'primary' capital accumulation, depriving producers of their own means of production, mainly land) in the pioneering capitalist economies, but also for its spread to other parts of the world (through colonialism) and for its replacement by a new system, namely, 'socialism'.

The role of non-economic force was incorporated in the Marxian concept of 'imperialist capitalism', particularly Lenin's theory of imperialism as the final stage of capitalism. Lenin did not share the views of some other Marxists who interpreted imperialism and colonialism as simply a policy of aggressive violence leading to colonial wars and military occupation of foreign territories. He nevertheless distinguished the 'imperialist', monopoly-capitalist stage, including 'territorial division among imperialist states of the world' from those of 'classical capitalism'. At the same time, and in contradiction with the above, Lenin's theory placed capital exports at the centre of the modern system of international capitalism.

The so-called 'Marxist–Leninist' school not only remained stuck with some original inconsistencies of Marxian theory, but also moved towards dogmatic oversimplifications cut off from reality. Foreign capital, particularly that of transnational corporations, was considered by it as an 'evil' to be exorcized, while the modern world system of market economies was deemed to be the manifestation of 'imperialist interests' and domination. Consequently, its representatives (like some radical nationalist scholars) interpreted the spread of capitalism – by means of foreign penetration into less developed countries – as only negative, harmful and development-hindering. In contrast, a sort of 'orthodox Marxism' overemphasized capitalism's positive role in developing the economies concerned, and considered imperialism to be the 'pioneer of capitalism'. Marxian theory, with its holistic and critical approach, has focused the investigation of social (and world) developments on inherent contradictions, which ensured progress, and on unequal relations (even if formally equal) among different classes or nations.

### Neoclassical Economics

Neoclassical economics also has its roots (like Marxian economic theory) in classical economics; it followed and reinforced the liberal principles of the latter, while rejecting its labour theory of value, replacing it with the concept of 'utility' and marginal productivity determining factor prices and incomes. Neoclassical economics combined the classical, production-oriented, cost and supply-determining 'objective' approach to market price formation, with the subjective, consumption-oriented, consumer needs and demand-determining approach.

Since its birth (more than a century ago), neoclassical economic theory has grown to include a great many, often very diverse, theoretical conceptions and methods. Owing to its great diversity, and the rise of newer branches or 'schools' of neoclassical economics, it is very difficult, if not impossible, to describe it as a homogenous 'body' with common features. Even those characteristics attributed to it (particularly in standard economics textbooks), as the most common and typical, seem to have been questioned by other neoclassical economists.

Neoclassical economics turned attention to the operations rather than the development of the market economy, to micro and macroeconomic phenomena and processes, that is, to pragmatic investigation of the market economy, demand and supply determinants, consumers' and firms' behaviour, entrepreneurial choices, allocative efficiency, etc. It has also enriched the literature on development since its beginnings. Along with its numerous developments in analysis and methodology (which can hardly be neglected by development economics), it has also elaborated a number of new theses, approaches or models relevant to development economics. Among others, these include the reformulated production function with the assumption of unlimited substitution between labour and capital; related new 'models' of economic growth; new price and income theories (Marshall, Böhm–Bawerk *et al.*); the conception of 'general equilibrium' as distinguished from partial equilibrium (Walras); the concept and method of 'opportunity costs' as a new approach to making choices between different products or industries, or even development alternatives in general; new thoughts on consumer attitudes, market segmentation, product differentiation, 'conspicuous consumption', 'inferior' and 'superior goods'; new theses about monopoly and market imperfections (Marshall, Chamberlin, Robinson); new approaches to technological progress, choice of technology; introduction of the time factor into economic analysis (Marshall); new concepts on the 'basis' of international trade and specialization (for example, the Heckscher–Ohlin theorem); the thesis about the 'natural' direction of international capital flows, namely, from capital-rich (more advanced) to capital-poor (less developed) countries; the idea of international equalization of factor costs, incomes and productivities (thus also of development levels) assumed to follow from internationally rational and mutually beneficial specialization or from free international factor mobility, that is, under some desirable conditions; and so on.

Neoclassical economics emphasizes the role of factor endowments and the related marginal productivity of each factor of production in the development or growth of the economy. Accordingly, the level of economic development of a country and its rate of growth depend not only on its natural resources, available labour and accumulated capital, that is, on factor endowments and the marginal productivity of these factors, but also on changes in the efficiency of these factors of production, determined by technological development, education, income distribution, social security, etc.

Most representatives of neoclassical economics share the belief that the market economy of capitalism is the best possible system and, thus, the final stage of historical development, which may, at most, be further improved by welfare measures or by eliminating 'market imperfections'. The previous historical process of development, leading to the rise of such a system, is mostly regarded as a unilinear one, involving the same stages or systems for all countries, which started with savage society and passed the stage of primitive agricultural systems to a combination of agriculture and handicraft production, and, finally, to the stage of modern factories, extensive trade and services in a capitalistic market economy.

Neoclassical economics has become the core component of what is misleadingly called 'mainstream economics', embodied in standard textbooks and taught all over the world nowadays. On the one hand, it has extended the scope of development issues and economic analysis to a much larger area with far deeper detail than any other stream of economics, and has also produced a number of refined analytical methods, sophisticated mathematical apparatuses, and a great variety of theoretical conceptions complementing or correcting one another. On the other hand, it has mostly become identified with its conventional textbook variant applying a narrow economistic approach, a short time horizon, a one-sided or fragmented viewpoint and overformalized mathematical expressions. It seems to get imprisoned in such oversimplified premises due to its perception of the capitalist market economy as an ideal system also operating harmoniously in reality. Ironically, realizing the gap between theory and reality, many 'students' of neoclassical economics have produced sharper critiques of prevailing reality than some of the radicals attacking neoclassical theory.

### The Historical School and Institutionalism

Besides neoclassical and Marxian theory, some other theoretical streams, such as the German 'Historical School' and 'institutionalism', have raised issues relating to development and economic systems in the nineteenth and early twentieth centuries, as still relevant to the economics of development and comparative systems today. They seem to be precedents of not only the later 'stage theories' (Aron, Rostow) and later variants of institutionalism (for example, Galbraith) or the 'new institutionalism' (Coase), but also of the concepts of development sociology (since Weber and Boeke), and some post-World War II theories of development and underdevelopment.

Both earlier and later branches of the German 'Historical School' attacked the presumptions behind classical and neoclassical economics, which abstracted from the non-economic motivations of human beings as well as from non-economic factors in economic development, and led to the idea of definable 'laws' governing social activities and the development of nations.

The American school of institutionalism expressed very similar views reflecting the historical conditions of a country (in this case, the United States) at the time of its increased efforts to catch up with the most developed nations, which involved a greater role for the state than after a successful 'take-off'. The most famous representative of this school, Thorstein Veblen, conceived of the historical development of society as basically involving institutions that undergo changes because people adjust to ever-changing conditions. However, since current institutions are products of the past, they can never fully meet the requirements of the present.

### Keynesian Economics

For John Maynard Keynes and his followers, it became obvious – in light of regular crises, particularly the Great Depression of 1929 – that the operations of the market economy are not as smooth and harmonious as assumed in abstract, idealized models. Instead, they 'normally' involved cycles with varying levels of disequilibria (or 'imperfect equilibria'). The socio-political consequences of deep crises or recessions – with large-scale unemployment, social distress and international conflicts in trade and finance, paving the way for fascism or communism and leading to world war – may endanger the very survival of this system.

The 'Keynesian revolution' implied a radical break with some fundamental premises and assumptions of both classical and neoclassical paradigms, rather than with their theoretical principles. While questioning the very premises and assumptions behind conventional classical and neoclassical theories, Keynesian theory offered a new approach to the relationship between economic development and equilibrium. It gave up the conventional assumption about such an interaction in all the partial markets between demand and supply, with a perfectly flexible price, as always, ensuring 'perfect equilibrium', and rejected the idea that in factor markets, both demand and supply depend on the same, namely the price, which flexibly responds to any changes in demand or supply. With regard to international trade, it postulated a cause–effect relation between changes in exports and national income, as well as between national income and imports (formulated in the concepts of export multiplier and marginal import propensity). It also pointed to the cyclical nature of the market economy (whether national or international) if not regulated by indirect interventions; to the consequences of 'demand constraints' on investment, national income and employment; to the role of psychological factors, expectations and speculation on the operation and development of the economy; to the role of money, monetary and fiscal policy in the development process; and to required activity by the state in the economy.

Large-scale unemployment is undesirable not only economically, because it reduces aggregate economic performance and the growth rate, but also socially, for depriving many people of their means of existence, and politically, for causing social unrest and fuelling radical political forces. The Keynesian conclusion is that governments must act to overcome it. In other words, the market economy cannot be left to operate spontaneously because its 'invisible hand' cannot ensure either maximum economic efficiency or social justice and equity.

It was Keynes's conviction that the state must intervene (but not by means of commands and direct instructions, as in 'socialist planned economies') and regulate – by counter-cyclical measures, including various monetary and, particularly, fiscal policies – the operation of the market economy. The Keynesian 'recipe' for indirect government interventions in the market economy is based on a consideration of the demand constraints caused by over-saving and liquidity preference, that is, the higher propensity of richer people to save and/or refrain from spending their incomes on consumption or investments. Consequently, the government should directly or indirectly encourage investment and spending, by measures such as fiscal policy, for example, financing from the central budget, public works, welfare programmes (for education, public health, social security, etc.) or other 'unproductive' (including military) expenditures, and also purchases from or support (for example, research and training) for private companies, and/or redistributing incomes through progressive taxation in favour of poorer people with lower savings propensity. All such measures should lead to increased effective demand, including monetary policy measures, for example, influencing the rate of interest to decline, thereby making money 'cheaper' and encouraging investors to borrow, while increasing the propensity to consume. Though such fiscal and monetary policies necessarily involve inflationary budget deficits and credit creation, the resulting increase in national income is supposed to cause growth in revenues, thereby eliminating the earlier debt incurred. As long as this occurs, inflation may not only support economic growth (in demand-constrained economies), but can also be temporary and kept within limits.

It follows that the growth of national income depends, on the one hand, on how much income is generated by production (for domestic and foreign markets) and investment, both induced by the propensity to consume, while investment is determined by the marginal efficiency of capital, and by how much of the income is absorbed by savings (depending on the level of income and influenced by the rate of interest) and imports. In the growth models of the Keynesian school, development of the economy basically depends on investment rates and the capital–output ratio. In case of large-scale unemployment, government spending is needed to overcome the constraints manifested in insufficient aggregate demand.

In view of the disequilibria and cyclical fluctuations of the contemporary world economy with regular oversupply and demand shortages, the Keynesian 'recipe' of counter-cyclical economic policies and state interventions generating additional demand with public expenditure and income redistribution in favour of the poor, with lower savings propensity, aimed at increasing employment and income levels, may also appear internationally relevant. Undoubtedly, a redistribution of world income or income increases in favour of poor nations, and the resulting increase in effective demand, would, *ceteris paribus*, expand world trade such that the economies of rich developed countries would also benefit from it.

International application of the Keynesian 'recipe' would require the operation, at the world level, of a welfare state, which does not yet exist. Besides the difficulties due to the absence of such a world state in implementing a demand-generating economic policy with income redistribution and public expenditure, Keynesian theory has also been criticized for reliance on aggregate macroeconomic indicators and psychological variables, for example, the propensity to import or the 'marginal efficiency of capital' and various expectations, which either blur important differences within society or cannot be properly measured and quantified. The most important criticism against Keynesianism or, more precisely, against its general application, is that it was elaborated for and reflects the problems of demand-constrained economies, and thus, can hardly be relevant to (less developed) economies in a 'Hayek situation' (where resource constraints increase competition for available factors of production) or 'shortage economies' (which suffer a regular supply constraint).

While the neoclassical theories, assuming more or less harmonious operation of the market economy, paid more attention to microeconomic phenomena, the Keynesian school shifted attention (back) to macro and international economics that involved some basic development economics issues. It also questioned illusions about 'laissez-faire' economics and rejected 'pseudo-mathematical methods', pointing instead to the complexity of reality. It predicted the 'euthanasia of the rentier' and called for reforms to reduce 'large income disparities'.

This short survey of the main schools of economics not only demonstrates their concern for development issues, but also highlights some important differences among them, including over:

- approach – whether economistic or interdisciplinary, whether 'stock', 'flow' or 'relation';
- nature of 'development' – whether economic or socio-political, harmonious or conflict-generating, unilinear or specific, endless or limited, self-sustaining or state-promoted;
- judgement of basic sources, most decisive factors and motive forces of development – which factor of production, activity or industry, what interests advance it;
- appraisal of the role of market spontaneity and/or state interventions, and the socio-political and institutional (system-related) factors in the development process;
- assessment of the prospects and results of development – whether accompanied by equality and justice or inequality and dominance, perhaps exploitation; whether bringing about benefits for all or only for some – classes or nations; and whether involving ever-lasting progress or leading to standstill or decay, break and transformation;

- views on contemporary and previous economic systems or 'stages' of economic development;
- conception of the relationship between the development process and equilibrium or disequilibrium in the economy;
- consideration of international conditions and effects of development;
- concepts of the world economy – harmonious or disequalizing operations, equilibrium mechanisms or aggravating disequilibria, mutually beneficial trade or unequal exchange, the 'laws' of specialization and international division of labour, the 'natural' direction of international resource flows, particularly capital exports and their expected results; and so on.

The list of issues identified in the above survey of the development theories of various schools of economics is, of course, far from comprehensive. The survey can also be extended to other schools, particularly those arising after World War II, or more recent ones. Nevertheless, the above survey seems sufficient to show that the problems of development were, indeed, part of economic theories (and the social sciences in general) from the outset, even before the appearance of 'development economics'.

Thus, what happened after World War II was only the separation (rather than the birth) of 'development economics' from the body of economics in general. Such a separation seems to reflect fairly well both an aversion towards 'mainstream' economics (or, at least, doubts about its applicability to underdeveloped countries) and the ideological effects of the Cold War. Economists dealing with the development problems of the less developed countries realized the irrelevance of many basic assumptions and premises behind many of the policies recommended by 'mainstream' economics in the west, while also rejecting the official 'Marxism–Leninism' of the Soviet bloc. The Afro-Asian and non-aligned movements, plus other efforts in the 'South' to remain outside the east–west conflict, reinforced this aversion to both western and eastern 'mainstreams'.

**Notes**

1 For a more detailed survey of the history of economic theories related to both development and international economics, see Szentes (2002).

2 For example, whether late-comer, less developed nations can and should follow the example of the more advanced, industrially developed countries (in a unilinear process of development); how penetration by more developed economic powers such as colonizers or foreign capital may promote development and modernization, while also subordinating the economy and exploiting the labour force of less developed countries; how market competition, even under conditions of equivalent exchange, by forcing technological innovations, leads to monopolization; what preconditions are needed for a dynamic equilibrium in the (national or world) economy, and why, in the absence of the latter, the market economy operates in a cyclical way; etc.

3 Contrary to the logic of Marx's conception of social reproduction and the primary role of human labour in it, particularly his stress on the quality of labour, in the Marxist literature, the source of new value, and thus of surplus too, has only been identified with labour performed in branches of material production, including weapons, narcotic drugs, unhealthy or environment-destroying products. On the other hand, even labour performed in important services, necessary for material production

itself or for the allocation and distribution of products, etc., has been characterized as a (secondary) source of profits, without creating new value.

The working class, or 'proletariat', which is supposed to create all value and be exploited by the capitalists, has mostly been identified with 'blue-collar workers' (that is, a nineteenth-century type of industrial working class). In sharp contradiction to the Marxian emphasis on reproduction of the human labour force (both its physical and intellectual qualities) as an organic and decisive part of the social process of reproduction, the role played in raising, caring and educating the new labour force – by mothers, physicians, nurses, teachers, scholars, etc. – has been deemed 'unproductive labour'. Such misconceptions made the Marxian view on the 'working class' quite anachronistic by the early twenty-first century.

4 The Marxian theory on social systems (social formations) incorporates a unilinear concept of development and a determinist perspective of history. According to this theory, human societies necessarily develop through the same stages as different 'social formations' (determined by their 'mode of production'). The Marxian thesis about the last 'stage' of social development – which was obviously a politically motivated, ideological vision about a future, alternative system – involved many utopian elements. This is one reason why the so-called 'existing socialism' in the former 'socialist' countries was linked, by public opinion, with the Marxian vision, despite some obvious contradictions between the two. 'Marxism–Leninism', the official ideology in these countries, was thus used to legitimize the system, to provide apologetic justification for their changing policies. Marx's vision about a future ideal society obviously belonged to the world of utopian thoughts and dreams, but has been used as a misleading ideology by those in power in 'socialist' countries. His predictions concerning the future of capitalism, with ever-sharpening contradictions and the eruption of a world revolution of the proletariat of all countries, have proved totally wrong. Since his time, capitalism has changed a lot (at least in the advanced countries), and revolutions (in less developed countries) aiming for a new, post-capitalist system have all failed. Although Marx addressed his theory to the working classes, he did not take into account how 'countervailing forces' (and not only revolutionary forces) would arise as capitalism advanced.

5 Strangely, Marx exempted future, post-capitalist society, as envisaged by him, as devoid of contradiction. Unlike all other historical social formations, his 'communist society' was supposed to operate without contradictions between social relations and productive forces, without 'class struggle', even classes, and state power. Thus, unlike the classical economists, who had some concerns about the limits of development and a 'stationary state', Marx was optimistic about the future of humankind.

The heavy emphasis by Marx on ownership provided an excellent opportunity for communist regimes to interpret the 'transition from capitalism to socialism' as a change in ownership structure leading to the predominance of state ownership. The same oversimplification appears in the widespread interpretation of systemic change in former 'socialist' countries today, the so-called 'transition from socialism to capitalism' as primarily and decisively determined by privatization.

Such misconceptions made the Marxian view on the 'working class' quite anachronistic by the early twenty-first century, hindering full recognition of substantial changes in social structure, class behaviour and the actual composition of the 'working class' in advanced market economies. They also strongly influenced, or were used to legitimize, the income and budget policies of the then 'socialist' countries, the 'egalitarian' wage system, budget expenditure and investment priorities.

Questions related to such misconceptions – for example, who are 'productive' in society?; whose work creates 'new value'?; how are incomes distributed?; which branches of the economy and what kinds of activities contribute directly to the growth of national income?; etc.– all belong to the sphere of development theory and policy as well.

#### References

Aron, Raymond (1962), *Dix-huit lecons sur la société industrielle* (Paris: Gallimard).
Boeke, Julius Herman (1953), *Economics and Economic Policy of Dual Societies* (New York: Institute of Pacific Relations).
Böhm–Bawerk, Eugen von (1902), *Capital und Capitalzins* (Insbruck: Wagner).
Chamberlin, Edward H. (1947), *The Theory of Monopolistic Competition* (Cambridge: Harvard University Press).
Clark, Colin (1957), *Conditions of Economic Progress* (London: Macmillan).
Coase, Ronald H. (1984), 'The New Institutional Economics', *Journal of Institutional and Theoretical Economics*, 140: 229–31.
Galbraith, John Kenneth (1952), *American Capitalism: The Concept of Countervailing Power* (London: Hamish Hamilton).
——— (1964), *Economic Development* (Boston: Boston University Press).
Hayek, Friedrich A. (1931), *Prices and Production* (London: Routledge).
———, ed. (1935), *Collectivist Economic Planning* (London: Routledge).
Heckscher, Eli F. (1919), 'The Effects of Foreign Trade on the Distribution of Income', *Economis Tidskrift*, 21.
Hegel, Georg W.F. (1961), *Vorlesungen über die Philosophie der Geschichte* (Stuttgart).
Keynes, John Maynard (1936), *The General Theory of Employment, Interest and Money* (London: Macmillan).
Lenin, Vladimir Ilyich (1948), *Imperialism: The Highest Stage of Capitalism* (London: Lawrence and Wishart).
Marshall, Alfred (1930), *Principles of Economics*, 8th edition (London: Macmillan).
Marx, Karl (1965), *Capital*, Vol. I, (Moscow: Progress Publishers).
——— (1966), *Capital*, Vol. II (Moscow: Progress Publishers).
——— (1967), *Capital*, Vol. III (Moscow: Progress Publishers).
Ohlin, Bertil G. (1933), *Interregional and International Trade* (Cambridge, Massachusetts: Harvard University Press).
Quesnay, Francois (1888), *Oeuvres économiques et philosophiques de Francois Quesnay* (Paris).
Ricardo, David (1821), *Principles of Political Economy and Taxation* (London: John Murray).
Robinson, Joan (1966), *Economic Philosophy* (New York: Pelican).
Rostow, Walt W. (1960), *The Stages of Economic Growth: A Non-Communist Manifesto* (Cambridge: Cambridge University Press).
Smith, Adam (1776), *An Inquiry into the Nature and Causes of the Wealth of Nations* (Edinburgh: MacCulloch).
Szentes, Tamás (2002), *World Economics I: Comparative Theories and Methods of International and Development Economics* (Budapest: Akadémiai Kiadó).
——— (2003), *World Economics II: The Political Economy of Development, Globalization and System Transformation* (Budapest: Akadémiai Kiadó).
Veblen, Thorstein (1957), *The Theory of the Leisure Class* (New York: Viking Press).
Walras, Leon (1910), *Éléments d'économie politique pure* (Lausanne: F. Rouge).
Warren, Bill (1980), *Imperialism: Pioneer of Capitalism* (London: New Left Books).
Weber, Max (1983), *The Protestant Ethic and the Spirit of Capitalism* (London: Allen and Unwin).

# Index

Abramowitz, Moses, 24
*Academia dei Pugni*, 24, 32, 35
Adelson, Candace, 28
Albertini, Rudolph von, 28
*Allegory of Good and Bad Government*, 40
American Economic Association, 49, 61
Amsden, Alice, 76, 125
*Anti-Physiocrat*, 59
Aoki, Masahiko, 76
Arida, Persio, 81
Aristotle, 4
Aron, Raymond, 152
Arrow, Kenneth, 76
Arthur, Brian, 9
Ashley, William, 2
Austrian School of Economics, 52

Bacon, Francis, xii, 5, 10
Bacon, Roger, 5
bad trade, 13
balance of trade, 4
Baran, Paul, 99, 138, 141
Barbon, Nicholas, 1
Barro, Robert J., 17, 92–93
*Bau und Leben der Sozialen Korper*, ix
Beccaria, Cesare, 24–26, 31–33, 35, 37–41, 49
Becher, Johann Joachim, 54
Beckmann, Johann, 57, 58
*Bemerkungen uber die osterreichische Staatso-konomie (Remarks on the economy of the state of Austria)*, 55
Berch, Anders, 7, 49
Bhagwati, Jagdish N., 117, 119
*Bibliografie der Kameralwissenschaften*, 57
Bielschowsky, Ricardo, 132
Birck, xviii
Birdsall, Nancy, 94
Bismarck, xv, 64
Bleaney, Michael, 140
Boeke, Julius Herman, 152

Böhm–Bawerk, Eugen von, 151
Botero, Giovanni, xii, xvii, 7, 13, 28–31, 39, 58, 61
Braudel, Fernand, 1
Brenner, Robert, 74, 77, 139
Brentano, Lujo, 61
Bretton Woods institutions, 12, 142
*Breve Trattato*, x, 29, 40
Brown, Judith, 28
Browne, Thomas, 4
Bruni, Luigino, 36
Bruton, Henry J., 135
Buchanan, James, xii, xviii
Bulmer–Thomas, Victor, 130
Burkhardt, Jacob, 39
Bush, George, viii
*Business Week*, 17

Calabria, Antonio, 29
Calvino, Italo, 39, 41
Cameralism, Germany, 2, 11, 49
Cameralist Economic Policy, 53–57
Campanella, Tommaso, 7, 39
capitalism
    definition of, 69–70
    dynamic economic system, 71
    Marxist approach to, 69–70, 73
    neoclassical definition of, 70
capital–labour ratio, 83, 85, 87
Capra, Carlo, 32–33, 36, 38
Cardoso, Fernando Henrique, 137
Carey, Henry, 49
Carey, Mathew, xiii, 2, 49, 60
Carli, Gian Rinaldo, 25
Carpenter, Kenneth, 55, 58
Cary, John, 13
Chamberlin, Edward H., 151
Chang, Ha-Joon, 100, 102
Chattopadhyay, Paresh, 140
Child, Josuah, 7, 19
Cipolla, Carlo M., 24

civil society, 35–36
Classical Development Theory, 88–92
Classical Economics, 146–48
classical individualism, 39
Clemence, Richard V., 49
Clement, Pierre, 13
Coase, Ronald H., 152
Colbert, Jean–Baptiste, 6–7, 13, 37
Cole, Charles Woolsey, 13
Colmeiro, Manuel, 3
commodity competition, 3
common good, synergic effects of, 5
*Communist Manifesto*, 62
communitarianism, 39
consumption, Duesenberry's theory of, 104
Crosby, Alfred W., 34
cultural continuity, and political economy of
    Italy, 39–41
Cunningham, W., 65
Custodi, Pietro, 32

da Vinci, 1
Daastøl, Arno, xxi, 4–5
Darnton, Robert, 32
*Das Adam Smith Problem*, 14
Davenant, Charles, 11
*De magnalibus urbis mediolani*, ix
de Santis, 3
Decker, Mathew, 12
Defoe, Daniel, 6, 16, 27
Delft, economic development in, 8
*Della Moneta (On Money)*, 31
*demand–pull* phenomenon, 10
dependency theory, xix
    critiques of, 139–41
    development of, 128
    intellectual sources and features, 137–39
    monopoly capital, 140–41
    nationalism, 141
    structuralism and, 139–40
*Der moderne Kapitalismus*, 50
*Der Teutsche Furstenstaat (The German Princi-
    pality)*, 53
*Destructive Influence of the Tariff upon Manu-
    facture and Commerce*, 14
development
    in history of economics, 146–56
    theories and policies of, 24–41
development economics
    activity-specific growth, 10–13
    capitalist transformation and, 69–79
    context-specific growth, 10–13
    dependency theory and, xix, 128, 137–41
    descriptive tradition, ix–x
    early contributions of, 99–126
    esoteric and exoteric theory, viii
    German economics as, xvii, 48–66

history of, vii–xxi, 146–56
in real world and theory, 125–26
international trade in, xix, 99–126
Italian tradition, 24–41
mercantilism and, xiii, xvi, 1–19
modern growth theory and, xviii, 81–95
neoclassical economics of, 99, 150–52
pioneers of, 81–95
prescriptive tradition, x
studies on, vii–xxi
*see also*, economics
developmental state, mercantilist economic
    policies of, 18–19
*Dialogues on the Corn Table*, 37
Diderot, Denis, 31
Dikshoorn, C., 34
diminishing returns to capital, 82–85
*Discourse on the Utility of Science and the
    Arts*, 34
Djiksterhuis, E.J., 34
Dobb, Maurice, 72, 74–75
double-entry book-keeping, 34
Drechsler, Wolfgang, 52
Duhring, Eugen, 49–50
Dutt, Amitava K., xix, 125
dynamic imperfect competition, 4

East Asian miracle, xvi
economic crisis in Argentina, 3
economic development
    activity-specific, 9
    manufactures/manufacturing and, 9, 37–
        39
    maxims of, 38
    protectionism and, 37–39
    synergic process, 9
economic growth, mechanics of, 87
economic scholasticism, xviii
economic tradition in Italy, xvii
economics
    classical economics, 146–48
    development in history of, xiv, 146–56
    econo-mystification and political economy
        of Italy, 34–35
    historical school and institutionalism, 152–
        53
    Italian tradition of political economy and,
        24–41
    Keynesian economics, 153–54
    knowledge and production-based canon of,
        xx
    Marxian economics, 148–50
    neoclassical economics, 150–52
    pluralism, xi
    types of, ix, 146–54
    *see also*, development economics
Ekelund, Robert B., 1–4

*Elements of Commerce*, 38
*Elements of Political Economy*, 32
Elizabeth, Queen, 10, 19, 27
Ely, Richard, 61
Enlightenment, Theories and Policies of Development in, 24–41
*Essay on Innovations*, 5

*Factories and Manufacturers*, 59
Fanfani, Amintore, 5–6
Fei, John, 91
Ferrara, Francesco, 33
feudalism, 72, 75
Filangieri, Gaetano, 32
*Financial Times*, 17
Fine, Ben, 140
FitzGerald, Edmund V.K., 132
Forbonnais, Francois Veron de, 38
Ford, Henry, 4
foreign direct investment, 104
*Foreign Policy*, 17
Foxwell, H.S., 62
Franci, Sebastiano, 24, 26
Frank, Andre Gunder, 137, 139
free trade, concept of, viii, 14, 37–38, 102, 114, 119
Frisi, Paolo, 35
*Furstenspiegel*, x, 50
Furtado, Celso, 132

Galbraith, John Kenneth, xiv, 152
Galiani, Ferdinando, 9, 25, 31–34, 36–37, 40, 61–62
Galileo, 1
Gates, Bill, 4
Gay, Edwin, 63
Gee, Joshua, 12
Genovesi, Antonio, 7, 25, 27, 31–36, 39, 41, 58
German economics, xvii, 5
    academic economics and specialization, 57–59
    as development economics, 48–66
    Cameralist economic policy, 53–54
    characteristics of, 50–52
    from Veit von Seckendorff to Wilhelm von Hornigk, 53–57
    historical schools of, 59–62
    in eighteenth century, 57–59
    in nineteenth and twentieth centuries, 59–62
    Morgenthau Plan and, 65–66
    nine points of economic policy of Hornigk, 55–57
    social problem, 62–65
    tradition, 50–52, 65–66

*Verein fur Sozialpolitik* and, 62–65
German Historical School, 61–63, 152
Gilbert, Allan H., 29
Goldhwaite, Richard A., 28
good governance, 77–79
good trade, 13
Goyeneche, Pedro Francisco, 7
Grafton, 5
Graham, Frank, xiii, 14
Grand Ducal Tuscany case, 27
Great Depression, 130, 153
*Greatness of Cities*, xii
Groenewegen, Peter, 32–34
growth and income distribution, theory of, 101
growth theory
    assessment, 92–95
    development and, 88–92
    endogenous growth model, 84–86
    exogenous growth model, 82
    old and new, 82–88
    pioneers of development economics and, 81–95

Haberler, Gottfried, 108, 112–13, 115, 118, 120–21
Habermas, Jurgen, 41
Hagen, Everett E., 113, 118–19
Hamilton, Alexander, 2, 15, 102, 118
Hamilton, Earl, 7
Harvard Business School, 63
*Hausvaterliteratur*, 50
Heckscher, Eli Filip, 2, 41, 102
Heckscher–Ohlin theory, 112, 119–20
Hegel, Georg W.F., 149
Henry VII (King), xiii, xvi, 16, 18–19, 27
Herder, Johann Gottfried von, 58
high-technology industries, 75–76
Hildebrand, Bruno, 61
Hilferding, Rudolf, 140
Hilton, Rodney H., 72
Hintze, Otto, 41
Hirschman, Albert, xiv, 54, 106–07, 130
*History of Economic Analysis*, 25
Hobbes, ix
Hoover, Herbert, 65–66
Hörnigk, Philipp Wilhelm von, 53–55
Huerta, Robert D., 8
Huet, Pierre Daniel, 7
human capital, vii, 35–36
Hume, David, xi, 9, 33
Humpert, Wolfgang, 57

*Il Caffe*, 24, 32, 35–36, 38
Ilardi, Vincent, 28
import-substituting industrialization (ISI), 128–31
Industrial Revolution, 1–2

Ingram, John Kells, 13
*Inquiry into the Principles of Political Economy*, x
institutionalism, issue of, 152
International Monetary Fund (IMF), xv
international trade
    development theory contributions to, 124–26
    in early development economics, 99–126
    theory of, 100, 108
    uneven international development and, 107–11
*Invisible Cities*, 39
invisible hand, concept of, xi
Italy
    from core to semi-periphery, 26–28
    political economy of, 24–41

Janssen, Theodore, 13
Jerome, St., 4
Jomo, K.S., vii
Jones, L.E., 87
Justi, Johann Heinrich Gottlob von, 9, 19, 52, 54, 57–59

Kaldor, x, 88
Kalecki, Michal, 138, 140
Kaplan, Steven L., 32–34, 38
*Kathedersozialisten* (Socialists of the Professional Chair), 62–63
Kauder, Emil, 32
Kay, Cristobal, 132
Keynes, John Maynard, 48, 138, 140, 153–55
Keynesian economics, 153–55
Khan, Mushtaq Husain, xvii, 69, 74, 76–78
Kim, Hyung-Ki, 76
King, Charles, 13–15
Klang, Daniel M., 41
Knies, Karl, 61
knowledge-intensive services, xv
Koyre, Alexandre, 5
Kristeller, Paul Oskar, 39
Krugman, Paul, xviii, 14, 34, 81, 92

*L'Encyclopedie*, 33
labour allocation, Lewis Model of, 114–15
labour supply, elasticity of, 82
Laclau, Ernesto, 139
Laffemas, Barthelemy, 13
Lal, Deepak, 125
Lall, Sanjaya, 139
Larrain, Jorge, 132
Laspeyres, Etienne, xvi, 6
Latin American structuralism, rise and decline of, xix, 128–43
Latini, Brunetto, 5
Lee, J., 92–93

Leeuwenhoek, Antoni van, 8
Leibniz, Gottfried Wilhelm von, 11, 19, 51–54, 61, 63
*Leviathan*, ix
Lewis, W. Arthur, xviii–xix, 81, 89–91, 105–06, 118, 123
Lincoln, Abraham, 66
List, Friedrich, x, xii, xiv, xvi, xviii–xix, xxi, 9–10, 13–14, 27, 31, 49, 60–61, 65–66, 102, 118
Litchfield, R. Burr, 28
Little, Ian, 135
Lluch, Ernest, 3
Locke, John, 3, 52
long-distance trade, growth of, 72–73
Lorenzetti, Ambrogio, 40
Louis XIV, 13
low-technology industries, 75–76
Lucas, Robert E., 87–88, 125
*Luxury and Capitalism*, 8

Machiavelli, 1, 5, 29
Magnusson, Lars, 2–3, 17, 30, 37
Malanima, Paolo, 27–28
Malynes, 3
Mandevilli, Bernard de, 41
Manilesco, 119
Mankiw, Greg, 93
Manuelli, R.E., 87
manufactures
    American system of, xviii
    economic development and, 37–39
Marini, Ruy Mauro, 137
Marino, John A., 40
market economies, 71–73
markets, liberalization of, 73
Marshall, Alfred, viii, xii, 123, 151
Marshall, George, xiv, 66
Marshall Plan, 66
Marx, Karl, xv, 49–50, 52, 70, 73–74, 138, 148–50
Marxian economics, 148–50
Marxism, 71, 73
Mazzotti, Massimo, 34
McCray, Patrick W., 28, 30
Medici Grand Dukes, case of, 26–28
*Meditations on Political Economy*, 35
Meier, Gerald M., 108, 119, 123
Menger, Karl, 52, 64
mercantilism
    as national benchmarking, 6–10
    debate on, 1–4
    destruction, 13–16
    dynamics and institutions, 10–13
    economic development and, xiii, xvi, 1–19
    economic policies, 18–19
    in Spain and Dutch Republic, 6–10

mercantilist dynamics and institutions, 10–13

Midas fallacy approach to, 1, 3

monetarists–productionists debate on, 3

nation-building and, 12

neoclassical economics and, 10–11

passage point for development, 16–19

renaissance wealth creation and, 4–6

rent-seeking approach, 3

state-building and, 3, 12

US economy and, 2

Mercier, Louis Sebastien, 33

Messbarger, Rebecca, 24

*Mesta* (organization of sheep farmers), 6

Meyen, Johan Jacob, 10, 58

Midas fallacy practice, 1, 3

Mill, John Stuart, xv, 64–65, 101

Miller, Judith A., 33

Minard, Philippe, 38

Misselden, Edward, 3

Mitchell, Wesley Claire, ix

Mizuta, Hiroshi, 49

Mola, Luca, 28

monoculture, issue of, 9

Montesquieu, 29

Morelli, Roberta, 28

Morgenthau, Henry, 65

Morgenthau Plan, xvii, 65–66

Mueller, Reinhold C., 28

Mun, Thomas, 13

Murfin, Andy, 140

Murphy, Kevin, 81, 92

Myint, Hla, 100, 121–22

Myrdal, Gunnar, xiv, xix, 17, 31, 99, 108–12, 118, 120, 126

*National System of Political Economy*, x, 102

Nelson, ix

neoclassical economics, 10–11, 150–52

*New Atlantis*, 5

New Institutional Economics, 73

Nietzsche, Friedrich, vii–viii, 32, 51–52, 62

Noether, Emiliana P., 32

normal profit, 3

North, Douglass, 73

Nurkse, Ragnar, xviii–xix, 81, 88, 90, 92, 103–05, 118

Ohlin, Bertil, 102

Okuno–Fujiwara, Masahiro, 76

Olson, Mancur, 73

Olson, Richard, 34

*On Crimes and Punishments*, 32

*On the Greatness of Cities*, 29

Oppenheim, H.B., 62

Ortiz, Fernando, 56

*Osterreich  ber alles, wann es nur will* (Austria

above everyone else, if only she had the will to), 4

Pack, Howard, 94

Palmieri, Giuseppe, 32

Parigino, Giuseppe Vittorio, 28

patents, institution of, 12

Paz, Octavio, 132

Perez, Carlota, 4, 10

perfect competition, 3–4

Perrotta, Cosimo, 2–3, 6, 12–13, 16, 28, 30, 56

Petty, William, 34, 55

Pfeiffer, Johann Friedrich von, 59

physiocracy, 33–34

Pigou, 123

Pinto, Anibal, 132

Polanyi, Karl, 75, 77

political economy

civil society and, 35–36

cultural continuity of, 39–41

economic development and, 37–39

econo-mystification, 34–35

from core to semi-periphery in early modern period, 26–28

from scholastics to enlightenment, 39–41

human capital, 35–36

institutions, 35–36

Italian tradition of, 24–41

manufactures and, 37–39

mathematics, 34–35

Medici Grand Dukes case, 26–28

methodology, 34–35

Naples and Milan schools of, 31–33

physiocracy and, 33–34

post-scholastic predecessors, 28–31

protectionism and, 37–39

Tudor Plan, 16, 26–28, 56

*Politics*, 4

Polo, Marco, 39, 41

Porta, Pier Luigi, 35

Porter, Jeanne Chenault, 29

Porter, Michael, xv, 13

Postlethwayt, Malachy, 15

Prebisch, Raul, 99, 108, 110, 118–19, 131–33

Pre-Smithian economics, 1, 4

Pritchett, Lant, 125

property rights

class relationship and, 70–74

growth and, 77–79

protection, institutions of, 12

protectionism and economic development, 37–39

Quesnay, Francois, 33–34, 41

Rae, John, 60

Rand, Ayn, 36
Ranis, Gustav, 91, 94
Raymond, Daniel, xiii, xviii, 14, 49, 60
real economy, 3
*Realokonomie*, 30
*Reason of State*, 29
Rebelo, Sergio, 87
Reder, Melvin, viii
Reinert, Erik S., vii–viii, xvi–xvii, xviii, xxi, 1, 4–6, 10, 12–14, 17, 27–31, 33, 35, 41, 48, 51, 53, 56–58, 60, 62, 64, 66
Reinert, Hugo, 62
Reinert, Sophus A., xvi–xvii, 1, 24, 29–30
renaissance wealth creation, origin of, 4–6
*Reports of the Secretary of the Treasury on the Subject on Manufactures*, 102
Ricardo, David, viii, xii, 18, 51, 59, 62–63, 64, 101, 122, 147
*Rise and Decline of the Free Trade Movement*, 65
Riva, Bonvesion de la, ix
Robbins, Lionel, xii, 15
Robinson, Joan, 151
Rodriguez, Octavio, 132
Rodrik, Dant, 94
Rolova, Alexandra, 28
Romer, D., 93
Romer, Michael, 87, 93
Romer, Paul, 85
Roover, Raymond de, vii, 26
Ros, Jaime, xviii, 81, 83, 93
Roscher, Wilhelm, xiii, xxi, 31, 54, 61
Rosenstein–Rodan, Paul, xiv, xviii–xix, 81, 89–91, 103, 106, 118
Ross, D., 94
Rostow, Walt W., 152
Ruestow, Edward G., 8
Ruffolo, Giorgio, 24, 27

Saad–Filho, Alfredo, xix, 128
Sabot, R., 94
*Sachsenspiegel*, 50
Sala-i-Martin, Xavier, 125
Salerni, Carlo, 25, 27, 37, 40
Samuelson, Paul A., 112
Santos, Theotonio dos, 137
Sawyer, Malcolm, 138
Scazzieri, Roberto, 35
Schaffle, Albert, ix
Schmoller, Gustav von, 12–13, 27, 50, 61–63, 65
*Schmoller's Jahrbuch*, 64
Schoenhof, Jacob, 14–15
Schumpeter, Joseph Alois, x, 17, 25, 29, 32, 41, 49–50, 52, 59, 62
Scitovsky, Tibor, 135
Scott, Maurice, 135

Seckendorff, Veit von, x, xvii, 25, 53–54, 63
Seligman, Edwin, 37–38, 61
semi-periphery of enlightenment, theories and policies of development in, 24–41
Serra, Antonio, x–xi, xiii, xvii, xxi, 3, 8, 14, 17, 28–31, 35, 39–40, 54, 58, 61, 66
Shleifer, Andrei, 81, 92
Singer, Hans, xiv, 108, 110, 118, 122, 133
Small, Albion W., 53
Smith, Adam, viii–ix, xi–xiv, 1–2, 4, 13–16, 32–33, 36, 41, 50, 52–53, 59, 70, 90, 100–01, 121–22, 147
  as misunderstood mercantilist, 13–16
Solo, Robert M., 82, 87
Sombart, Werner, x, 8, 30, 50, 52, 60, 62
Soros, George, 4
*Spectator*, 32
Spooner, F.C., 32
Steadman, Philip, 8
Steindl, Josef, 138
Steuart, James, x–xii, 13
Stiglitz, Joseph, xv
Stokey, Nancy J., 125
Stolleis, Michael, 53
structuralism
  critiques of, 135–37
  dependency theory and, 139–40
  left critique, 136–37
  neoclassical critique, 135–36
  principles and policies, 132–35
  rise and decline of in Latin America, 128–43
Sugden, Robert, 36
Sugiyama, ChuLei, 49
Sunkel, Osvaldo, 132
*supply–push* phenomenon, 10
Sweezy, Paul, 72, 138, 141
synergic common good, 5
Szentes, Tamás, xix

*Tableau Economique*, 33
Tavares, Maria da Conceicao, 132
Taylor, Lance, 81
*Teutsche Furstenstaat*, x
*Theory of Economic Development*, 49
*Theory of Moral Sentiments*, xiii, 15
Thorp, Rosemary, 130
Thunen, Johan Heinrich von, 58
Tollison, Robert D., 34
trade
  classical theory of, 102, 111, 121, 123
  comparative advantage theory of, 101, 111
  development issues in mainstream theory of, 111–21
  free trade, viii, 14, 37–38, 102, 114, 119
  gains from, 112
  intervention, 119–20

losses from, 113, 115–16
   theory of, 100–02
   wage rigidity and, 113
triple-level rent-seeking, 4
Tron, Andrea, 25, 27
Tubaro, Paola, 34–35
Tudor Plan, 16, 26–28, 56
*Types of Economic Theory*, ix

US economy, mercantilism and, 2
United Nations Economic Commission for
   Latin America (ECLA), 131
*Universal Relations*, 29
Uztariz, Geronymo de, 7

Veblen, Thorstein, viii–ix, 8, 16, 153
Venice, 19
Venturi, Franco, 27, 32, 34, 36–37
*Verein fur Sozialpolitik* (Association for Social
   Policy), 62–65
Vermeer, Jan, 8–9
Verri, Alessandro, 35
Verri, Pietro, 25, 27, 31–33, 35–41
Viner, Jacob, 112, 117–20
Vishny, Robert, 81, 92
Vries, Alessandro, 24
Vries, P.H.H. de, 40

Wade, Robert, 76

Wagner, Adolph, 61
Wallerstein, Immanuel, 24, 27, 137
Walras, Leon, 151
*War and Capitalism*, 8
Washington Consensus, xv, 55, 66, 142
*Wealth of Nations*, viii, xi, xiii, 14–15, 32
Weber, Max, ix–x, 62, 152
Weil, D., 93
Will, Georg Andreas, 33
Williamson, Oliver E., 69–70
Winter, ix
Wolf, Martin, 17, 19
Wolff, Christian, 11, 51–52, 54
Woo-Cumings, Meredith, 76
Wood, Ellen Meiskins, 70, 74, 77
World Bank, xv, 10, 126
World Trade Organization, 126

Xenophon, tradition of, 50

Young, 90

Zanden, Jan Luiten van, 26
Zanier, Claudio, 28
Zincke, Georg Heinrich, 9, 57
Zinobi, Chevalier de, 37
*Zollverein*, 60